PARENTS
WHO KILL

PARENTS WHO KILL

MURDERERS OF NEWBORN, PRE-TEEN AND TEENAGE CHILDREN

CAROL ANNE DAVIS

Author of the bestselling *Children Who Kill*

First published in paperback 2009
by Pennant Books

British Library Cataloguing-in-Publication Data:
A catalogue record for this book is available on request from
The British Library

ISBN 978-1-906015-37-4

Pennant Books' True Crime series is edited by Paul Woods.

Designed & typeset by Envy Design Ltd

Printed and bound in Great Britain by Clays Ltd, St Ives plc

Pennant Books
PO Box 5675
London W1A 3FB

www.pennantbooks.com

ABOUT THE AUTHOR

Carol Anne Davis was born in Dundee, moved to Edinburgh in her twenties and now lives in south-west England. She left school at fifteen and was everything from an artist's model to an editorial assistant before going to university. Her Master of the Arts degree included criminology and was followed by a postgraduate diploma in adult and community education.

A full-time writer since graduating, her crime novels *Sob Story*, *Kiss It Away*, *Noise Abatement*, *Safe As Houses* and *Shrouded* have been described as chillingly realistic for their portrayals of sex and death.

She is also the author of the true crime books *YOUTHFUL PREY: Child Predators Who Kill*, *SADISTIC KILLERS: Profiles of Pathological Predators*, *COUPLES WHO KILL: Profiles of Deviant Duos*, *CHILDREN WHO KILL: Profiles of Pre-teen and Teenage Killers* and *WOMEN WHO KILL: Profiles of Female Serial Killers*.

Carol's website is located at www.carolannedavis.co.uk

For Ian
1957–2009

CONTENTS

ACKNOWLEDGEMENTS

I'm indebted to Dr Marc Feldman for answering my questions about mothers who deliberately harm their children, sometimes fatally, in order to gain attention. Dr Feldman is a clinical professor of psychiatry at the University of Alabama and an international expert in Munchausen's (and Munchausen's-by-proxy) syndrome. He is also a respected author whose latest book is the revealing *Playing Sick*.

I'm also grateful to crime scene investigator Paul Millen for explaining gun residue to me, an intriguing aspect of the Neil Entwistle case. Paul has over thirty years' experience in the management and scientific investigation of crime, and his work has been commended by the Commissioner of the Metropolitan Police. He was responsible for the development of the prestigious diploma in Crime Scene Investigation awarded by the Forensic Science Society, and was later elected vice president of the society. He is also author of the book *Crime Scene Investigator*.

I'd similarly like to thank Jerzy Morkis, editor of the Scottish newspaper *East Fife Mail*, for keeping me up to date with details of the Robert Thomson case and for answering my questions. Thomson's frenzied murder of his children, followed by an attempted suicide, received far more coverage in his native Scotland than it did in the English press.

Last, but certainly not least, I'm delighted that Gregg Olsen, one of

America's foremost true crime authors, granted me an interview. Gregg visited Tanya Reid in prison following her convictions for child abuse and murder and wrote a revealing book, *Cruel Deception*, about this particularly troubling case.

INTRODUCTION

Ask a member of the public to describe a murderous mother and they will usually describe a teenage girl who hides her pregnancy from her parents, gives birth alone in her bedroom and leaves the infant to die of exposure in a nearby park. In reality, mothers also kill in their twenties, thirties and forties, and their reasons are equally diverse. Within these pages you will find women who murdered their offspring for insurance money, to garner attention or in order to enjoy a new romance. A few killed their children (and sometimes committed suicide immediately afterwards) whilst in the throes of post-natal depression, whilst others believed that their hapless progeny were possessed by demons.

Some fathers who kill are also religiously motivated, believing they are sending their child to a better place. In other cases the motive is financial. Chillingly, however, the most common reason is revenge on the children's mother, because she has either left or else is planning to leave. In similarly disturbing but more poignant instances the motive is mercy, when terminally-ill children face an agonising and protracted death.

There is also a section here on couples who killed their children together, in the belief that they were ridding them of demonic possession, or by administering physical discipline, or as a result of gross medical neglect.

In previous books I've split British and American killers into distinct sections, because their modus operandi were different – for example, British sadists usually kill close to home whilst American sadists often transport their victims for hundreds of miles, assaulting them repeatedly en route. But vengeful fathers who kill in Britain or in the States are amazingly similar, threatening their exes and even phoning them whilst in the act of murdering the children. Similarly, there is little distinction between a neglectful mother in the UK or USA and cases from France and Australia show the same character traits. As a result, I've grouped these killers in themed chapters according to their reasons for murder rather than by country of origin.

The fourth part of the book examines ways of preventing some of these murders and is followed by an appendix of useful addresses.

PART ONE
MURDEROUS MOTHERS

CHAPTER ONE

TELL NO ONE

Thirty infants a year are killed in Britain, mostly by their mothers. These women often conceal their pregnancies and give birth alone in their bedrooms or in semi-public settings such as a college bathroom or a hotel.

They do so for a variety of reasons. Sometimes the baby is the result of an affair which they've had whilst their husband was working away from home, and to admit to the pregnancy will end the marriage. In other instances, the girl is single and from a religious family which opposes pre-marital sex. Women with a previous history of mental illness are more likely to panic when they find out they are expecting an unplanned and unwanted baby, as are those who are already under stress from previous experiences in their lives.

The stereotype is of a young teenage – or even younger – girl who has little understanding of biology, but many mothers who kill their children at birth are in their late teens or early twenties. They tend to be passive individuals with a desperate need to appear perfect to their parents and friends.

Though impoverished, uneducated girls are the most likely to give birth in secret and dispose of their babies immediately afterwards, it's not unusual for high-school pupils and university students to do likewise, preferring the extended pain of a medication-free birth to admitting the impending arrival of an illegitimate child.

If a mother murders her baby in its first twenty-four hours, the offence is one of neonaticide. In fact, most of these women snuff out the baby's life – usually by strangulation or suffocation – when it gives its first cry. Others abandon the infant in a dustbin or under a bush in the park so that it dies of exposure. In America, such infants are often disposed of down the garbage chute. Some American prosecutors make no allowance for the new mother's state of mind, so girls who kill their newborns can be given lengthy sentences for murder in the USA.

The Infanticide Act, passed in Britain in 1922, recognises that childbirth and lactation can cause enormous hormonal shifts which result in temporary mental illness and can cause a mother to kill her baby. (The act isn't applicable in Scotland, but Scottish judges tend to sentence along similarly compassionate lines.) As such, women who commit neonaticide in the United Kingdom face, at worst, the charge of manslaughter.

The case which follows – that of British mother Caroline Beale – made headlines throughout the world when she secretly gave birth during a holiday in the United States and was caught attempting to take her dead baby back into Britain. The American legal system demanded a twenty-five-year sentence whilst British authorities pleaded for clemency, given her obvious fragility and confused state of mind.

CAROLINE ANN BEALE

Unlike many women who are charged with neonaticide, Caroline – born in June 1964 – was from a good, loving family. She left school at sixteen and went to college to take a course in community care. Attractive and well-liked, she went on to work in health administration and, at twenty-two, began dating Paul Faraway, the son of a teacher and a judge's clerk who made sporting rifles for a gunsmith. The following year they set up home together in Essex and got engaged.

Throughout the rest of the 1980s and the early 1990s, the couple's lives were comparatively uncomplicated. But, in the summer of 1993, Caroline's best friend Alison had a recurrence of the cancer which she'd been treated for in 1991. She began to feel tired all the time and didn't respond to chemotherapy. Later, surgeons had to remove her ovaries.

In March 1994 Caroline realised that she was pregnant (she'd conceived in January), but didn't tell anyone and tried to put it to the back of her mind. She knew that Alison had wanted children but could no longer have them, so perhaps, on a subconscious level, she didn't want to upset her ailing friend. She continued to visit Alison in hospital, though she sometimes had to cut the visits short as she was deeply distraught at how badly the illness had ravaged her.

Caroline could see that her friend wasn't going to get better – but Alison didn't realise this and continued to make plans for the future. By May 1994 she was so ill that she was moved to a hospice, where she lost her sight. Caroline continued to visit her friend, though it was harrowing to see the previously vibrant clothes designer lying motionless and unable to recognise anyone. The following month, Alison died at age thirty-one.

Caroline was overwhelmed by the death, and had crying jags which lasted for hours at a time. This went on for week after week. She began to sleep for eleven hours at a stretch, a common symptom of clinical depression. Her employers were so concerned that they offered her compassionate leave.

Her boyfriend arranged for her to accompany him and his brothers on holiday to America, but, in the weeks leading up to the trip, Caroline continued to behave oddly, sleeping for long periods, eating more than usual and appearing despondent. No one knew that by now she was almost nine months pregnant, as she disguised it with layers of baggy clothing. She later said that she'd had a dream in which Alison said that she was lonely and wanted the baby for company. This convinced Caroline that her baby would be born dead. Her relationship with Paul was going through a difficult period and they had stopped having sex, so she was able to hide the fact that her previously flat stomach was now heavy and round.

A lonely labour

On their arrival in New York on 14 September, Caroline was again tired and moody. Paul's brothers kept asking her what was wrong, but she repeatedly insisted that she was fine and they understandably assumed that she was still recovering from her bereavement. She spent much of their sightseeing visits staring unfocusedly into the distance and was always keen to return to their Manhattan hotel. Paul told her that it was time she got over Alison's death, but, when she remained unenthusiastic about touring the city, he decided to give her some space and increasingly went out on his own, leaving her watching TV in their room.

At 5pm on 22 September 1994, Caroline went into labour after encouraging the men to go out for the evening. She spent the next six hours in agony, giving birth in the bath where, at one stage, she may have passed out. She cut the cord and left the baby floating in the water whilst she went into the toilet to expel the afterbirth. She later said that the baby wasn't breathing so she put it into a plastic bag, placed the package in a duffle bag and put it next to her bed. The following morning she toured New York City with her boyfriend and his brothers, carrying the bag containing the dead baby the entire time.

That afternoon, the men went for a final drink at JFK airport in New York before their return flight, whilst Caroline went to the ladies'. A security guard who was scanning the terminal for anything suspicious saw her hanging around and noticed that she looked frightened. He also wondered if she was smuggling something under her coat. After conferring with a female officer who thought Caroline had a money bag strapped to her stomach, he told her to remove it and put it through the metal detector. But the English tourist refused and tried to return to the ladies' room.

When security staff persisted, she admitted that the bag strapped to her stomach contained a baby and protested that she didn't want her friends to see it.

Staff took her into a side room, opened the bag and saw the corpse of a seven-and-a-half-pound baby girl. By now Caroline was shaking uncontrollably and begged them not to tell her boyfriend. (The prosecution would later speculate that it was not his baby.) She became even more distressed when they handcuffed her. Consequently, she was detained as an emotionally disturbed person and taken to Queens General Hospital, where detectives handcuffed her to the bed.

Informed of what had transpired by detectives, Paul and his brothers were understandably stunned. Paul tried to contact Caroline but she had apparently said that she didn't want to see him. Back in England he went into shock. He began writing to Caroline on a weekly basis and they would later talk on the phone. Her parents were also very supportive, working tirelessly to provide her with the best legal help.

Meanwhile, zealous prosecutors decided that Caroline Beale should be charged with second-degree murder and she was sent to Riker's Island, one of America's toughest jails. It was the last place that a young woman in the throes of a nervous breakdown deserved to be, though her vulnerability was recognised and she was put on suicide watch.

Visitors found that she was desperately thin, with a ghostly complexion. She shook constantly and cried so much that she often became incoherent. Meanwhile, Paul became ill with glandular fever and their already-failing long-distance relationship broke down.

After eight months Caroline was let out on bail but forbidden to leave America before her trial, a daunting edict for a woman desperate to return to her family. She stayed with some of her American supporters but they noted that she was hoarding her antidepressants, and feared she would commit suicide.

The rationale

Talks were going on behind the scenes between the defence and the prosecution. The latter said that the baby had been born alive because air had been found in her lungs. They claimed the infant had taken a few breaths before being suffocated, and speculated that the motive was to conceal the pregnancy from Paul as she might have been impregnated by another man. (Paul had chosen not to give a blood sample, as was his right, so they couldn't determine who the father was.)

The defence noted that, if Caroline had dumped the body in New York, it would never have been traced to her. Instead, she'd carried it around all day and then attempted to board a plane back to England still carrying the corpse, the actions of a woman who was mentally ill. According to a professor of pathology, the baby suffered none of the marks consistent with the haemorrhages sometimes seen after suffocation.

Several experts believed that the baby girl had died at birth, possibly being strangled by the umbilical cord, and that air had been artificially introduced into her lungs when Caroline picked her up.

An empathic American journalist described her as a "non-malevolent, unsophisticated, tragic figure", a viewpoint which was increasingly shared in Britain and throughout the States as her story made headline news.

By now Caroline had been in America for eighteen months and was desperately missing her family, terrified of being sent back to jail. She reluctantly agreed to plead guilty to manslaughter – a crime that she did not believe she had committed – in exchange for her return to Britain and psychiatric help. If she'd gone to trial and been found guilty, she could have been jailed for up to twenty-five years.

After the plea bargain, her father articulated what many people had been thinking: "I personally think that this has been a cruel and medieval prosecution that does no credit to a civilised society." In turn, the judge retorted, "Any law that grants a blanket exemption from prosecution or punishment for those people who kill their children when their children are under one year of age is a law which is primitive and uncivilised."

Back home at last, Caroline returned to work, writing supportive letters to several of the women who supported her in Riker's. Her baby, whom she named Olivia, was cremated in the States and her ashes were returned to England.

Caroline's experiences were harrowing – but, two years after her imprisonment, another mentally-ill 'tell-no-one mother' in Britain would be treated very differently . . .

EMMA GIFFORD

Though her father was a millionaire and she benefited from private schooling in England, Emma had her share of childhood misery. Her Swedish-born mother was an alcoholic and her father was frequently away on business trips. It was his second marriage and he would go on to marry for a third time.

By age thirteen, Emma was clinically depressed. She was outwardly obedient and passive but deeply disturbed. After leaving school, she went to Edinburgh University to study English and drama, but dropped out after a year and tried to commit suicide. Though she recovered physically and, for a time, mentally (most mental illness is episodic, as sufferers tend to lack the strategies to cope with stressful life events), she didn't return to complete her course.

In 1994, when she was nineteen, she became pregnant by her student boyfriend but concealed the pregnancy. He only became aware of the baby after she gave birth in a London hospital. Both families agreed that the best thing was to have the baby adopted, but Emma was deeply distressed by this and spent hours preparing a 'life book' for the infant that she was giving up.

The following year she became pregnant again. Her boyfriend, who was still a student, begged her to have an abortion and she told him she had done so. They split up and her mental health deteriorated markedly. She secretly continued the pregnancy, hiding it from staff at the florist's where she worked.

In May 1996 she gave birth to a baby boy, whilst alone in the bathroom of her Kensington flat. She took him into the lounge and attempted to breastfeed him, but couldn't. She later explained that he was coughing and didn't appear well. She fell asleep and awoke the following day, with the baby, still breathing, beside her. She phoned her work and said that she couldn't come in, but didn't tell them why.

Bleeding heavily and once again suicidal, she smothered the baby with a flannel, a pillow and some clothing.

Emma went to work the following day, then phoned her older brother Kris and said that she wanted to kill herself. He immediately drove to her flat to collect her and brought her back with him to his home in Kent. He had no inkling that the plastic bag she was clutching contained the corpse of her infant son. The following day, she returned home and put the tiny body in a freezer, then continued with her normal life.

A few weeks later, Emma's brother found the frozen cadaver and the young woman made a full confession to the police, admitting, "I was afraid. I didn't want people to know that I was pregnant. I didn't know what to do." The police could see that she was mentally disturbed and they were sympathetic, as she also appeared to show genuine remorse.

On 21 December 1996, her sixty-year-old father accompanied her to the Old Bailey, where she was sentenced to three years probation and ordered to receive psychiatric counselling. The judge was understanding, remarking on the lonely birth and adding, "this is not something which should be allowed to cloud your entire future." He also warned her against having further children whilst under the supervision order. The defence reassured him that she had been fitted with an IUD contraceptive device.

STEPHANIE WERNICK

Born into an affluent Jewish family in 1970 in New Jersey, Stephanie fared less well at school than her twin, Tracy, and two older siblings. Academic excellence was important to her parents so she was often grounded for failing exams. They eventually hired a tutor to ensure that she got her high-school diploma, and also sent her to a private college in Long Island as her grades were so low.

Enjoying her freedom for the first time at college, Stephanie began to drink and have sex like almost everyone else. By the following spring she was pregnant, but would later claim that she didn't know.

By the onset of her second year at college she was gaining in size and began to wear increasingly baggy clothes. Several of her dorm mates asked her if she was pregnant but she vociferously denied it, fearing what her family would say.

On 17 December 1990, days before college broke up for the Christmas vacation, Stephanie – now aged twenty – went into the bathroom and, after over an hour and a half in labour, delivered her baby son into the toilet. Looking under the door, her friends saw a pool of blood around Stephanie's feet but she told them she was just having an unusually heavy period. They thought that they heard a baby whimper, but the sound wasn't repeated and they assumed that they must have been wrong.

Meanwhile, Stephanie stuffed seven balls of toilet paper down the baby's throat, tore away the umbilical cord and briefly left the toilet cubicle to put the baby into a trash bag. When one of her friends returned, she called to her from the locked cubicle to say she'd disposed of her bloodsoaked clothes in the trash, asking her friend to please take it down the hall to the garbage room. Her friend obliged, though she was surprised at the weight of the ruined garments. Meanwhile, Stephanie showered, reassured her dorm mates that she was fine and went back to bed.

A grim discovery

Back at the garbage room, a janitor noticed a bloodied towel on top of one of the trash bags. He called to the cleaner and together they opened the bag to find the body of a baby boy. The policeman who was first on the scene attempted to revive the infant, but the toilet paper was wedged so far down his throat that hospital staff would need forceps to remove some of it. Their belated attempts at cardiopulmonary resuscitation were in vain.

The house mother and the police awoke the girls to say that a baby had been found, some of them admitting that they thought Stephanie had given birth. She denied this, claiming, "My parents would kill me." But when detectives arrived on the scene she phoned her father, who told her not to talk to anyone.

At the medical centre, she told staff that she was frightened and asked, "What will happen to me? . . . What's going to become of me?" She said that she had menstruated regularly and had no idea that she was pregnant. In fact, women who are in denial about an impending birth are more likely to continue to menstruate each month – even if it's only very light bleeding or spotting, proof of the mind's effect on the body.

Indicted for manslaughter, Stephanie Wernick moved to a different college and began a new relationship whilst she awaited trial. Her lawyer insisted that she required psychiatric treatment and two psychologists concluded that she had poor motivation, with very little insight into what she'd done.

At her trial, she wept continuously and was allegedly too distraught to testify in her own defence. Her attorneys said that she'd had a brief psychotic episode during which she'd disposed of the child, but that she'd then returned to normal. The prosecution claimed that she was immoral, that the birth of the child was an inconvenience, and that she was a shallow and sociopathic young woman who thought only of her own comfort. They noted that she exhibited no fear of any likely consequences and seemed incapable of remorse. Found guilty, she was sentenced to one to four years in prison.

SABINE HILSCHINZ

It's easy to feel sympathy for the pregnant girl who is afraid to tell her parents that she's been sexually active. She kills and disposes of the infant in a desperate attempt to keep their love. She may even fear physical reprisals if she admits to her condition. As a teenager, for example, Rose West – now in prison for aiding her serial-killer husband – was battered by her father when she told him that she was pregnant by her lover, Fred.

But occasionally a woman will commit repeated acts of infanticide, using it as a kind of retrospective contraception. She's willing to cause pain, however fleeting, to infant after infant rather than use birth control or remain celibate. Understandably, the law judges such women more harshly than the 'tell-no-one' teenager and sentences them accordingly.

Sabine Hilschinz grew up in East Germany, the product of a housewife mother and railwayman father. She married a police cadet called Oliver who later joined the Stasi, the Ministry for State Security. Sabine herself trained as a dental nurse though she had an IQ of 120, which is university-level. The couple had three children together, and at first she was devoted to them.

But Oliver's work took him away from home for weeks at a time, and Sabine couldn't cope with the demands of motherhood. Bored and lonely, she regularly went drinking by herself, leaving her little ones at home alone. Soon her social drinking had escalated into alcoholism and she spent much of her life in a vodka-induced haze. The German authorities, who were monitoring the family, became so alarmed at the children's failure to thrive that they eventually took all three into care.

Serial murder

In October 1987, Sabine found that she was pregnant by one of the men she'd brought home after a night at the pub. She told no one of her condition, concealing it by wearing increasingly baggy clothes. Oliver noted that she was gaining weight, but they'd agreed not to have further children (and it's not clear if they were still having sex together), so it didn't occur to him that she might be expecting again. In May 1988, she awoke in the marital bed next to her snoring husband and realised that she was going into labour. Tiptoeing into the bathroom, she gave birth over the toilet and let the baby drown in the water.

Whilst her oblivious spouse remained fast asleep next door, Sabine cut the umbilical cord and put the tiny corpse into a plastic bag before placing it in a large plantpot and covering it with soil. She put herbs in the pot and set it on their apartment balcony.

Three years later, in 1992, she gave birth to another illegitimate child, this time in a hotel room. She left the baby to die, brought it home in her suitcase, wrapped it in a plastic bag and hid it inside another large flowerpot, which she seeded with herbs and placed alongside the previous pot.

The following year she had another secret birth, concealing the corpse in an empty fish tank in her garage and topping it up with sand. The next year she gave birth again and put the corpse into a large paint can. She hid another of her unwanted babies in a bucket and covered it with clods of earth. She got pregnant every year, until she had secretly given birth to and disposed of nine newborns, the last born in 1998.

Eventually, the mother from hell moved house. Lacking room for all of the makeshift coffins, she took them to her mother Eva's house in Brandenburg and stored them in the older woman's shed. In the same timeframe she left Oliver and started a long-term relationship with an older gentleman called Johann, giving birth to his baby daughter. He found her to be an exemplary mother and a loving common-law wife.

But Sabine's previous less-than-motherly actions were about to catch up with her. In 2005, Eva decided to springclean her shed and garden. Too old to wrestle with heavy plantpots and a fish tank filled with sand, she paid a younger neighbour to clear the place. To his horror, he found nine tiny skeletons and called the police. They arrested the thirty-nine-year-old and asked her why she hadn't used contraception. She explained that, after disposing of the first baby, she'd realised that a gynaecologist would know that she'd recently given birth and might ask questions about the child's whereabouts, therefore avoiding any contact with the medical profession. She failed to explain why she hadn't opted for celibacy or a non-procreative form of sex.

Police broke the news to her husband, who was so shocked that he vomited. He told them that she'd grown – and presumably used – herbs from the plantpots containing the corpses. A pathologist confirmed that all nine infants had died within minutes of birth.

In June 2006, Sabine appeared at Frankfurt-on-Oder court charged with the manslaughter of eight of the nine babies. Because of

Germany's statute of limitations she couldn't be charged with the death of the first child, as it had died in 1989.

Sabine declined to give evidence but had previously told her lawyer she'd only murdered one of the infants, leaving several of the others to die of neglect. She said that the babies were fathered by her husband, Oliver, and that she'd hidden the pregnancies from him because he didn't want any more children. But no one who knew her believed this, as she'd brought numerous men back from bars and clubs whilst Oliver was working away from home. He said that he'd noticed she had a weight problem – but it obviously hadn't occurred to him that she'd get pregnant again, when she'd been such a bad mother that all three of her children had been taken into care.

Sabine Hilschinz was sentenced to fifteen years in prison. Her lawyers appealed but, in April 2008, a German court upheld her sentence, noting that she appeared to have been fully aware of her actions and the consequences if she was caught.

UNKNOWN MOTIVES

Sometimes a mother murders her children and takes her secrets with her to the grave – as in a recent British case where a woman in her seventies died, having gone through three marriages which produced eight known children. In May 2008, one of her adult daughters was clearing out her late mother's house in Manchester when she found an egg crate hidden at the back of a wardrobe. The crate held two towel-wrapped toy boxes which she opened to reveal two decomposing babies. The remains were at different stages of decomposition, indicating the children hadn't died at the same time. The crate also contained a newspaper from 1956.

Police said that they'd have to test the DNA of the remains to establish that they were indeed the dead woman's children, adding that her family were deeply shocked as they were aware that the infants were probably their siblings. They would never know why she had killed two of her infants, yet let others live.

An eighteen-year-old boy had a similarly gruesome experience in Wenden near Frankfurt in May 2007, when his forty-four-year-old mother was away from home and he went rooting deep inside the family freezer in search of a pizza. Instead, he unearthed three tiny corpses wrapped in plastic bags.

His alcoholic mother, Monika Halbe, admitted secretly giving birth to a baby in 1986, and to two more between 2003 and 2007. She said that she had hidden the babies, but that she hadn't murdered them. However, the prosecution countered that the first had died of suffocation or neglect, and that one of the others had been drowned.

She was jailed for four years and three months for the most recent deaths, but wasn't tried for the baby born in 1986 because of the statute of limitations, more than twenty years having elapsed.

There have been similar cases elsewhere in Europe, with families belatedly realising that their mothers were, effectively, serial killers.

CHAPTER TWO
HORMONAL HELL

Giving birth can be a challenging experience which leaves the new mother physically and emotionally exhausted. This low state is compounded five days later when oestrogen and progesterone, which have been up to a thousand times their normal level, drop back to their pre-pregnancy state. Such huge changes in the endocrinal system cause spontaneous bouts of weeping in three quarters of women, a condition colloquially known as the 'baby blues'.

The majority of mothers recover within a couple of days, but up to ten percent go on to suffer post-natal depression with symptoms which include fatigue, insomnia, anxiety and loss of appetite. Thyroid problems brought on by the pregnancy can also create a low mood and lethargy. Half of this depressed ten percent will require psychiatric care, either in hospital or on an outpatient basis.

Fortunately, only two mothers in a thousand actually suffer a psychotic episode in which they lose touch with reality, as a result of post-natal (also known as post-partum) depression.

Women who come from families with a history of psychiatric illness are up to eighty percent more likely to suffer an episode of severe post-natal psychosis than women without such histories. Unfortunately, a new mother who suffers such a depressive episode is fifty percent more likely to suffer a recurrence in subsequent pregnancies.

Though they have originally looked forward to motherhood, a small number of these temporarily-psychotic mothers kill their babies and, sometimes, themselves.

In other instances, clinical levels of depression are not necessarily hormonal, being caused instead by the woman's situation: a poor marriage or relationship, bad housing, poverty or the lack of a supportive mother figure can all contribute to feelings of anger and hopelessness.

DANIELLE WAILS

A Newcastle barmaid, Danielle had a history of failed relationships which included violence. She was known to social services and to mental health charities.

When she was twenty, she found out that she was expecting her first child – her sister-in-law would later say that she'd deliberately become pregnant in order to hold on to her new boyfriend, twenty-two-year-old Robert Gallon. But, a few weeks later, she said that she wanted a termination as she couldn't cope with a child. Her boyfriend looked shocked and talked her out of it, promising that they would be a family. He had already fathered a son, now aged two, that he didn't see because the mother had moved away, but he liked the idea of fatherhood.

The couple moved in together and Danielle gave up work, but she called Robert so often at the building site where he worked that his boss became furious. She also bombarded his family with phone calls and texts and wanted to know where he was at every moment of the day, often accusing him of being with other women. She would even phone various Newcastle pubs, asking if he was there and telling the bar staff to send him home. Meanwhile, Danielle went on drinking binges throughout the pregnancy and became deeply depressed, professing that she no longer had a life.

In March 2005 she gave birth to a son, Alexander. But she was unable to cope with his crying and repeatedly sent texts to her boyfriend, asking for him to come home from work and help out. When he couldn't, she alternated between tears and threats. Danielle also went to her doctor to tell him how useless she felt and he was sympathetic, explaining that she had all of the symptoms of post-natal depression. He prescribed antidepressants but she only took them for ten days, later explaining that they'd made her feel drowsy and she was afraid she would fall asleep whilst bathing the child.

Threatening suicide

One day, when Robert was caring for Alexander, she arrived home drunk and caused a scene. He called the police and they let her off with a caution. On another occasion she phoned him at work and said that she'd thrown the baby down the stairs. He raced home to find the infant unharmed.

The couple continued to argue, so Robert moved out to live with his grandmother when Alexander was six weeks old. Danielle then threatened to take an overdose, saying that she'd done so before. As the house had been rented to Robert by his employer, Danielle had to be re-housed by a Catholic charity at a hostel for single mothers on the other side of Newcastle.

For the next two months she lived alone, frequently sending texts to Robert Gallon. She made up stories about being mugged whilst out shopping and, when that didn't win him back, pretended repeatedly that the baby was ill. Her own mother had seven children to care for, so she couldn't babysit as often as she'd have liked, but Danielle was given various appointments with social services. Unfortunately, she often didn't turn up.

On Father's Day that June, she texted Robert again and he came round after work to spend the evening with his child. He continued to visit Alexander, but before long Danielle's jealousy resurfaced and she kept asking him if he was seeing other girls. She told him that the baby was a 'devil' when he wasn't there, and it was obvious that she hadn't bonded with the child. In August she phoned him when the infant wouldn't stop crying, and a neighbour overheard her screaming, "Do you want me to throw this bairn down the stairs? Do you want me to stot its head?"

On Saturday 27 August 2005, she sat alone, brooding. She needed to be with someone, preferably Robert, but the baby had become an obstacle and her life was an endless round of nappies, bathing and feeds. She could hear Alexander in the next room, screaming, and sent his father yet another text. It said, "You hurt me so bad. I can't think of anything else to do. I'm sorry. I hope you remember that me and the bairn love you. It's best I leave this way. I love you, always have and always will."

She'd hoped that her veiled threats would bring him around, but he didn't respond. So she called and sent texts to him all of the following day, but he'd had enough of her manipulation and stayed away.

Arson

That evening, she laid her four-month-old-son on the settee and set fire to an armchair in the room with her cigarette lighter. As the flames took hold, she phoned 999 from her mobile and screamed at the operator to save her baby, saying that he was at the other side of the lounge from her and they were separated by a wall of flames. The horrified operator could hear little Alexander shrieking as the fire spread. Tearing the cord from the landline, Danielle Wails used it to tie her wrists then ran into the hall and began screaming for help through the letterbox.

Firefighters kicked in the door and put out the flames, whilst an ambulance took her and her badly-burnt baby to hospital. There she was questioned by police and told them that two masked men had burst into the house, kicked the baby and punched her in the face. She'd regained consciousness to find herself tied up and the house on fire, and had only managed to phone 999 by using her tongue to press the buttons on her mobile phone.

Within hours, Robert was informed by Danielle's mother about the fire. Police confirmed that the baby had died of his injuries and he went to Danielle to comfort her. The couple reconciled and went to stay at her parents' house.

For the next three days, Danielle was almost constantly in tears. Robert and her family were hugely sympathetic. The police, meanwhile, spent these three days searching for the intruders and investigating the crime scene. Danielle had said that the intruders had locked her in – but they found her key in the laundry basket. The fire alarm had been checked by the charity the previous week, yet now the batteries were found in a kitchen drawer. She said that she hadn't heard the intruders enter the premises because the radio was playing, but no radio was found at the property. She'd described how the men had viciously knocked her unconscious, yet she had only light bruising to her face.

It was clearly a fabrication, so the police arrested Danielle on suspicion of deliberately starting the fire and murdering her son. She vehemently denied this throughout hours of questioning, but was charged and remanded in custody. Several of the other female prisoners hissed, "Child killer!" at her in prison and she was put into isolation for her own safety.

Ironically, women who have abused and neglected their own children are the prisoners most likely to attack a mother who has killed. It's easier for them to scapegoat someone else than to examine their own shortcomings.

Confession

The following month, handcuffed to a police officer, she attended Alexander's funeral and read out a poem which said they would be reunited in an afterlife. Robert visited her, hoping for answers, but eventually caused a scene and was barred from the prison.

As her trial date neared, her legal team challenged her: her story didn't add up; there was no sign of the supposed masked men. Belatedly, she admitted that she'd started the fatal fire by herself.

At Newcastle Crown Court in August 2006, with her family and friends there to support her, Danielle pleaded guilty to infanticide. Two psychiatrists testified that she had been suffering from post-natal depression at the time she murdered Alexander, her mind disturbed after the birth. Her QC echoed this, saying that she was comparatively isolated and had struggled to care for her son.

The judge noted that she had already spent over a year in jail and sentenced her to a three-year community order, which included three years probation and supervision at a bail hostel. After the trial, Det Supt Barbara Franklin, who led the enquiry, said, "Danielle can only be described as an attention seeker."

En route to the hostel by train, Danielle Wails went on a drinking binge and gave an interview to a woman's magazine. (The previous month, the baby's father had told his side of the story to a different woman's weekly.) The magazine stated that she wasn't paid for her story, but the authorities were enraged as she'd given the interviewer information which she hadn't given to the police or the courts. A local MP demanded an enquiry as to why Danielle hadn't been escorted all the way to the bail hostel, and she was briefly returned to jail for breaking her bail conditions by abusing alcohol.

SHERYL LYNN MASSIP

Twenty-four-year-old Sheryl and her husband were elated when she gave birth to their first son in March 1987. The couple returned to their home in Anaheim, California, with their new baby, Michael, only to find that colic made him cry for up to eighteen hours a day. Sheryl took him to the doctor several times but was told that he was healthy, and that he would grow out of the almost-intolerable wailing. (Most babies only suffer from colic for the first three months of life.) Meanwhile, she was so exhausted that she couldn't eat or sleep.

After a month of this mayhem, the former beautician became so confused that, according to her later testimony, she began to hear voices telling her that Michael was in pain and that she should put him out of his misery. Afraid for what she would do, she tried to return him to the hospital where she'd given birth, but they turned her away.

On 29 April, whilst in the grip of a full-blown psychosis, she decided to kill the child for his own good. She threw the six-week-old infant in front of a moving car, but the driver managed to swerve and miss him. After picking the baby up, the unhappy mother took him into her garage where she grabbed a blunt object and hit him over the head. He was still alive as she put him behind one of the rear tyres of her vehicle and backed over him. Sheryl then disposed of his body in a nearby trashcan.

When her husband got home from work, she appeared dazed and told him that Michael had been kidnapped. At the police station she elaborated on her story, telling them that her son had been taken by a black 'object' with orange hair and white gloves who wasn't really a person. Shortly afterwards, the psychosis passed. She became deeply distraught and made a full confession. At her trial in November 1988, she pleaded insanity.

There's little doubt that she'd suffered a full-blown psychotic episode and had been deranged at the time of the death; yet the jury rejected her plea and found her guilty of second-degree murder. However, a sympathetic Superior Court judge, Robert Fitzgerald, ultimately rejected the jury's verdict and found the unfortunate young woman not guilty by reason of insanity.

Care in the community

Californian law at that time stipulated that a criminal defendant given such a sentence had to spend at least six months in a psychiatric hospital, but the judge rejected the requested period of commitment and ordered Sheryl to spend a year as an outpatient at a counselling centre. Afterwards, she was required to attend various treatment programmes, all of which she completed successfully. She divorced and later remarried, having a daughter with whom she forged a loving relationship.

In May 2008, Sheryl, now forty-five and living in San Bernardino County, asked for a court order which would recognise that she is now sane and release her from further treatment. A leading mental health authority supported her application, stating that she no longer requires therapy. At the time of writing, the deputy district attorney had yet to decide whether or not to oppose her request.

BEVERLY BARTEK

Beverly and her husband badly wanted children, but he was sterile. They opted for artificial insemination and, on 3 May 1986, she gave birth to a daughter, Laura, in a Nebraskan hospital. A few days later, the nuclear family returned to their Lincoln home.

Thirty-three-year-old Beverly went on maternity leave from her job as deputy superintendent of a wildlife centre, but found it almost impossible to sleep. On the rare occasions when she did drop off, she had terrible nightmares. She lost weight and became obsessed with the idea that artificial insemination was immoral, and that her husband would leave her because Laura wasn't his biological child. As the days progressed, her mental health worsened and she apparently heard a voice telling her that her infant daughter was evil, and that she had to die. On 24 May she visited her physician and told him of her paranoid delusions, but he said that she shouldn't worry. It was just the baby blues.

On 26 May, Beverly drowned her twenty-three-day-old daughter in the sink. Medics estimate that it takes as little as sixty to ninety seconds for a small baby to die by drowning. Forty minutes later, she made a confused call to the local emergency services, who arrived to find the infant dead, wrapped in a nightdress, a nappy and a towel.

The distressed mother was charged with first-degree murder and spent a month in a psychiatric hospital, after which she was allowed home on the proviso that she was supervised by her husband and mother. She remained under psychiatric care.

When the case went to trial, five psychiatrists testified that she had been psychotic when she murdered her daughter. The judge found her not guilty by reason of insanity, but opined that confining her to a psychiatric hospital would serve no useful purpose. She was free to go.

Changing times

Though, in the aforementioned modern cases, transgressing mothers were treated leniently, those who killed their newborns in the early part of the twentieth century often spent the rest of their lives in institutions. This could have happened in the British case which follows, had the woman's husband not petitioned repeatedly for her release.

BETH WOOD

Beth's first baby, a son, was born in March 1902 in Romford, England, nine months into her marriage to her husband Bert. The couple initially lived with Bert's parents but Beth and her mother-in-law often clashed, being similarly strong-willed. Later, they rented a home of their own and, in 1907, had their second child, another boy. In February 1913 the couple had a daughter and, in July 1916, Beth gave birth to yet another son.

By now, Beth was back in the shadow of her hated in-laws as her husband had gone into business with his brother. But life was comfortable for the couple and their four children, who enjoyed the luxury of a five-bedroomed terraced cottage with a large backyard, where the little ones could play.

Unfortunately, the Woods' daughter, Maisie, developed the highly-infectious disease diphtheria in March 1918, a month after her fifth birthday. She was rushed to hospital and the house was fumigated; council workers burned the child's toys, clothes and furniture, lest the disease spread. Maisie was placed in the isolation unit of the local infirmary where, later that month, she died.

Beth was too distraught to attend the funeral and stayed at home with her baby son, telling him repeatedly that Maisie had gone to Heaven. Her grief was compounded the following month when her sixteen-year-old son left home to join the Territorial Army, and she expressed fears that she'd never see him again.

In retrospect it's clear that Beth was suffering from clinical depression, finding the simplest task too much of an effort, but well-meaning relatives suggested to Bert that he should impregnate her. Another child was what she needed to take her mind off of Maisie's death.

Internal injuries

In late 1918, Beth became pregnant for the fifth time. She was now forty years old and in poor physical and mental health, convinced that she was going to die and that Bert would have to cope with the children without her. She cried every day and worried about whether her secondborn son, due to leave school the following year, would be able to find employment in those difficult post-war times. She suffered from insomnia, and so would rise early and scrub the floors and the front step until she was exhausted. Her diet was meagre and, when she did eat, it was a less-than-nutritious slice of bread with margarine.

On 16 August 1919, Beth went into labour three weeks early. She was in pain throughout the night, though attended by a caring and experienced midwife. Everyone was expecting her to have a single baby during the home birth but, when her daughter was born, the midwife could see another baby girl in the birthing canal and it was breech. She manually moved the baby into a head-down position, causing Beth further agony.

The second baby was born and, unaware that a third child was still in the womb, the midwife gave Beth a dose of the medicine ergot to help expel the placenta. This made the third baby's heart stop beating. The uterus contracted violently and, fifteen minutes later, the dead or dying baby was born, whereupon Beth haemorrhaged massively. The midwife tried desperately to revive the infant which, like its siblings, weighed only three pounds, but to no avail.

Beth almost lost consciousness during the grisly birth, and had to be taken to hospital in a taxi for a blood transfusion. The doctor told her that, once her health had recovered, she would need a major operation to restore her lacerated perineum, the area between her rectum and vagina, which was badly torn. On her return home she was told to rest in bed for a month, but found it impossible to relax and began to fret about the impending operation. She told Bert that she feared the surgery, especially as it might leave her incontinent. In the space of eighteen months she had lost two children and now had premature twins to nurture, yet she had nothing left to give.

For several days Beth remained in the marital bedroom, following doctor's orders, but still directed the entire household from her sickbed. In retrospect it seems she was either going into a manic phase or reacting to the ergot that she was being given regularly to prevent post-partum bleeding. Ergot can produce dramatic mood swings, even hallucinations or full-blown psychosis, in some patients. Desperately thin and undernourished, Beth Wood must have been particularly susceptible.

Drowned

When the babies were ten days old, she awoke some time between midnight and 4am with a terrible feeling of foreboding. Whilst the rest of the household slept, she took both of her infant daughters from their crib, dragged the tin bath into the backyard and filled it with cold water from the butt. She would later remember that the cold had made her feel more energised than she had for months. Then she put the babies, still clothed, into the full bath and went back to bed.

At 4.30am she woke her sleeping husband and said agitatedly that she'd left the babies downstairs. He explored the downstairs rooms, then went out into the yard and found them, drowned, in the tin bath. He confronted Beth but she denied resonsibility, saying that she'd merely bathed them and left them downstairs. Increasingly confused, she began to weep.

The police were summoned and Beth was taken to the local hospital, by which time her mental health had deteriorated further. She talked to babies that only she could see, complained of pains in her head and retreated into a world of her own.

Murder charge

A fortnight after the murders, the coroner held an inquest. When he saw how weak Beth was, however, he said that she did not have to give evidence. She could only walk by leaning heavily on a nurse and was still too sick to have the operation on her perineum.

Unfortunately, it would be 1922 before the law was changed to allow for a manslaughter charge in such post-natal depression cases, so Beth was charged with double murder. On 17 October 1919 she appeared, still desperately frail, before the local magistrate. She was remanded to Holloway Prison until her trial and was allocated a cell in the hospital wing, where she spent most of her time weeping and expressing both grief and remorse.

Whilst she was in prison, the babies – named Queena and Freda – were buried next to their sister Maisie. In those impoverished days, insurance companies refused to insure a child under three months old for fear that the parents would be motivated to murder it. So the Wood family had to pay the cost of the double funeral from their savings and didn't have enough left over for a headstone – though one was bought at a later date.

On 31 October 1919, Beth went on trial at Essex Autumn Assizes, knowing that the jury could find her guilty – in which instance she would face the death penalty. She pleaded not guilty. The prosecutor was sympathetic, outlining the death of five-year-old Maisie, the dead newborn triplet and the injurious birth. The defence echoed these statements, noting that Beth had borne no malice towards her babies, and had drowned them whilst in an enfeebled state of mind.

The judge told the all-male jury that, if they believed Beth had intended to drown the girls, they must find her guilty of murder – only then could they deal with whether she was responsible for her actions. The jury found her guilty, but said that she was *not* responsible.

Incarcerated

In a compassionate society, the courts would surely have decided that Beth had suffered enough and allowed her to return to her loving husband and sons. Instead, she was sent to Broadmoor, the psychiatric hospital, where she joined a hundred other women who had murdered their children in the grip of post-natal psychosis (in those days known as puerperal insanity). Some of these women would remain there for the rest of their lives . . .

Though she recovered physically and mentally, Beth had no memory of drowning the two girls. She told other inmates that she must have done it because everyone said that she had, and she sometimes expressed the wish that she'd been given the death sentence. Meanwhile, her husband sank into a deep depression which lasted a year. The children had to be raised by his mother and an unmarried sister. After this, he moved his family into a new house and began to petition various legal bodies for his wife's release.

On 4 December 1921, forty-three-year-old Beth Wood was allowed home to her ecstatic husband and sons. Prematurely grey and somewhat depressed, she remained an inveterate worrier for the next thirty years.

Bert died when Beth was seventy-one and she remarried to an old friend, but her mind began to unravel. When she tried to set fire to her underclothes, she was committed to a psychiatric hospital. Beth was frequently visited by her concerned relatives, but soon she no longer recognised them. She died of a pulmonary embolism on 15 September 1957, aged seventy-nine. Her memory has been kept alive in her great-granddaughter Sian Busby's beautifully-written book on the subject, *The Cruel Mother* – subtitled *A Family Ghost Laid to Rest.*

CHAPTER THREE

MENTAL BREAKDOWN

Though hormonal changes – and generalised stress – in the post-partum months are the most common cause of mental breakdown in mothers, a small percentage develop a severe mental illness that isn't necessarily associated with childbirth.

VIVIANE GAMOR

An intelligent woman who was studying for a Masters degree, mother-of-two Viviane Gamor became delusional in 2003. The mature student – who lived in Hackney, east London – insisted that she had met various famous people and would talk at length about these fictitious relationships. She began to stare at strangers intently for no apparent reason. More chillingly, she shaved off the hair on one side of her baby daughter's head.

Over the next two years, Viviane's mental health deteriorated further. She changed her name by deed poll to Mother Nature Viviane and said that Jesus was her twin.

In early 2006, she was sectioned under the Mental Health Act for threatening her half-sister with a knife. The father of her son and daughter, Gabriel Ogunkoya, took the bewildered children to live with his parents; they were also cared for by him and his girlfriend. Yet, despite the crucial role he played in his children's lives, the authorities didn't tell Gabriel why his ex-partner had been sectioned, or that she'd been diagnosed as a paranoid schizophrenic.

Unsupervised access

Viviane seemed to respond well to medication and, after five weeks, the authorities let her out. A condition of her release was that Hackney social services would oversee any contact that she had with her children. But staff shortages meant that the supervision only extended to the first visit, after which a social worker mandated that she should be allowed unsupervised access to Antoine and Keniece. The children's father was so alarmed by this that he sought legal counsel, but the solicitor said that, if he kept them from their mother, he would be virtually kidnapping them. Gabriel was so concerned that he gave his ten-year-old son a mobile phone and told him to call at any time.

The twenty-nine-year-old's first two unsupervised access visits in January 2007 with her children passed without incident – but, unknown to Hackney social services, she'd stopped taking her medication. On 24 January, she was seen by a psychiatrist who said that she had a positive outlook and did not pose any further risk. Two days later, during the children's third overnight visit, she flew into a psychotic rage and began to beat ten-year-old Antoine with a hammer. Neighbours heard his agonised screams and called the police. They arrived at Viviane's flat, but by then she'd killed her son. She had also wrapped clingfilm around the face of her three-year-old daughter, Keniece, suffocating her to death. Viviane told horrified police officers, "I don't care. They're not mine." She was sent to a psychiatric facility.

From the start, Viviane freely admitted both killings and later pleaded guilty to manslaughter due to diminished responsibility. She appeared, flanked by psychiatric nurses, at the Old Bailey in June 2008 wearing a red leather jacket and a scarlet t-shirt. Viviane seemed indifferent to the proceedings and was detained indefinitely under the Mental Health Act.

Afterwards, grieving father Gabriel said, "I obeyed the law and let them go. I wish I had not done that. The system that I obeyed has frogmarched my children to their deaths. They assessed her and found nothing wrong. This is pure negligence which will not be tolerated."

In August 2008, an inquiry concluded that the National Health Service should have taken more account of Viviane Gamor's bizarre behaviour towards her children – but, surprisingly, it failed to identify a single decision which could have prevented their deaths. The children's father, now thirty-three, branded the inquiry a whitewash and said, "My family and I feel totally let down. It is a system which has failed my children."

DEANNA LANEY

A religious obsessive, Texas housewife Deanna Laney named her three sons after biblical characters. As the years passed, her mania deepened until she believed that she was hearing messages from God. He told her to kill the boys and said that, if she resisted, they would meet a yet more unpleasant death. Reading her bible more obsessively than ever, she began to lose weight and would later say that she smelled sulphur, interpreting this as the presence of the Devil. Over time she saw signs that God wanted her to kill the boys with rocks, and she hid one away in her baby's room.

On 11 May 2003, Deanna put the three children to bed at 9pm before retiring for the night herself. But she awoke at 11pm and went to her fourteen-month-old, Aaron, who was asleep in his cot, fetched the rock and brought it down hard on his skull. He began to scream. Her husband woke up and asked her what was wrong. Calling out that everything was fine, she put a pillow over the baby's face to muffle the noise. He was left partially blind, with permanent motor-control disabilities, as the result of this brutal attack.

A double murder

Leaving little Aaron with severe injuries, Deanna then woke six-year-old Luke and told him to follow her into the garden. He did so. She ordered him to lie down with his head on top of one of the largest stones in the rockery. When he was supine, she picked up another rock and smashed it into his head. Though he sustained massive injuries, however, the unfortunate child did not die right away. When he did expire, his mother was unconcerned; her god had promised that the little boy would be resurrected on his birthday, in two months time. She then dragged him into the shadows, where his brother wouldn't see him, and put a large boulder on his chest.

Thirty-nine-year-old Deanna then fetched eight-year-old Joshua from his bed and led him to the garden where she brought a rock crashing down on his skull, fatally injuring him. Pulling him into the shadows to lie beside his brother, she placed another large boulder on the child's chest.

Returning to the house, the devoted choir singer calmly phoned the operator and said that she'd killed her three boys. Detectives arrived to find the oldest two dead and the baby fighting for his life. When they asked her why she'd done it, she replied, "I was told to do this by God." A week later, she told a court-appointed psychiatrist, "I know that murder is illegal under man's law, but I was answering to a higher authority."

Deanna maintained her religious arguments during her trial in May 2004, telling the jury, "In our faith we believe the word of God. This word is infallible. I feel the Holy Spirit springs up within me when I speak of Him." She also said that she expected to become, "God's witness to the end of time." Her husband, who had promised to stand by her, broke down several times as jurors were told of his sons' painful and frightening deaths.

The jury took seven hours to find her not guilty by reason of insanity, and Deanna was shipped off to a mental hospital indefinitely. Afterwards, her brother-in-law, a pastor, said that she wasn't responsible as she had been possessed by a demon at the time.

CHAPTER FOUR

BRAND NEW BOYFRIEND

Childfree organisations – like the British Organisation of Non-Parents (BON) – warn women not to have children if they aren't prepared to end up as single parents. After all, even the most committed mother can lose her partner to death or divorce. Single mothers who find that they cannot cope often tend to relinquish custody to the child's father, to their own parents or, much more rarely, to the state.

But Susan Smith and Diane Downs rejected these options in favour of murdering their children and pretending that a stranger did it. This gave them the opportunity to reinvent themselves as free and single, something which their new boyfriends desired.

Both women had difficult childhoods which included sexual abuse. They were left with borderline personalities, in which they swung from the emotional state of 'motherhood is everything' to wanting their offspring permanently out of the way.

Borderline personalities can put on a wonderful act, in this case acting out the role of the perfect mother, but deep down they are completely self-absorbed and have very little to give to other adults, far less a needy child. Mothers suffering from this syndrome feel totally adrift as single parents, and will do anything to attach themselves to a man and to keep him, even when he wants to leave.

SUSAN VAUGHAN SMITH

Susan was born in 1971 in the small town of Union, Southern

Carolina. Her mother was a teenage bride and housewife, her father a mill worker and volunteer fireman.

Susan was their third child and their first daughter, and was very close to her father. He nurtured her, teaching her how to speak and how to read. But the couple divorced shortly before her seventh birthday and, one month later, he put a shotgun to his temple and committed suicide.

(As a teenager, Susan would form intense attachments to men whom she regarded as father figures. But, when they couldn't fulfil her many unmet needs from childhood, she would angrily end the relationship and go in search of another man.)

When Susan was seven, her mother married a man from a wealthy family called Bev Russell, who was very active in the Christian Coalition. Susan's mother, Linda, was also religious, a stalwart at the local Methodist church. Outwardly they were a respectable family, but by age thirteen Susan was so unhappy that she took an overdose of aspirin. When she recovered she threw herself back into her school activities, joining numerous after-school and leisure clubs.

When she was fifteen, Bev started coming into her room at night and fondling her. Unsure of how to react, Susan would pretend to be asleep. At sixteen, she told her school counsellor and Bev admitted the offence. The family went for counselling but the abuse wasn't reported to the police. Susan continued to spend her evenings and weekends in frenetic activity, as if, by filling every waking moment, she wouldn't have time to think about everything that had occurred.

At eighteen, she started dating an older married man and was deliriously happy – but when he ended the affair, she took an overdose and spent several days in hospital. She once again went into therapy.

At nineteen, Susan became pregnant by David Smith, a year her senior, who already had a fiancée. Susan was working as a checkout girl at the local supermarket and David was the assistant manager. The couple had a church wedding in March 1991 and their first son, Michael, arrived in October. Susan was a good mother, though she worried constantly about money and was very jealous when David spoke to other women, sometimes hitting him and accusing him of cheating on her.

Two days after their first wedding anniversary, the couple split up but they later reconciled and procreated a second son, Alex. But, shortly after his birth in September 1993, they split up again. Susan no longer wanted David, but she hated to see anyone else with him and did everything she could to break up his relationship with his girlfriend. By now she was having full consensual sex with Beverly, her stepfather, who was still married to her mother. She also had relationships with various other men in town.

A new start

In September 1994 Susan filed for divorce, though this was against David's wishes. She took a secretarial job with a fabrics firm and began dating Tom Findlay, the boss's son. She often left the children with friends whilst she went out to party, sometimes spending her evenings at a popular country and western club. But when Tom realised she wanted a serious relationship, he admitted that he didn't want to settle down with someone who already had children. He wrote her a very complimentary farewell letter, telling her that she'd "make some man a great wife". He could have played her along, but instead he'd decided to be honest. Yet he would be left with feelings of guilt over what happened next.

For, instead of finding someone who was happy to join a readymade family, Susan decided to get rid of her existing one. If she was single, she reasoned, then Tom – who was both affluent and attractive – would hopefully want her again . . .

On the evening of Tuesday 25 October 1994, a week after the break-up, she drove fourteen-month-old Alex and three-year-old Michael to John D Long Lake. Parking on the bank, she got out of the car, took off the handbrake and watched the vehicle roll into the water, eventually sinking out of sight. Racing to a nearby house, she begged them to contact the police, saying that she'd been carjacked at nearby traffic lights by a black man who made her drive into the countryside at gunpoint, whereupon he'd taken control of her Mazda and driven away with both of her sons.

Police, aided by hundreds of concerned local people, mounted a huge search of the area; photographs of the boys and descriptions of what they were wearing were broadcast on national television. Susan and David, who had no reason to doubt his wife's version of events, made a televised plea for their safe return. Susan claimed, "I have prayed that whoever has them, that the Lord will let him realise that they are missed and loved more than any other children in this world." After further religious sentiments, she added, "I just feel in my heart that you're okay."

For nine days, Susan stuck to her story whilst her son's corpses decomposed in John D. Long Lake. Divers had searched parts of the lake, but it was an enormous stretch of water and they failed to find the Mazda. Meanwhile, Susan slept a lot, becoming upset when she was asked to take a lie-detector test by the police. David told her that, when they got the boys back, they would reconcile as a family. She replied that they could do so even if they *didn't* get the boys back.

Lie detector

But the authorities were increasingly aware that Susan's story wasn't adding up. She failed two polygraphs and, despite careful questioning, could give only the vaguest details of the supposed carjacker. Still she stuck to her story, telling reporters, "whoever did this is a sick and emotionally unstable person." After a lot more religious rhetoric, she added that she had put her faith in "the Lord".

Finally, Sheriff Howard Wells, who had been outwardly supportive, told her that her story didn't add up. Why were three hours of her evening unaccounted for? Why was she allegedly driving to a friend's house when she was carjacked, on a night when her friend was out? Why had no one else seen a black man acting suspiciously in this overwhelmingly-white community? He said that they were going to have to contact the media and tell them the truth – for by now he believed that Susan knew something about her sons' disappearance.

At this stage, Susan broke down and asked if she could have his gun so that she could shoot herself. She confessed, showing detectives where the car had entered the water. They fished it out, still containing the children strapped into their car seats, from the bottom of the lake.

The toddlers' faces were so bloated after nine days in the water that they had to have closed caskets, their distraught father unable to kiss them goodbye. His mother, a Jehovah's Witness, tried to console him by saying that he'd "see them again on Resurrection Day".

Sheriff Wells also looked for a supernatural solution, saying on national television: "I think we need to continue to pray for these two children, and pray for this mother and this family."

However, the public were incensed that Smith had blamed a black man for the carjacking, seeing this as act of racism. But Susan hadn't previously been a racist; in fact she had briefly dated a black man during her teenage years, despite the fact that this was frowned upon in her racist neighbourhood.

As well as wrongly labelling her a racist, sectors of the media also said that she'd lied about being sexually abused as a teenager, coming to this conclusion as Susan had apparently retracted her claims. In reality, she was probably trying to spare her mother the shame of being married to an abuser, for appearances were vitally important to Susan's religious family.

Awaiting trial, the double killer spent her time reading the Bible in her cell at the Columbia Women's Correctional Centre. She wrote David a note saying that her life would be hell from now on, and that no one cared a damn about her. When he visited her, she said that, when she got out, she'd like to have further children with him. He was lost for words.

After much thought, David gave his support to a campaign to seek the death penalty for his wife. He explained this decision in a later book, *Beyond All Reason*, emphasising that it was Michael and Alex – *not* their mother – who were the victims: "They are the ones who died awful, unspeakable, senseless deaths, suspended upside down in their car seats, as the water seeped into the Mazda and rose above their little heads."

Trial

Six months after the murders, Susan Smith went to trial. The defence portrayed her as a victim of her unhappy childhood and cheating husband. David Smith was understandably enraged at being portrayed as the bad guy – after all, he had been a loving parent to his sons.

Her stepfather, Bev Russell, took the stand and admitted abusing her when she was fifteen and continuing an inappropriate relationship with her. He said that it had ended shortly before she drowned her sons. Looking at Susan, he said, "My heart breaks for what I have done to you." The prosecution, determined not to paint Susan as a victim, got him to admit that the sex had been consensual, though this didn't make it right on account of her age and the fact that he was *in loco parentis*, married to her mother.

Susan's attorneys alleged that she'd planned to die with her boys, but had jumped out of the car at the last minute. She'd told them that she'd had second thoughts, but that the car had sunk immediately, before she'd had time to free them from their seats. This contradicted the prosecution's reconstruction of events, showing that the car had skimmed along the water for some distance and floated due to an almost-empty fuel tank, before sinking slowly to the bottom of the lake. The children had taken at least five minutes to die.

The judge said that the jury could go for the lesser charge of involuntary manslaughter if they preferred, but they found her guilty of murder. She was sentenced to life, which effectively means that she won't be eligible for parole for thirty years.

In Broad River Correctional Institute, Susan received numerous letters from religious practitioners who said that they were praying for her. She has remained deeply religious and also exceptionally needy, a woman who uses her sexuality to gain acceptance and a semblance of love.

Around 2000, or possibly earlier, she began an affair with a prison guard married to a former prisoner, who had spent thirteen years working as a corrections officer. The relationship came to light during a medical in September of that year, when Susan was found to have contracted a sexually-transmitted disease. Both she and the fifty-year-old-guard admitted the relationship, and he was promptly fired. Susan Smith was told that she could also face sanctions, such as losing her much-coveted job in the prison library, or forfeiting the time she was allowed to spend in the prison grounds.

DIANE DOWNS

Christened Elizabeth Diane Fredrickson shortly after her birth in August 1955, Diane was always known by her middle name. Her mother was a teenage bride, her father, who was six years older, a strict disciplinarian. The couple, who were fundamentalist Baptists, went on to have another four children who they raised on various Arizona farms. When she was five, Diane's father opted for a change of career, beginning to work his way up the ladder of the US Postal Service.

When Diane was twelve, her mother began working nights and she was left with her father. She would later tell her husband how, during this period, her father began to sexually molest her, coming into her bedroom at night for a year. Eventually she became so insomniacal that her father took her to the doctor for sleeping tablets. Afterwards, he drove her into the desert to molest her but a Highway Patrolman allegedly saw her crying, with her shirt unbuttoned, in the front seat. He approached the vehicle and asked the crying teenager what was happening. She said that she'd had an injection from the doctor. The officer took her father to one side and spoke sharply to him. He would never touch his daughter inappropriately again.

The family continued to attend church three times a week, their social life also revolving around religious functions. Their home life was rigidly authoritarian, and perhaps explains Diane's later hatred of – and determination not to follow – rules.

Marriage

At fifteen, Diane fell in love with a boy called Steve Downs who was seven months her senior. After school, he joined the navy and Diane went to bible college, where she studied to be a Christian missionary. She also taught at Sunday school. When Steve returned from his tour of duty they married. She was only eighteen and immature for her age.

Diane had too many emotional needs for a teenage boy to satisfy. Almost immediately, she decided to have a baby so that she'd have someone of her own to love. Without telling Steve, she stopped taking her birth control pills and, nine months after the marriage, gave birth to their first daughter, Christie Ann.

But a baby can only take from its parent, and needs to be constantly nurtured. Diane soon tired of the role of caregiver. She joined the Air Force and was shipped to Texas, leaving Steve to care for their six-month-old child.

After just three weeks she was sent home with terrible blisters on her feet. Almost immediately, she decided to have another baby and, within days, was pregnant again. Christie was only fifteen months old when her sister Cheryl was born.

Steve was appalled. Their finances were already poor, so he decided to have a vasectomy. But the operation didn't work and Diane got pregnant for a third time. Steve persuaded her to have an abortion, after which he had his second vasectomy operation.

Psychiatrists say that most women recover their equilibrium quickly after a termination, with neurotic women being the exception. Diane fell into the latter category, convincing herself that she had to have another baby to replace the terminated cells.

Two years later she left Steve, taking the children, and moved back to live with her parents. Being back in their home again just made her miserable though.

The couple reconciled and she asked Steve to have the vasectomy reversed. He refused, doubtless aware that Diane enjoyed pregnancy more than motherhood. Determined to get her way, she seduced a nineteen-year-old youth and became pregnant by him. The baby, Stephen Daniel Downs, was born on 29 December 1979 and soon became known as Danny, his middle name.

Steve let everyone think that Danny was his biological child. He adored the boy and treated him the same as his two daughters. But Diane fell into a deep depression. She began to hit the children, just as she'd been hit by her father throughout her childhood.

A disordered personality

Yet she still loved the *idea* of motherhood – to the extent of offering herself as a surrogate mother, telling doctors it was important to her that the adoptive parents were Christians. The clinic put Diane through a series of tests, where she scored highly on IQ and physical health but did badly on the psychopathology scale. She told the psychologist about her parents being strict and distant, about the incest and how it had left her with no enjoyment of sex. The psychologist's findings that she could shut down her feelings at will were reinforced by a second opinion; both psychologists believed she was suffering from Histrionic Personality Disorder.

But the clinic was so desperate for surrogates that they accepted her. Artificially inseminated, she became pregnant at the first attempt and was delighted, telling acquaintances that for the first time she had a purpose, and that her aborted child might be reincarnated in the new baby. She also began sending frequent letters to the anonymous parents via care of the surrogacy office, giving them updates about the pregnancy.

Her marriage ended. By 1981, she was divorced and working as a mailperson – she loved the job, and was in a high-energy state throughout the pregnancy. Yet she ignored her existing children, not letting them into the lounge in case they made it untidy and preferring to party at night, rather than spending time with them.

Cheryl became clinically depressed and told the neighbours – who often fed her when she was locked out of the house – that nobody cared. Christie was also incredibly sad, and acquaintances noted that, in trying to take on the role of mother to her siblings, she was becoming old before her time.

Acquaintances said that all three youngsters were emotionally starved and physically neglected, sometimes playing outside in light clothing and bare feet in the winter. Diane hit the children so hard that a co-worker suggested she go for counselling, but she continued to party instead.

In May 1982 she gave birth to her surrogate baby, a daughter, and immediately handed her over to her new parents. She received $10,000, which she used for the deposit on a new mobile home. Three weeks later, she went back to work and began a new series of short-lived affairs with co-workers. She would act submissive and giggly until she got her boyfriends into bed, where she would scratch them until they bled. They were left with the impression that she hated men.

They were also confused by her bizarre behaviour, as she read the Bible every night and quoted it to them chapter-and-verse, and yet continued to have extramarital sex, which her religion forbade. On her postal route she refused to deliver soft porn titles such as *Playboy* and *Penthouse*, as they offended her, yet she was heard to call her children "fucking bastards", and would push them away when they wanted a hug.

Diane had sex with at least two of her co-workers, and then started an affair with a third, Dave (not his real name). Dave never wanted children and had had a vasectomy. Now that his second marriage was going through a bad patch, he thought that he and Diane could have a casual fling. But he was alarmed to note how often she dumped her offspring on others, and equally confused when, during a daytrip, she asked them repeatedly, "How much do you love Mommy?" Trying to extricate himself, he suggested that she give her marriage a second chance.

Threatening suicide

But Diane remained fixated on Dave, the first man whom she'd ever been orgasmic with. She knew that he'd never wanted a family, so she suggested that they could get married and that she'd keep her children out of his way. Dave reminded her that he had no intention of leaving his wife, but this was a message which Diane chose not to hear.

In September 1982, she gave the children's father full custody and began to study at night school for a pre-med course. (But she soon gave it up, as she wasn't able to spend any time with Dave.) That same month, she gave Dave a sexually-transmitted disease which she'd contracted during a previous relationship. He ended the affair. Hysterical, Diane grabbed her ex-husband's gun from his house and threatened to shoot herself.

A few days later, Diane mounted an all-out attempt to get Dave back. She had his name tattooed on her arm and said that this meant that she was permanently his woman. She came to work bra-less and flirted outrageously. Soon, he restarted the affair. Ecstatic, she sent him handwritten poems and cards and letters, the hallmarks of a lovelorn teenager rather than the twenty-seven-year-old mother that she actually was.

In January 1983, Steve moved house and the children went back to live with Diane. She told Dave that, if he moved in with her, she'd get a full-time nanny. In the same timeframe she opened her own surrogacy clinic in town. (This fitted with her image of herself as a potential doctor.) The following month, she asked Dave who he loved best – her or his wife. When he said the latter, Diane became so violent that he finished with her again.

Downs took this incredibly badly and started phoning his home and workplace on a daily basis. Within weeks they had reconciled and he gave her a signal that they were serious by getting a matching tattoo. In April she moved to Springfield, Oregon, on the understanding that he would soon join her there. Her idea was that her parents could babysit for the children – permanently, ideally – and she and Dave could get Springfield postal routes.

But, free of Diane's influence, Dave decided that he wanted to reconcile with his second wife. He began to send back Diane's letters and gifts, marked 'return to sender'. Though her postal job kept her busy during the daytime, she turned to marijuana and alcohol to get through the lonely nights. She returned to Arizona at the end of April, to try to win Dave back, but he said he "didn't want to be a daddy", and that it was over. He drove away before she could create another scene.

She wrote to him, "Do you ache for me in the same way that I ache for you?" On another occasion, she tried to coax him back by stressing how, "the kids are terribly independent and require very little care." It was a sociopathic statement, given that her youngest child was three years old.

For the first half of May, Diane brooded about how she could get her lover back when he so clearly didn't want a readymade family. If only she didn't have the children . . .

Murder

On 19 May 1983, Diane took all three of her offspring – Daniel, aged three, Cheryl, aged seven, and Christie Ann, aged eight – out for a drive in Springfield. She parked in a rural location where she shot the children, and then herself, before disposing of the gun (probably in the adjacent river). But all three children were still alive, so she sat in the car and waited for them to die.

Eventually, another vehicle went past; she realised that she'd have to drive on or it would look suspicious. Driving slowly to the local hospital, she parked and screamed for the nurses, telling them that a bushy-haired stranger had carjacked her, shot her in the arm, shot the children and then fled.

Medics found that Daniel, the toddler, had been shot once, the near-contact wound creating holes in his chest and back. He was crying weakly. Christie, who was close to death, had been shot twice in the chest and once through the right thumb, presumably as she put up her hands to defend herself. She died on the operating table, but surgeons managed to revive her. Shortly afterwards, she had a stroke which left her paralysed. Cheryl, who had been shot twice in the back at point-blank range, was dead on arrival and could not be revived. Medics were surprised to find that the wounds had clotted, suggesting that the shootings had occurred much earlier than the children's mother was suggesting, negating her claim that she'd driven swiftly to the hospital. Her own wound to her left forearm had broken the limb, but she'd been able to drive with her right hand.

Detectives arrived, by which time Diane had been told that Cheryl was dying (though of course she'd been dead on arrival at the hospital). Diane told them not to revive Christie if she too died, in case she'd sustained brain damage. She agreed to go with them to show exactly where the carjacking took place. As they passed her vehicle – a red Nissan Pulsar MX which she'd bought three months before – she said that she hoped it didn't have any bullet holes in it. She remained equally impassive as she showed them where the shootings had taken place. Meanwhile, back at Springfield hospital, her father was equally unemotional as he identified his dead granddaughter, though several of the nurses were in tears.

Diane told detectives that the stranger had stood in the centre of the lane and that she'd stopped the car to help him. He'd then leaned in and shot all four of them, after which she'd pretended to throw her car keys into the lane and he'd stumbled after them. When his back was turned, she'd driven off at speed.

She phoned Dave the following day and told him what had happened, also telling him that she loved him. He expressed his sympathy for the tragedy but warned her to stay away.

Reality check

Meanwhile, nurses noted that Christie exhibited severe anxiety when she was visited by her mother, her heart rate accelerating from 104 to 147. She appeared terrified of Diane.

Detectives were also concerned. It would not have been possible to see the children, curled up in the backseat – or sleeping under a sweater on the floor beside the front passenger seat, in Cheryl's case – from the passenger window, so how had the stranger noticed them? Why hadn't

Diane mentioned that she had access to a .22 Ruger, the murder weapon? Why had that weapon, which her husband confirmed she had borrowed, suddenly disappeared?

They were also aware that Diane's wound could easily have been self-inflicted, and noticed that she had yet to shed a tear for her dead child and the little girl's critically injured siblings. As one detective put it, "Mother's attitude totally fucked," though she told the authorities that Cheryl was "in heaven" and was "probably an angel". They were convinced that Christie could name the killer, but the little girl couldn't speak and was still too weak to write.

Increasingly convinced that Diane Downs had shot all three of her children, and that Christie would ultimately be able to identify her as the killer, the police made sure the little girl always had an armed guard and was never left alone with her mother. Meanwhile, she and her brother Danny, who would never walk again, were transferred into the care of the local authorities.

Police tried to gently question Danny about the shootings, but his eyes filled with tears and he whispered that he wasn't allowed to talk about it. Later, he told nurses, "I can't stand up – my mommy ran over me with the car."

Meanwhile, Christie was slowly opening up to the authorities, admitting that her mother had often slapped her and Cheryl across the face, and had also spanked Danny. Asked who had shot them, she stammered, "I think . . . I think Mom." She had frequent nightmares, still had great difficulty in speaking and never asked to see her mother. And yet, when asked to write down the names of people she loved, Diane topped the list.

The investigation continues

By now, Diane had told detectives that she'd seen the bushy-haired stranger before and that he'd used her name, so it couldn't have been a random shooting. She added that her ex-husband or Dave's wife might have hired someone to kill her and the kids.

Detectives pointed out how bizarre it was that the man had managed to shoot three little children in the centre of their bodies, despite their being in a darkened car, and yet had only shot Diane, the largest and closest body, in the arm. She then alleged that she knew who the killer was, and that he had deliberately tried to kill the children in order to devastate her. On another occasion she said that there were two men present who were wearing ski masks, and that she'd pulled one of the masks off. Later, she decided that this version of events was only a dream.

Incredibly, she deliberately got pregnant for the sixth time, seducing a casual boyfriend at her most fertile time of the month. She would later tell author Ann Rule (who wrote an impressively-detailed book about the case, *Small Sacrifices*), "for nine months I had love again . . . Someone I could love who was with me." She had somehow blotted out the fact that she was so bad at actual motherhood that her children were emotionally and physically neglected, and that she'd attempted to take all three of their lives. She and her parents also placed a bizarre birthday poem for Cheryl in the local paper, writing, "Jesus loved you . . . he took you to heaven."

Fortunately, by now Christie was beginning to heal emotionally and was able to confront the reality that her mother had shot her and her siblings. Asked to play the role of her mother in a reconstruction, she stood outside the car and pointed her finger at the dolls representing herself, her brother and her sister. After pretending to shoot them, she burst into tears.

Trial

On 28 February 1984, Diane was arrested for murder and attempted murder. She pleaded not guilty to all charges and was remanded in custody.

At the Lane County Courthouse the jury heard Diane's version of events, which the prosecution swiftly demolished. The defence said that Diane had been molested by her father and that this had changed her ability to connect with people; the jury shouldn't be misled by her endless talking and fixed smile.

Prosecutors noted that it had taken her over twenty minutes to drive the four-mile journey to the hospital, yet she'd said that she'd sped all the way.

Christie, her arm still paralysed, took the stand weeping and admitted that her mother had shot Cheryl. Asked what had happened next, she said that Diane had shot Danny, then gone to the back of the seat and . . .

She broke down at this point and the prosecutor gently asked her, "Who shot you?" Christie replied, "My mom." When she admitted that she still loved her mother, the entire courtroom – including the usually dry-eyed Diane – was in tears.

Taking the stand, Diane Downs said that her father had never let her cry, and that she'd learned not to show emotion. She spoke about his sexually molesting her when she was twelve, and said that she hadn't told anyone until she turned sixteen.

She denied that the children had been a barrier to her relationship with Dave – but the prosecution produced a letter in which she'd told him, "The nanny will take responsibility for most of the kids' spare time."

Diane now told the court that a deity might have wanted the children dead in order to punish her, because Baptists should put "God first", yet she'd put her children first. (In reality, she'd always put herself and her boyfriends first.) She also expressed faith that, "God will make Danny walk again."

Diane had told detectives that the shooter stood outside the car and was only five foot eight – but he'd have needed arms like an orangutan in order to shoot the children at almost point-blank range. Christie's version, that their mother had shot them from inside the vehicle, made much more sense. Diane had the motive, a weapon identical to the murder weapon, and the opportunity. She'd arranged for the shooting to take place next to the river so that she could immediately dispose of the gun. Then, realising that the children were still breathing and with no means to finish them off, she'd driven at a snail's pace to the hospital and told the doctors not to artificially resuscitate them.

The prosecution said that Diane had failed at everything – marriage, motherhood, her attempts to become a doctor, her efforts to start her own surrogacy clinic. She'd seen the prospect of a childfree life with Dave as a new start. When that had failed she'd deliberately become pregnant, trying to recreate herself as the ideal mother. Diane shook her head at the accusations whilst caressing her swollen stomach again and again, still using impending motherhood as collateral.

The jury were out for twenty-two hours, then returned with two guilty verdicts for attempted murder and one for murder. Diane smiled and said that the verdicts were a surprise. Ten days later she gave birth to a daughter, who was immediately given up for adoption. Strangely, she asked that her own parents be allowed to adopt the infant – but why give a girl baby to the father whom she claimed had molested her as a child?

At her sentencing, she told the judge that she would serve her time and then track down the "bushy-haired stranger" who had maimed and killed her children. The judge sentenced her to life plus fifty years, adding, "The Court hopes that the defendant will never again be free."

After the trial, one of the prosecutors who had become close to Christie and Danny, and who admired their courage, adopted them.

Prison

During her first few months in Oregon State Women's Correctional Centre, Diane received dozens of letters from male prisoners. Still a fantasist, she said that she planned to become a teacher or a counsellor for teenagers, and that she'd be paroled in five to seven years. Instead, she had to settle for working in the prison kitchen, a coveted job but still far from glamorous. But she did successfully study for an arts diploma, graduating at age thirty-one.

The following month – on 11 July 1987 – she clambered onto a picnic table in the penitentiary grounds and threw herself onto and over the perimeter fence. Amazingly, the armed guards didn't see her. The alarm went off, but as it was often activated by birds or strong winds no one investigated immediately. Half an hour elapsed before they realised Diane had gone.

Meanwhile, the attractive killer had hitched a lift for a mere half-mile and moved into a rundown apartment owned by another prisoner's husband. She spent the next few days frantically having sex with him, desperate to become pregnant again. On 21 July, police arrested her without incident. She said that she'd escaped in order to track down her children's killer, whom she now claimed was an Indian called Samasum Timchuck.

On her return, Diane pleaded not guilty to escaping and was sentenced to an additional five years. An ongoing security risk, she was transferred to Clinton, a New Jersey high-security prison.

Diane Downs will become eligible for parole in 2014. Meanwhile, she has retained her health and enjoyed a sexual relationship with a prison guard. She is currently housed in the Valley Prison for Women, Chowchilla, California. Her surviving children, aided by their kind and compassionate adoptive parents, have worked hard to overcome their disabilities and both graduated from college. Christie married and had a son in 2005, whilst Danny, who remains partially paralysed due to the bullet which entered his back, has become a computer specialist. Cheryl was cremated and her ashes were scattered in Arizona.

Chillingly, both Diane Downs and Susan Smith continue to express the desire to have further children.

CHAPTER FIVE

THE IGNORED

The mothers in the previous chapter wanted to return to the single life and deliberately killed their children in order to do so. Those in the following cases also desired their independence and partied as if their babies didn't exist, leaving them to die of gross neglect.

SABRINA ROSS

A former teenage prostitute, Sabrina Ross had a drug problem for most of her adult life. In her late twenties she gave birth to a son, Rio, who was born with a methadone dependency. She lived with him in a flat in Bristol, England, and promised social services that she'd beat her addiction if they would allow her to retain custody.

But Ross regularly smoked crack cocaine in front of the baby and would pass out for two hours at a stretch, leaving him uncared for. When he learned to crawl he would explore the flat, and she once found him clutching an empty methadone bottle. She would later admit to police that she sometimes forgot to put the cap back on the bottles after taking some of the liquid heroin substitute.

One evening in July 2007 she went out three times to buy drugs, leaving fourteen-month-old Rio alone for a total of nine hours. During that fatal evening, she shared sixteen rocks of crack cocaine and two heroin wraps with a friend.

The following day she found Rio in his cot, clutching a Winnie the

Pooh toy. He was cold and stiff and had been dead for several hours. When autopsied, his body was found to contain methadone, morphine and cocaine.

On 27 June 2008, Sabrina Ross – her face pitted with the acne of the typical drug addict – pleaded guilty to manslaughter at Bristol Crown Court. Mr Justice Roderick Evans told her, "Rio was inhaling class A drugs and there is reason to believe he ingested methadone. It was gross neglect that ended his life. Your child looked to you for protection and you breached that trust. No term of imprisonment can give Rio his life back." Ross wept as she was sentenced to five years. She has another baby which has been taken into care, though its age and gender have been withheld from the public to protect its identity.

In July 2008, a report on behalf of Bristol Safeguarding Children Board said that Rio's death was "clearly avoidable". It noted that individual agencies should have shared information about Sabrina Ross.

JENNIE BAIN DUCKER

A learning-disabled student with a poor attention span, Jennie dropped out of high school in Tennessee, USA. By sixteen she was married and pregnant, but she miscarried and the marriage broke up. At eighteen, she married for the second time and occasionally worked in a factory and in a restaurant, but she was sacked from the latter for often failing to show up for her shift.

By now she was exhibiting signs of manic depression, staying awake for several days then collapsing with exhaustion. She also made several suicide attempts during this time.

By twenty, she'd given birth to two sons – Devin and Dustin – and split up from their father. She hated to be alone, and would drive around looking for friends or acquaintances to keep her company. At one stage she hired a babysitter for her children and then didn't return home for twenty-five hours.

All-night party

On 6 June 1995, Jennie spent part of the day with one of her boyfriends, his child and her children. She returned home with her sons but went out again in the early hours of the morning, having decided to spend some time with another boyfriend in his room at the Holiday Inn.

She drove to the motel with her two sons and left them strapped in the locked car, clutching bottles of milk for sustenance. Dustin was a year old whilst Devin was twenty-three months.

For the next couple of hours, Jennie, her boyfriend and two of his friends partied. She drank double the legal driving limit before falling asleep at around 5am. As the young mother continued to sleep, the morning sun rose and the car got hotter and hotter. By midday, when she awoke, the temperature in the car was 128 degrees and the boys had cooked to death.

In court, she claimed that she had planned to speak to her boyfriend about their relationship and then leave, that she hadn't wanted to party. But her boyfriend's buddies disputed this, saying that she hadn't told them that her children were locked in the car outside. She also stated that she had periodically checked on her sons by looking down at the car from the motel room's second-floor balcony – but, as the car had tinted windows, it would have been impossible for her to see any signs of distress.

She was originally charged with first-degree murder, but this was later reduced to the charge of aggravated child abuse. The judge described her behaviour at the trial as "hostile", and she was sentenced to eighteen years with the proviso that she'd become eligible for parole after six.

CHAPTER SIX

MURDER-SUICIDE

Suicide is the most frequent cause of death amongst young mothers, a percentage of who also murder their children. (Twenty-eight percent commit suicide, the rest dying of various pregnancy and post-natal complications such as pre-eclampsia and haemorrhaging.) Often the motivation is pure, with the woman believing she is taking the child or children to 'a better place'. These mothers are often suffering from puerperal psychosis, an extreme form of post-natal depression. Two women in a thousand are sufferers, and those with a previous psychiatric history are more susceptible.

SUSAN TALBY

A nurse by profession, Susan and her salesman husband Richard married at St Oswald's Catholic Church in Peterborough, UK, in 1999. Their first son, Joseph, was born in April 2002, followed by Paul in September 2004. After Paul's birth Susan suffered from post-natal depression, but appeared to have made a good recovery and went to work at a branch of the fashion store Next. The family lived in a semidetached house in Peterborough's desirable Werrington village. Susan regularly visited her mother and brother who lived nearby. The children also saw Richard's parents most weekends and sometimes stayed with them for several days. The little boys played football with their dad and with neighbourhood children. In short, Susan had a good support system in the community.

In late February 2007, Richard prepared to leave on a business trip. His last memories relating to his family would be of happy domesticity, as his wife was playing Scrabble with four-year-old Joe whilst Paul, two, tucked into a sausage roll.

Familicide

Some time later, Susan, aged forty-one, wrote a suicide note. She suffocated the children whilst they slept, then went to the landing and hanged herself.

When Richard returned he found the bodies. Distraught, he made herculean efforts to revive them but it was too late. The thirty-eight-year-old was comforted by neighbours and relatives. Police said that they were not treating the deaths as suspicious, that it was clearly a murder-suicide.

The following month, Richard Talby released photographs of a smiling Susan with the children, explaining that he wanted people to remember them in happier times. He paid tribute to his wife, recalling the many good times that they had shared. "I loved Sue, Joe and Paul with all my heart," he testified.

DAKSHA EMSON

Daksha was born in Tanzania in 1966, the eldest daughter of a traditional Indian couple. When she was four they moved to India, emigrating later to England when she was nine.

Daksha was a beautiful child who did very well at school, but felt different to the rest of her classmates in London. At eighteen, whilst attending medical school, she attempted suicide for the first time. She was diagnosed with depression but later displayed signs of mania, whereupon her diagnosis was changed to bipolar affective disorder (manic depression) and she was treated with Lithium and Prozac. She stabilised on the drugs, graduated with honours and began studying to become a consultant psychiatrist, gaining an MRCPsych and working in Guy's and St Thomas's Hospitals. In 1991, she married David, a fellow psychiatrist.

When she wanted to have a baby, Daksha discontinued her medication for fear that it would harm the foetus. In July 2000, the thirty-four-year-old gave birth to a daughter, Freya. But, though she initially bonded with the infant and referred to her as 'precious', she became increasingly depressed. She also felt upset and isolated after her father fell out with her husband and refused to visit her home again.

Clinical depression

Aware of the stigma of mental illness, Daksha told no one about the full extent of her affliction. She kept a diary in which she wrote, "Feel flat all the time . . . Feel useless as a wife, as a mother, as a woman. See no hope for the future . . . I'm a useless mother. I'm no good."

She was due to resume her course of antidepressants on 10 October, but on the 9th, when Freya was three months old, she stabbed the baby and herself at her Newham home. The wounds did not prove fatal, but she then doused them both with a flammable liquid and set them alight. The three-month-old died at the scene but Dr Emson was rushed to the burns unit where she eventually expired, without regaining consciousness, on 27 October 2000. The murder-suicide was later described as a psychotic episode. A subsequent enquiry showed that the east London borough of Newham did not have a perinatal psychiatric service, suggesting that this service become available for all local mothers. Daksha's husband later said she had "taken the baby back to God".

Culture clash

It's not only post-natal depression which can make a woman kill her children and herself. Sometimes the stresses come from external factors – everything from financial problems to marital difficulties. Young Asian women who have been raised in Britain also face the culture clash between their Western ambitions and the traditional demands of their extended families. Torn between two very different cultures and believing in an afterlife, they may see familicide as the only answer – the suicide rate among young Asian women is almost three times the national average.

NAVJEET SIDHU

Navjeet was raised in Southall, close to west London, and grew into a competent and happy young woman. In 1998 she landed a job as a receptionist at the Asian station Sunrise Radio, where her colleagues found her to be assertive and cheerful. That same year she had an arranged marriage to Manjit Sidhu, who had been born in India. Some of her friends thought that the marriage was unhappy, but the couple had a daughter and a son together and both parents doted on them. They set up home in Greenford, a nearby west London suburb, where for a time Navjeet's mother lived with them. Manjit worked for the Post Office whilst Navjeet continued her reception work with Sunrise.

But Navjeet never fully recovered from the birth of her second child, Aman Raj, in 2003. (Aman is the Punjabi word for 'peace'.) The following year she became a full-time housewife and seemed driven to be the perfect mother, always taking her offspring to the park and to play centres. She seemed to find it difficult to relax.

In January 2005 Navjeet went to India to spend time with her relatives and, when she returned to London, she was very quiet. Friends noticed that her unhappiness had deepened but she would not say what was on her mind. She spoke to a former colleague who got the impression that she was somewhat isolated and lonely. Another noticed that she looked depressed and worn-down. Her GP had given her tranquillisers for depression, but apparently there was a breakdown in communication between doctors and social workers regarding her case.

In early summer 2005, Navjeet confided in a friend that she was pregnant for the third time and unsure if she could cope with three young children. She was also worried about the family's finances.

Murder-suicide

In July 2005, Navjeet's medication was changed without explanation to a different type of antidepressant. On 31 August she phoned her husband and told him that she was leaving him, taking the children and "going far, far away". Distraught, Manjit left his work and drove around the neighbourhood, searching for her. Meanwhile, the twenty-seven-year-old mother, by now four months pregnant, took a bus to Southall train station. She pushed twenty-three-month-old Aman in his pram whilst five-year-old Simran held her hand.

Navjeet was seen at the station mid-morning, hanging about on a section of the platform deemed out of bounds to the public. A concerned employee asked what she was doing and she replied calmly that she was showing her children the fast trains.

The young mother left the area at his insistence but returned at 1pm, when he'd gone. Holding both children she jumped in front of the Heathrow Express train, which was moving at 100mph. The horrified driver saw her but could not brake in time. Navjeet and her daughter died instantly, but Aman, though terribly injured, initially survived.

Manjit had seen his wife re-enter the station at lunchtime and had driven around trying to find a parking space for his BMW. He finally parked and raced onto the platform, only to find his wife and daughter dead, and his baby son being tended to on the tracks. But Aman had been badly crushed. Two hours later he died of his injuries.

The devastated man later issued a statement to his deceased wife and children: "I love you with all my heart and I know that one day we will be together forever."

Further tragedy

Unfortunately, Navjeet's mother, Satwant Kaur Sodhi, never got over her daughter's death and returned repeatedly to Southall station, the scene of the murder-suicide. She'd stand for hours and cry until concerned friends found her and brought her home. On the morning of Tuesday 21 February 2006, the fifty-six-year-old went to the station and threw herself under the Bristol to Paddington train which was travelling at 95mph. She died instantly. It was later reported that her son-in-law, Navjeet's husband, was also suffering from depression and had returned to India.

Intolerable isolation

Many new mothers feel isolated, especially if they have to live on sink estates with little money and poor access to inexpensive transport. But a walk to a nearby community centre or branch library can provide a much-needed break from home. Mother-and-toddler groups provide an opportunity for interaction with other women. The Samaritans are also on hand, operating a twenty-four-hour service that anyone who is lonely or distressed can call.

Unfortunately, women who speak no English cannot avail themselves of such services, and their isolation – whenever their bilingual husband is at work – is total. This level of loneliness often leads to mental illness, with occasionally fatal results . . .

MUSAMAT MUMTAHANA

Musamat was born in Bangladesh in 1984. Nothing is known of her early life, but by 2006 she was living in Birmingham, UK, with her husband, Shuhal Miah, and their sons, two-year-old Raheem and one-year-old Nahim. Both boys had been born in Birmingham. The young mother was very isolated as she didn't speak English. On the rare occasions when she went out she wore a burkha, which made it difficult for the neighbours to get to know her; though she was only twenty-two, they thought that she was pushing thirty. Her life revolved around caring for the children in the family's recently-renovated, three-storey, semidetached house.

Shuhal, her sociable twenty-six-year-old husband, spoke excellent English and was well-liked in the neighbourhood. As a businessman he often worked long hours. But Musamat began to crack under the strain of being alone, and, in mid September 2006, a neighbour heard screaming coming from her Handsworth residence. The neighbour considered calling the police, but the screaming stopped and she decided not to intervene.

On Wednesday 4 October 2006, Shuhal returned from work shortly before 9pm. Unusually, Musamat didn't let him in. A neighbour helped him gain access to the residence, where he found that she had hanged both of their infant sons and then herself. Police took him, shocked and clutching a baby blanket, to stay with relatives. He later issued a statement, saying, "I have suffered the most tragic loss that anyone could imagine, this being the deaths of my wife and my two beautiful children." He added, "My wife was the most beautiful, gentle person and my two beautiful sons were my pride and joy who had their whole world to live for. Sadly, this is now not to be."

DR SHIRLEY JANE TURNER

Though women regularly kill both their children and themselves, it's virtually unknown for them to murder their boyfriend or husband during the same bout of self-destructiveness. But Shirley Turner – who divided her time between America and Canada – represents a weird variant of this. She murdered her boyfriend before she realised that she was carrying his baby; then, when their son was thirteen months old, she killed the child and herself.

Early unhappiness

Shirley Turner was born in Kansas in January 1961 to an American father and a Canadian mother. Her parents separated when she was seven and her mother took her to live in Newfoundland, Canada. They were reliant on welfare and desperately poor. Mother and daughter were not close, but Shirley found solace in her studies as she had a good memory and a high IQ.

Two failed marriages

She gained top qualifications at school and did equally well studying chemistry at university. But, in her third year, she was so desperate for love that she dropped out to get married. The couple had a son in 1982 and a daughter in 1985. But Shirley was increasingly unstable, and the relationship ended in divorce in 1988. She remarried and had a daughter with husband number two in 1990, but, by the following year, that marriage had also ended. The father retained custody of their child.

Two years later, her older children went to live with their father and Shirley returned to her studies, beginning medical school in Newfoundland in 1993. She was so confrontational – at times hysterical – that one of her lecturers refused ever to be alone with her. But she was an exceptional student who graduated with honours and became a family doctor, albeit not a particularly popular one.

Unfortunately, her love life remained erratic. She hit one boyfriend in the face after he broke up with her in the spring of 1999. Thereafter, she phoned him so often that he contacted the police. But the calls continued, and in some of them she whispered, "You will die." He moved from Newfoundland to Philadelphia for work purposes, whereupon Shirley took a plane to his new hometown and hired a rental car from which she spied on him for the next two days. She then took a non-fatal overdose of sleeping pills and climbed the three flights of stairs to his flat, punching each step with both hands and leaving a trail of blood. He was out, so she sat in the corridor writing letters to him in which she stressed that she wasn't evil, but that she wanted to be cremated and needed him to return her rental car. He came home with his flatmate and found her, sleepy but conscious. She was taken to hospital and released the following day.

In the summer of 1999, thirty-eight-year-old Shirley became friends with a doctor who was twelve years her junior, Andrew David Bagby. The couple met in Newfoundland, though he later relocated to Latrobe, Pennsylvania, and she to Council Bluffs, Iowa, both in the US. She told him of her two failed marriages and three children, assuring him that she didn't want a serious commitment – just a good social life and some fun. But, despite her protestations that she only wanted a casual fling, Shirley was so needy that she immediately fell in love.

In September the couple attended a Bagby family wedding and stayed with his parents in California. She was watching television with them when the terrorist attacks on the Twin Towers were televised. Shirley remained indifferent to the horrific loss of life, ignoring the carnage and continuing to talk about the telephone service which she'd arranged for her new apartment. She behaved irrationally whenever she went out with Andrew and his friends, becoming enraged if they didn't like her choice of bar or if he went someplace without telling her first. After she caused a scene when presented with a large bill in a restaurant, his friends flatly told Andrew she was 'nuts'.

By mid-2001 Andrew had already tried to end the relationship, but she kept calling him and turning up at his Pennsylvania apartment. On 20 October that year, he took her to another family wedding and slept with her. It was an entirely wrong signal to send to someone whom he no longer wanted in his life. Three days later he told a friend that he and Shirley had once again broken up, and that he was now dating a radiographer.

Andrew's murder

On Monday 5 November, Shirley Turner arrived unexpectedly at Andrew Bagby's Pennsylvania apartment as he was getting ready for his 7.30am hospital shift. He left her in the flat, having agreed to meet her after work at 5.30pm, before she returned home. Friends suggested that he shouldn't meet her alone, but he said that he'd be fine. Meanwhile, Shirley phoned her practice nurse and lied about her whereabouts, telling the woman that she was in bed in Iowa with a migraine and wouldn't be coming in to work.

Late that afternoon, she met Andrew in the parking lot of Keystone State Park. When he got out of his vehicle, she shot him once in the chest and once in the cheek. He fell forward onto his face, badly injured, and she fired the next two shots at his rectum. Bending down, she shot him in the back of the head. She tried to shoot him again but the gun was empty, so she settled for kicking him in the face. Shirley then drove back to Iowa, dumping the gun en route, and began to phone Andrew's family and friends, asking if they'd heard from him. She endeavoured to sound like a concerned lover rather than a murderess.

Questioned

Andrew's body was found at 6am on the following morning. His belongings were untouched, so it was clear that this wasn't a robbery. The shots to the face and the rectum suggested that the killer knew the victim and wanted to humiliate him.

Detectives were immediately suspicious of Shirley. She told them that she and Andrew were in love, yet several of his friends and relatives said that, on the Monday that he died, he'd told them she was a "psychotic bitch" and that he'd been increasingly determined to extricate himself from the relationship. The female doctor admitted to having a .22 calibre pistol and said that it must be in her car; yet, five hours later, she phoned the police and reported the weapon missing. Similarly damning, Shirley's pistol often malfunctioned and an unspent casing had been found next to Andrew's corpse.

She said that she had been in bed, suffering from a migraine, in Iowa at the time of the murder, but her mobile phone records showed that she'd made calls from Pennsylvania. The police also found that she had a history of harassing ex-boyfriends and had lost custody of all three of her children, because of her emotional coldness.

A week after the murder, as detectives continued to put together a case against her, she fled back to Canada. Later that same month she found that she was expecting Andrew's child.

In Canada, Shirley received treatment for anxiety and depression from a psychiatrist who she had previously worked for. When she was arrested, he paid her surety money and she was let out on bail, pending a hearing regarding her extradition to the US on the murder charge. Still extremely disturbed, she turned up at the home of Andrew's ex-fiancée, Heather, and accused her of committing the murder. When her own twelve-year-old daughter arrived for a short access visit, she refused to send her back.

Meanwhile, Andrew's parents were so determined to support their future grandchild that they gave up their jobs in California and relocated to Canada. They forced themselves to be civil towards Shirley whenever she called. On 18 July 2002 she gave birth to a baby boy, calling him Zachary Andrew Turner. The Bagbys paid for his care, as Shirley wasn't working, and babysat for him as often as possible – hoping to get full custody when his mother went to jail.

On 14 November, Shirley's order of committal was finally heard in a Newfoundland court and she was sent to a women's prison. The Bagbys took Zachary to visit her every weekend, as stipulated by the court order. But in January she was bailed and took the baby back. By now, it was clear that Zachary preferred being with his grandmother, Kate Bagby, rather than with his mother, a fact that wasn't lost on Shirley. She often changed her mind at the last minute about their babysitting arrangements and said that he'd have to be fostered if extradition went ahead, and she was imprisoned in the USA.

In mid-July, Shirley met a medical technician in a pub and quickly went to bed with him. Her mood darkened at Zachary's first birthday party when he chose to cling to his grandma over her. She told him that, now that he was one year old, he couldn't expect to be coddled forever and that it was time he became more independent. Then she phoned a friend and wept, complaining childishly, "He likes her more than me."

Fatal attraction

Later that month, Shirley's boyfriend finished with her and she went into bunny-boiler mode – phoning him at all hours of the day and night. She told him that she was pregnant, then that she'd had an abortion. A few days later she stated that she hadn't had an abortion after all, but a miscarriage. Later still, she claimed that the miscarriage was a false alarm and she was continuing with the pregnancy.

He told her to stop calling, whereupon she appeared to retreat into a fantasy world. She told a friend that she and her new man were working things out.

Late on Sunday 17 August 2003, she drove to his house with Zachary in the backseat. His vehicle was parked in the driveway and she pushed a bloody tampon under one of the wheels, presumably her way of telling him that the pregnancy was a false alarm. She also lodged two photos under another wheel, one of herself with Zachary and another of her in bra and briefs. Leaving her boyfriend's house – and probably en route to his workplace – she ran her car into a ditch.

At this point, she gave the baby several of her tranquillisers and walked to the coast, following the road until she reached a marina. At 3am she jumped into the North Atlantic ocean, clutching her thirteen-month-old child. Their bodies were washed up on Manuels Beach the following day.

Changing the law

By now the Bagbys – having lost both their beloved son and grandson – were so distraught that they could barely function. But they regrouped, and David wrote a book, *Dance with the Devil*, about the failures of the Canadian judicial system. He now speaks out for victims' rights.

The couple also helped set up an American scholarship – the Dr Andrew Bagby Family Medicine Scholarship Fund – in their son's name, which allows medical students to spend a month working with family doctors in a clinical setting. Two years later, a similar fund was established in Newfoundland, Canada.

SUSAN BIANCARDI

After killing her sixteen-year-old daughter and attempting to kill her fourteen-year-old, Susan turned the gun on herself but it jammed. Prior to the shooting, she hadn't seriously hurt or neglected her children, she wasn't a Munchausen's-by-proxy mother and didn't have a hormonal or financial reason to kill them. As such, she fits best into the murder-suicide category where a mixture of long-term unhappiness, psychiatric problems and external events conspire to convince the woman that she and her offspring would be better off dead.

Early difficulties

Susan Biancardi married in 1970, and in 1972 moved with her husband, Philip, to Beverly, Massachusetts. She became clinically depressed during her first pregnancy in 1974, which resulted in a beautiful baby girl whom she christened Marcia. Two years later she gave birth to another equally attractive child, Audrey. The family were regularly seen around the neighbourhood, going out on walks together or to the icecream parlour. Susan even helped the local children put on a backyard play, making all of the costumes on her sewing machine.

Though she went on to suffer intermittently from depression, and sometimes seemed to be living off her nerves, she was a good mother to her children when they were young. She paid for them to have music and dancing lessons, and encouraged them to participate in sports and drama. Later, she was very proud when Marcia made the cheerleading team.

Susan was also a good worker at the local town hall, where she was head clerk in the assessor's office. She kept excellent records, gave helpful tax advice and was especially attentive towards elderly visitors. She brought in home-baked cookies for her colleagues on a regular basis and kept them up-to-date with her daughters' accomplishments. She also taught at the local Sunday school.

But behind the Superwoman image was an increasingly unhappy wife. In 1984 Susan filed for divorce from Philip, citing "cruel and abusive treatment". She later changed her mind and reunited with him.

In 1987, thirteen-year-old Marcia began dating an older boy of whom Philip and Susan disapproved. This led to numerous family altercations. The following year, Susan filed a complaint against the youth, alleging that he'd raped her daughter and contributed to the delinquency of a minor. The charges were investigated and dismissed. But Marcia loved the boy and continued to see him throughout the rest of the 1980s, hoping that her parents wouldn't find out.

Disturbed behaviour

Meanwhile, Susan's life increasingly revolved around religion and she often attended the Second Congregational Church in Beverly, taking her daughters to lengthy prayer sessions. But this couldn't quell the deep sadness inside her, and she turned to drink, the alcohol clashing with the tranquillisers that she was already on. She began to see two psychiatrists and told them that she was exhausted, but couldn't sleep.

All three of the women in the Biancardi household were becoming increasingly disturbed, with both girls having terrible nightmares. 'Little Audrey', as Susan called her, aged fourteen, often slept in the same bed as her mother whilst her father was working nights. Their mother was always phoning the girls to check up on them.

Marcia was becoming a young woman who needed an increasing level of independence, the right to make her own choices. Yet when her mother found out that she was still seeing her boyfriend, she was incensed. She fell into a deep depression, stopped eating and lost over two stone in weight. Her marital troubles continued and Philip left their bed, sleeping alone in the attic. Susan told a friend that she was going to leave him and take the girls.

It was clear by now that she favoured her younger daughter, Audrey, who was surprisingly mature for her age and very much the family peacemaker. When Susan and Marcia came to blows it was the fourteen-year-old who stepped between them to prevent anyone getting hurt.

Susan admitted to a relative that she now hated Marcia. In January 1990 she slapped the teenager across the face and threw her out of the house, for refusing to relinquish the phone to her sister. Schoolfriends noticed that Marcia was deeply unhappy, though she tried to hide this with bright chatter and by practising with the hockey cheerleading team. She also sang in the school choir.

On 11 February 1990 Susan cancelled the sixteen-year-old's beloved riding lessons, telling her instructor that Marcia had a bad attitude. She asked the riding school to sell the teenager's riding boots and hat, saying that she no longer needed them. But on the 13th she bought each of the girls a bunch of roses and helped them wrap Valentine's Day gifts, to take to their friends at school the following day.

Murder and attempted suicide

That same night, Susan was as insomniacal as ever. At midnight she left her bed, which she was sharing with Audrey, and walked up the stairs to the attic, where she took her husband's sixteen-gauge bolt-action shotgun from its usual storage space behind a bureau. She walked back down the stairs and into Marcia's room, put a blanket over the muzzle and held it three inches from her sleeping daughter. Susan then shot the sixteen-year-old through the torso and hurried back to her room.

Marcia, who was naked, staggered from the bed and began to scream that there was blood everywhere. Audrey woke up and Susan told her to stay where she was, whilst she returned to Marcia's bedroom. Marcia yelled, "Mother, stop!" and Audrey raced down the hall to find her sister, covered in what she thought was tomato ketchup. Susan told her that Marcia had had a bad dream, and to go back to bed.

Audrey went back to bed as ordered, unaware that she'd just witnessed a St Valentine's Day massacre. Seconds later, Susan approached the bed and pressed the muzzle of the gun into Audrey's side, pulling the trigger. But the shotgun jammed and Audrey managed to push it away. She noticed that her mother's eyes were wide with fright; jumping out of bed, she raced back to her sister's room to find Marcia slumped against the door, moaning. She had lost a lot of blood.

The fourteen-year-old raced down the hall to call the police but saw her mother in the bathroom, pointing the gun at her own stomach. She pulled the trigger, but again the shotgun misfired. Susan warned Audrey not to tell the truth about what happened to her sister. When police arrived, Susan told them that Marcia had committed suicide.

The police were suspicious, as the sixteen-year-old had phoned her best friend that night and made plans to go dancing – hardly the actions of a girl who was suicidal. They also found out that Susan had previously slapped her oldest daughter and claimed to hate her, but couldn't prove that this hatred had resulted in murder. Susan's friends believed her version of events and she returned to her old life, buoyed up with a heavy intake of alcohol.

For the next year, Little Audrey kept the terrible secret. But then she broke down, walked into a police station and told them what had happened that fateful night. Weeping, she begged them to get psychiatric help for Susan, describing her as "a good mother".

Drink-driving

On bail, whilst awaiting trial, Susan continued to drink and was arrested for drunken driving. She later said that people looked at her as if she were a monster, and that she felt monstrous at the time. On reflection, however, she knew that she was very ill.

Trial

At Essex County Superior Court in March 1992, Biancardi's defence team claimed that she was psychotic at the time of the killing, though the prosecution noted that she'd been lucid enough to lie to the police about Marcia committing suicide. The defence also said that she was now suffering from psychogenic amnesia, unable to remember the homicide.

Audrey spoke up for her mother, saying that illness had made Susan Biancardi fire the fatal shot, and that she had no control over her actions. She pleaded with the judge to give her homicidal mother psychiatric treatment rather than imprisonment. But in first-degree murder cases Massachusetts law doesn't allow for judicial input at the sentencing stage, so Biancardi was sentenced to life in prison without parole. She began to serve out her sentence in Framingham State Prison, often on the psychiatric unit.

Her husband Philip understandably divorced her, citing "irretrievable breakdown". He later remarried.

Second trial

Three years after her trial, Susan's life sentence was overturned by the Supreme Judicial Court, which noted how the original jurors hadn't been told that, if they found her not guilty by reason of insanity, she would have been sent to a psychiatric facility rather than freed immediately. She was granted a second trial, but decided to plead guilty to second-degree murder to avoid going through the court system again.

Maternal

As the years passed Susan became a mother figure to many of the younger prisoners in Framingham State Prison, though staff noticed that her idea of motherhood revolved around being in control. They also noted that she found it difficult to handle stress. But Audrey – whilst admitting that she still missed her sister and that her mother had done a terrible thing – continued to love her unconditionally.

Parole request

In January 2007, almost seventeen years after the murder, fifty-nine-year-old Susan Biancardi applied for parole. Audrey supported her application, saying that she was a wonderful mother whom she still loved dearly. An aunt who had been recently widowed said that Susan could come and live with her if she was freed.

During her parole hearing, Biancardi apologised to Audrey, to her ex-husband Philip and to Marcia – the daughter she shot dead. She said that she was sorry for the murder, though she couldn't remember it. She stated that she was now a different person and would never put herself through the type of pressure that she'd put herself through prior to the homicide. She said that she had been diagnosed as bipolar and had been taking her medication consistently for the past seven years. As with all bipolar patients, she was capable of swinging from depression to manic elation. (Psychiatrists tend to disagree as to whether the syndrome has a biological or psychological origin.)

The board discussed her case then voted six to one to turn down her request. They stated that she "continues to struggle with interpersonal relationships and is still developing skills for handling conflict and stress, exactly the conditions that led to the horrific and brutal murder of her daughter." They also noted that she still has significant mental health problems. Susan Biancardi remains in the mental health unit at MCI Framington.

CHAPTER SEVEN
FOR YOUR OWN GOOD

Though leaving bruises on a child can land a parent in court, many mothers and fathers still physically chasten their children. Ill-educated and immature parents are especially likely to do so, assuming that their child is being bad when he does something perfectly natural such as soiling himself or refusing food. When light blows don't bring about the desired results, such parents resort to hitting harder. Physical abuse is the most common cause of childhood homicide.

When children under the age of five are murdered the culprit is most often the mother, with children in their first and second year of life being most at risk. Women who have been raised by unloving or abusive parents – and who have been unable to resolve such conflicts in their past – often grow up to feel incompetent and powerless. As such, they are incapable of coping with a relentlessly crying baby. These women often have a mental illness, ranging from depression to schizophrenia, which may also predispose them to assault their child. Children with health problems are especially at risk.

Left alone for hour after hour with a sobbing infant, a small percentage of these mothers silence their son or daughter permanently, sometimes hitting them with household objects or battering them into the furniture, floor or walls. Babies who die from such acts of physical abuse often have fading bruises and healing fractures, evidence of previous assaults.

A 1973 study by Peter Scott found that over-inhibited mothers were the most dangerous when they eventually lost control. This is delineated in the first case, where a mother shook her baby for the first time with ultimately fatal results.

MARTINA McHATTIE

Martina, who suffered from low self-esteem, had an affair with a co-worker in 2003 and became pregnant. He ended the relationship when she refused to have an abortion. Largely unsupported, as her mother had died and her father lived abroad, she gave birth to Reece in April 2004.

Martina cared for the baby without incident until October, when he began teething and often cried uncontrollably. The young mother would later admit that her stress just built and built. Late in the afternoon on 21 October, she phoned an ambulance and said that the six-month-old was having difficulty breathing. Paramedics arrived at her Wakefield, UK, home to find the baby limp and unresponsive, his lips turning blue. He was taken to Pinderfields Hospital but soon transferred to the intensive care unit at Leeds General Infirmary, where his condition remained critical.

Two days later, Martina swallowed five packets' worth of paracetamol whilst at the hospital, then told a nurse. She was treated in casualty. When asked why she'd overdosed, she told medics that she knew Reece was going to die.

On 24 October her fears came true. At the autopsy, a neurologist found brain swelling, haemorrhaging and bleeding to Reece's eyes, consistent with Shaken Baby Syndrome, and the police were called in. The young mother told them she'd been running a bath when the infant had fallen from the settee and onto the floor, a distance of fifteen inches. They were suspicious as his injuries suggested that he'd been thrown against a hard object, but there was insufficient evidence to prosecute.

Chaotic years
Throughout 2005 and 2006, Martina McHattie remained unstable and guilt-ridden. She self-harmed, overate and again tried to commit

suicide. In July 2007 she engaged in sexual activity with a fourteen-year-old boy. That same year, she admitted to police that she had shaken Reece in order to make him stop crying, explaining that her inability to soothe him had made her feel inadequate.

Court

At Leeds Crown Court in May 2008, she pleaded guilty to manslaughter and said that she had caused her son's death because she was unable to cope. The defence explained that she had been a perfect mother prior to shaking the child.

The judge, Peter Collier, took pity on her, saying, "I am satisfied that you will live with the knowledge and guilt every day of your life and I also know it's very unlikely you will be able to bring up a child of your own." He sentenced her to twelve months, suspended for two years with a supervision order.

The twenty-six-year-old returned to court in July 2008 and was given a twenty-six-week prison sentence, suspended for a year, for sexual activity with the fourteen-year-old boy.

TANYA DACRI

Tanya was just nineteen and her husband Philip twenty-one when they had their first child, a daughter, in January 1988. When the baby was six weeks old she was taken to the local hospital in Philadelphia, having almost drowned in the bathtub. Medics found that she was bruised and undernourished, so they alerted social services. The baby was put into foster care and thrived, but was returned to the couple within months under the mistaken belief that babies should always live with their biological parents. The nuclear family was subsequently monitored by child welfare workers for a while.

Creating a second victim

In November 1988 the Dacris had their second child, a son whom they called Zachary. As before, Tanya found that she couldn't stand his crying. She hit him repeatedly – by the time he was a month old, he'd suffered two separate breaks to his collarbone and had five broken ribs.

The abuse continued apace and, on 6 January 1989, she again attacked the infant, leaving him bruised and with a hairline fracture. Unsurprisingly, Zachary's crying intensified. The following day, she drowned him in the bathtub. When her husband phoned her from work, she told him that she'd put an end to the baby's cries.

He came home and found his dead son wrapped in a plastic bag. (His reaction is not on record.) The following night he returned home to find that Tanya had dismembered the infant, cutting him into six pieces with a kitchen knife. She had wrapped each limb and the head in brown paper bags, weighed down with the barbells Philip used to get fit. Deciding to stand by his woman, he drove her to the river and helped her dispose of the grisly packages.

Three days later, Tanya told the police a tale which they initially believed. She said that she'd parked on the outskirts of a busy shopping mall and that two black men had snatched Zachary from her arms. She added that she feared her father had organised the kidnapping, as she'd recently filed sexual abuse charges against him for incestuous acts that had allegedly occurred in the past.

Detectives investigated but could find no one in the car park to corroborate her story. They intensified their questioning of the seemingly-distraught couple. Tanya and Philip would eventually admit what had happened, and told them where to find Zachary's butchered remains.

On 12 January, divers recovered five of the parcels – the final package, containing his torso, washed up two days later. An autopsy showed the extent of the abuse which he'd suffered during his two months of life.

Tanya Dacri pleaded guilty to an open charge of murder, which meant that a lesser verdict of third-degree murder was a possibility. At first it seemed as if she'd be treated compassionately on mental health grounds, with psychiatrists suggesting that she was a borderline personality who had suffered a brief psychotic episode. But when the prior abuse of her daughter – and the earlier blows which Zachary had endured – came to light, the judge found her guilty of first-degree murder and she was sentenced to life in prison without the possibility of parole.

Her husband, who had helped her dispose of Zachary's body and colluded in her kidnapping story, was given nine to twenty-three months in the county jail.

CHAPTER EIGHT
SICK AT HEART

Most hospitals are familiar with the Munchausen's patient, a man or woman who has deliberately made themselves ill in order to enjoy medical attention. Some of these patients will go to extreme lengths to develop symptoms, even ingesting faeces and broken glass.

Rarer, thankfully, is Munchausen's-by-proxy, henceforth abbreviated to MBP, as identified by British paediatrician Sir Roy Meadows in 1977. In MBP, women fabricate or deliberately cause health problems in the children in their care. (Very few such cases are caused by men.) A third of MBP mothers have some form of medical training, such as American children's nurse Genene Jones, who drugged and killed several of her little patients. Others harm their own offspring and persuade medics to perform unnecessary procedures and operations on them.

These mothers, often lonely and isolated, want to be recognised as worthwhile, even important. They mask feelings of low self-esteem and inadequacy by presenting themselves as model parents who rarely leave their child's side. Doctors and nurses are initially impressed by the mother's attempts to research and understand her child's medical problems and her refusal to leave the sickroom for hours at a time.

In reality, the MBP mother is the parent from hell who only pretends to love her offspring. She really views him or her as an object which will bring her closer to the doctors and nurses with whom she craves a relationship.

Though Roy Meadows got an important statistic on Sudden Infant Death Syndrome wrong at the trial of Sally Clark in 1999, he did sterling work for years in protecting children from cruel MBP parents. He has noted MBP as a form of child abuse rather than a mental disorder. Other experts have since backed this up, noting it as a deviant behaviour on a level with burglary. Nevertheless, the American Diagnostic Manual, as used by many US psychiatrists, has listed it as a psychiatric condition since 1980.

It's vital that more doctors become knowledgeable about MBP, as nine percent of victims die and many are left permanently disabled. Moreover, when challenged, some women will stop harming their children. Unfortunately, others move to another part of the country and start the abuse all over again.

TANYA LEIGH REID

Tanya's mother was ill throughout her formative years, so she was partially raised by a devoted older sister. Tanya was accident-prone, and so was no stranger to hospital herself. Shy and slightly overweight, she had occasional fainting spells in her teens and also suffered from stress-related stomach pains. She lived in Dumas, Texas, with her parents and three sisters, and was a choir girl at the local Baptist church.

A couple at her church thought that she'd make the ideal babysitter and so, on 29 October 1974, they invited the seventeen-year-old schoolgirl over to look after their four-month-old son, Scotty, whilst they attended a religious event. Tanya arrived with her homework as the couple left. Shortly afterwards, she phoned her mother to say that the baby had woken from his nap and appeared to have a cold which was making him breathless. Her mother suggested phoning the baby's parents to see if he was on any medication, and Tanya agreed that was what she'd do – but her next call was to the emergency services, explaining that the baby had stopped breathing.

A police officer in the vicinity raced to the house, to find Scotty blue and unresponsive on the couch. He gave the baby mouth-to-mouth resuscitation and Scotty resumed breathing; the child was taken to hospital where he stabilised.

One month later, Tanya was given a Good Neighbour Award from the local Chamber of Commerce for her quick response to Scotty's apnea episode (loss of breathing). The presentation was held at a local restaurant where she photographed for the local paper, which lavished praise on her deed. More than a decade later, she still treasured the thank-you note and gift which Scotty's parents sent.

But Tanya's own life was restricted, as her father forbade his daughters to date the same boy twice. Eventually, she ended up dating her next-door neighbour, Jim Reid. He was several years her senior, a successful but quiet man who was also her parents' friend.

Bernadette's birth

Tanya left school and began to train as a licensed vocational nurse. A month into her training – on 25 November 1977 – she and Jim married, though she'd later admit that she was already having second thoughts, claiming, "Daddy was domineering, then I went into a domineering marriage." Yet instead of seeking solace in the nursing work that she professed to love, she quit and took a job at the factory where Jim was a supervisor. She worked there for just over a year before becoming pregnant. Again, she apparently had fainting spells which ensured that her co-workers made a fuss over her and that her boss allowed her to take early maternity leave.

Bernadette (a pseudonym to protect her identity) was born on 15 October 1980 and was a beautiful, healthy girl. Fortunately, the Reids were living close to Tanya's parents at the time of Bernadette's birth, so the new mother got lots of attention and support. Bernadette was a colicky baby, but otherwise fine.

Morgan's death

By the time the Reids had their second daughter, on 17 May 1983, they had moved to Illinois where Tanya was unemployed and bored. They called the little girl Morgan Renee. The baby appeared healthy, and yet in August she apparently had a seizure. Tanya had her admitted, limp and sweating, to hospital where she swiftly revived.

Over the next few weeks, Morgan was readmitted to the children's ward on an approximately fortnightly basis. The baby would arrive looking blue and breathless but would stabilise quickly in hospital, kept in for observation for several days and allowed home in good health, only to apparently stop breathing once again. Nurses noted that Tanya quickly became frustrated with the baby girl, and once saw her slapping the child on the leg – though she stopped as soon as she realised that she was being observed.

Tanya had struggled to find common ground with other young mothers in the neighbourhood, but now she regaled them with horror stories of what she'd endured with Morgan. She claimed she couldn't leave the baby alone for even a moment in case she died.

In January 1984, the Reids returned to Texas. Tanya spent a week with relatives, during which Morgan thrived. But, shortly after moving into her new home, the baby was rushed to hospital, blue-tinged and unresponsive. She quickly recovered but was kept in from 10-26 January for observation and tests, after which she was sent home with a clean bill of health.

But, on 6 February, the former licensed vocational nurse called the hospital to say that her daughter had endured yet another attack. They raced the baby to intensive care but she was brain-damaged. The hospital reluctantly switched off her life-support. The nine-month-old girl laboured for breath until the following day, then died. Some of the nurses were in tears, but Tanya was dry-eyed.

At the autopsy, the pathologist found bleeding in the baby's skull but wasn't familiar with Shaken Baby Syndrome. The body bore no external injuries, so he wrote that there was no evidence of child abuse. The authorities then determined that this was a Sudden Infant Death Syndrome case, and Morgan was buried at the family plot in Texas.

Matthew's suffering

Tanya continued to tell the regulars at her local church of her loss, claiming that it was God that had "taken an innocent child". Neighbours were surprised at how often she left her surviving daughter, Bernadette, with a babysitter.

Fifteen months after Morgan's death the Reids had a son, Matthew. By now they were living in Illinois and Tanya was once again isolated and bored. Three weeks after his birth, she called paramedics and explained that he'd had an apnea episode and that she'd used her nurse's training to resuscitate him.

Over the next few months she'd claim that he suffered from seizure after seizure. Concerned medics routinely hospitalised the blue-tinged, sweating and panicky baby. Tanya remained at his bedside, talking to doctors, nurses and other patients about her child's condition. The lonely housewife had the sympathy and attention that she craved once more.

It was hard for Tanya to make friends, as the family moved around because of Jim's job. In autumn 1987 they moved to Iowa and she again attempted to befriend other mothers, but her endless chatter and pushy nature were offputting to most of them. She craved adult conversation and talked non-stop to Jim when he got home from a hard day at the office. But Jim was an introvert, who understandably wanted to relax. He later admitted that she was impossible to please and that he only stayed for the sake of the children, whom he adored. He had no inkling that she might be responsible for their health problems, as they only occurred when he was at work and when there were no other witnesses around.

As the months passed, Tanya continued to phone the Iowa emergency services to say that Matthew was having the same breathing difficulties as his late sister. By age two he could only say a couple of words, so he had several home visits by educational specialists. But at two-and-a-half they were able to determine that only his language skills were delayed; his motor and social skills were normal, so the home visits came to an end.

Tanya was enraged and told everyone that her son needed special attention. She had previously told a paediatrician that her deceased daughter, Morgan, had suffered from Fragile X syndrome, a genetic condition usually found in boys. She also spoke at length about the various anti-seizure medications that Matthew was on and seemed more interested in talking about medical intervention than in alleviating her child's distress. Medics noticed that she often tried to keep them talking whilst her toddler son fought for breath.

Within two days of being told that Matthew was functioning normally, Tanya phoned an ambulance to say that he'd stopped breathing and had turned blue. A paramedic entered the house to find her bending over him, apparently giving mouth-to-mouth. His lips were violet, yet the paramedic got him breathing almost immediately.

A fortnight later Tanya phoned the emergency services again, saying that Matthew had had another seizure. This time paramedics arrived to find her apparently giving her son artificial resuscitation, but when they moved her out of the way they found that he was breathing of his own accord.

A terrified child

At the hospital, nurses noted that the little boy seemed afraid of his mother and only ever uttered the words, "Mom go." (A babysitter had noticed that Matthew screamed whenever Tanya was around, yet he was a relaxed, happy child when she wasn't there.) This time, doctors were suspicious and asked her if anyone other than herself had witnessed the apnea episodes. Tanya lied and named several people, saying that she'd give them the address of a doctor who had witnessed an attack. But of course she never did.

On another occasion she carried Matthew into hospital and, oblivious to his cries, started to talk in depth about a possible diagnosis. Doctors noticed that he had small scratches on his face which appeared to have been made by his own nails, as if a pillow or hand had been pushed over his face and he'd tried to pull it away. They were baffled as to how he could have seizures when he was on anti-epileptic medication, and began to question Tanya more closely about the events leading up to Matthew's attacks.

The next time that she called an ambulance, she requested that they take her son to a different hospital. A detective who accompanied paramedics noticed that Tanya was more interested in talking to them than in her son, as he lay gasping for breath on the ground.

The authorities asked to see the autopsy report for Morgan, Tanya's dead daughter. They realised that she'd been shaken or slammed against a surface, so that the small blood vessels leading to her brain had torn and leaked. They now believed that Tanya Reid was an MBP mother, who had murdered her secondborn and might do the same to her third any day.

In March of 1988, Matthew was given to the care of foster parents, and then to Tanya's relatives. He began to catch up developmentally, didn't suffer any more seizures and enjoyed general good health.

Trial

It was February 1989 before Tanya Reid was brought to trial in Iowa for abusing Matthew. Medics testified to his numerous hospitalisations, and how they'd eventually become afraid to send him home. They described how he was so terrified at seeing his mother that he'd scream and race away in the opposite direction. Once she had approached whilst he was sitting in a high chair and he'd tried to flip himself over the back of it.

Doctors noted that the little boy only became ill in the daytime, when his mother was around, or during the specific evenings that his father worked late. The baby monitor showed that he'd never had an apnea episode during the night, when he and the rest of the family were asleep. Most crucially, babies usually stop experiencing apnea by six months, whereas Matthew was still suffering at eighteen months.

Tanya took the stand and suggested that the bleeding around her daughter Morgan's brain could have been caused during resuscitation attempts, but medics rejected the explanation. She was asked if she'd ever had another child stop breathing in her care, other than her own children, and said no. The prosecution then reminded her of how she'd been given a Good Neighbour Award for saving the life of Scotty, the infant that she was babysitting. Tanya muttered that she'd forgotten about the award.

The defence countered that Morgan hadn't died immediately when her life-support machine was switched off. They said that victims of Shaken Baby Syndrome have swollen brains, and die quickly when taken off of a ventilator. They also said that both Morgan and Matthew had slightly abnormal brains, suggesting a congenital defect. A psychologist for the defence said that Tanya's responses to standard psychological tests were normal, and there was no suggestion she was an MBP case. In contrast, five doctors for the prosecution had said that they believed she was committing MBP crimes.

On 28 April 1989, the judge found her guilty of felony child endangerment of Matthew. She wept as she was sentenced to ten years in an Iowa women's prison. Shortly afterwards, Jim divorced her – though he remained in contact – and got custody of both children. He later remarried. Meanwhile, Tanya found love in another woman's arms.

The second trial

In December 1993, Tanya Reid went on trial for Morgan's murder. Again she took the stand in her own defence and again she was found guilty. This time she was sentenced to sixty-two years, with the proviso that she serves twenty before becoming eligible for parole.

But, in February 1995, the appeals court overturned her murder conviction, arguing that the judge had not proved beyond a reasonable doubt that Tanya killed her daughter with her own hands. The prosecution said that they would retry the case.

In 1996 she was retried at a different venue – Lubbock in Texas – before a jury and found guilty. For the next twelve years she remained behind bars, supported by her extended family, although Matthew –

who suffers from permanent hearing loss which he believes is due to his mother's actions – understandably wanted nothing to do with her.

In September 2008 she was paroled and returned to live with her relatives in Texas.

Cruel deception

In October of that year I interviewed top crime author Gregg Olsen, who spoke extensively to Tanya Reid and wrote a book about the case, *Cruel Deception*. Gregg's other best-selling books include *Starvation Heights*, *Abandoned Prayers* and *If Loving You Is Wrong*. More recently, he has ventured into realistic crime fiction with *A Cold Dark Place* and *A Wicked Snow*. His website and blog can be found at www.greggolsen.com.

I started off by asking him why Tanya had insisted on taking the stand to defend herself. Was this an extension of her attention-seeking behaviour, or did she truly believe that she could convince a jury of her innocence?

"Tanya couldn't stop herself from telling her side of the story during her first two trials," Gregg said, "though she wisely stayed off the witness stand during her third time out. She also had a judge, not jury, decide the case. Tanya was the kind of woman who seemed so sure that if she could just explain things, tell people, show her love for her children with her tears, they'd conclude she couldn't possibly have harmed anyone. She saw herself as the quintessential mother. The problem in her testimony wasn't in her delivery, but in the facts themselves. So yes, I do believe that she enjoyed playing the martyr, the victim of a witch hunt by child abuse professionals who just didn't like or respect her."

We discuss his 1993 visit to Tanya in an Iowa prison, where she acted as if she'd done nothing wrong. Did she try hard to convince him of her innocence?

"Really, she was so pathetic that she didn't have to try to convince me of anything. I told her that I didn't know what happened, but I was sure that she hadn't meant to kill her baby. She sobbed and sobbed and thanked me for that – without admitting guilt, of course. We'd talked on the phone and corresponded before I wrote the book and there was never any doubt that she wanted to win me over to her side. She needed an advocate, which, of course, I could never be."

I ask him how she behaved during the visit. Was she just like the girl next door or was there anything unusual about her demeanour? Was she flirtatious? Confrontational? Shy?

"Again, she cried through most of it. I think she was absolutely stunned that she didn't get an acquittal. I think she was convinced that the jury would see things her way – that she was a caring mom with children suffering from some strange seizure disorder that had yet to be fully understood by medical authorities. In her shock of the conviction, and her panic over her future, I think I saw a very frightened and remorseful woman. She knew what she did. She probably would have given anything to rewind that part of her life and deal with her compulsion for attention in some other way."

A psychiatric explanation

Keen to understand more about this perplexing syndrome, I turned to Dr Marc D. Feldman, Clinical Professor of Psychiatry at the University of Alabama. Dr Feldman is listed in *The Best Doctors in America* and *The Guide to America's Top Psychiatrists*. He has written several books about his experiences with Munchausen's and Munchausen's-by-proxy patients – including *Patient or Pretender*, *The Spectrum of Factitious Disorders* and *Playing Sick* – and has appeared on everything from CNN to Court TV. He maintains a website at www.munchausen.com.

I asked him to describe the worst MBP case that he was aware of in which a mother harmed or killed her children. "Probably the worst of which I am aware is the Marie Noe case in Philadelphia, though it was never formally adjudicated as MBP; that's because no MBP expert was given the opportunity to review the records or interview Mrs Noe. However, based on the facts of the case as I know them, I do believe it has all the features of MBP."

Dr Feldman went on to outline the case: "Marie Noe had ten children between 1949 and 1968. Two died without having left the hospital, and there is no suspicion that Mrs Noe was involved in their deaths. However, the remaining eight children died after lifespans ranging from weeks to more than a year, with the deaths being attributed by coroners to various medical ailments that, in retrospect, were not credible. This occurred before there was an awareness of the form of maltreatment called MBP and, indeed, child abuse as a whole was scarcely recognised by the professional and lay communities. There was disbelief that a mother would deliberately act in such a way as to cause harm to her child. This is among the reasons that the remaining eight children died as a result of suffocation by Mrs Noe without her culpability being publicly considered.

"In 1998, after a magazine interview by the writer Stephen Fried who was interested in the serial deaths, Marie Noe finally acknowledged that she had killed at least some of the children, and possibly all. She could never fully put into words why she did what she did, but it is notable that she also had a history of gratuitous lying and falsely claiming multiple sexual assaults that struck people as dubious. She also seemed to enjoy the trappings of the funerals, and these features are consistent with the pursuit of attention and sympathy in many MBP cases. Startlingly, she received no jail time; instead, she was on house arrest for five years (which she violated without consequence) and instructed to cooperate with doctors who would be allowed to interview her. As I noted, no MBP experts were among the selected interviewers. As of this writing, Mrs Noe is alive and still living in her original home in Philadelphia. Her husband, Arthur, affirms her innocence despite her having admitted to the MBP."

Nine percent of MBP children die. Do these murderous mothers feel any guilt at this stage or are they too disengaged to have feelings for others? Tanya Reid seems impervious to the fact that she killed one of her children and permanently damaged another, and it seems that Marie Noe is equally blasé.

Dr Feldman confirms that he's also found this to be the case. "Many of the perpetrators seem to have disengaged from the children they abused, treating them as objects to be manipulated rather than individuals to be nurtured. For this reason, guilt does not seem to be among the common responses to identification and confrontation; rather, they engage in a pervasive and often entrenched denial of their culpability, including the fatal abuse of the child."

So what did he make of those MBP mothers who induced repeated symptoms in one or more children, yet allowed another child to develop naturally – such as Tanya Reid, who repeatedly harmed Morgan and Matthew but spared Bernadette, her oldest child?

The psychiatrist explained, "It's true in all forms of abuse that a mother may target all of her children, or only one. There may have been a failure of mother-infant bonding for various reasons in that case, or the mother may have become more needy and attention-seeking as the number of children increased, thus targeting the youngest, and most vulnerable, child. I have not come across cases in which the younger children in the family are spared while older ones are abused; instead, the reverse is true in those cases in which only one child is victimised."

In his landmark book *Patient or Pretender*, Dr Feldman noted that in 1988 fifty-five percent of nurses in an American study hadn't heard of MBP. Are US trainee nurses and doctors now educated about this syndrome in medical school?

"There is a stunning lack of professional education about MBP. To my knowledge, it is considered a very tangential part of medicine and not covered in any depth. I think that these days more people, including doctors and nurses, have heard the term, but lack an understanding of its detection and implications. In the US, the government and private/public foundations have not funded any research into MBP, and the only educational efforts that occur are the ones arranged by speakers now and then who have become MBP-knowledgeable on their own. That is how my own education about MBP was acquired."

I tell him that there is equal ignorance about the topic in Britain, with numerous online forums suggesting that doctors and detectives are being overzealous in accusing mothers of sick children of fabricating their symptoms. Why is the general public so unwilling to believe in MBP?

Dr Feldman notes that MBP experts in the UK have been targeted by groups promoting the concept that MBP doesn't exist. "They have this belief despite open admissions of the maltreatment by some (few) perpetrators and despite the confirmatory videotapes that were originally acquired there. Many professionals have been publicly derided for their work in the field and threatened with endless lawsuits or legal challenges and personal smears, and because of these groups, which generally contain MBP perpetrators hiding from the charge of MBP, there has been a chilling effect on all child protection work. The two main figures who have been victimised have been Dr David Southall and Dr Roy Meadows; their reputations have been ruined as a result. There have also been overzealous lawyers and biased members of the media who seek to make their reputations by denigrating the entire field of MBP. Fortunately, these efforts have been much less successful in the US, and in some cases the doctors have been able to work together with those who claim, despite the lack of evidence, that MBP is being over-diagnosed."

So how can professionals differentiate between genuinely concerned mothers and MBP mothers? As Dr Feldman writes in *Patient or Pretender*, "One way to differentiate between caring mothers and potentially lethal mothers is by being suspicious of a mother (or father, grandparent, foster parent or other) who shows a peculiar eagerness to consent to having invasive procedures performed on the child." He also notes that the children remain sick whilst the mother remains by their hospital bed, but recover when she goes home. "The mother returns after a couple of days and the child gets sick again. The symptoms closely parallel the mother's presence."

PREVENTING COT DEATH

Though a small number of murders are wrongly labelled as unexplained infant deaths, most Sudden Infant Death Syndrome cases are genuine and parents are devastated when their loved and cared-for baby suddenly dies. Two hundred and fifty babies a year in England and Wales die of SIDS, the causes of death being difficult to ascertain.

A ten-year-study, reported in *The Lancet* of May 2008, found that many of these dead infants were carrying potentially-harmful bacteria. Scientists have speculated that these could trigger a chemical storm which overwhelms the baby and results in his or her demise.

Babies born to smokers are much more at risk from Sudden Infant Death Syndrome than those born to non-smokers – around thirty percent of cot deaths could be avoided if the mothers hadn't smoked when they were pregnant. But making sure that the baby isn't exposed to smoke *after* its birth can still make a huge difference. Infants who are exposed to one-to-two hours of smoke a day are more than twice as likely to die, and those exposed to a smoky home all day are eight times more likely to die.

Experts say that, to reduce the risk of cot death, parents should lay a baby on its back to sleep (hence the aptly-titled Back to Sleep campaign). But they shouldn't let the infant sleep in bed with them as it's all too easy for a baby to suffocate. They should also avoid sleeping with a baby on a sofa or armchair, as it's possible to inadvertently crush or smother the infant to death. The free booklet *Reduce the Risk of Cot Death*, from the Foundation for Sudden Infant Death, offers further advice, and the foundation's address is listed in the Appendix.

CHAPTER NINE

CAPITAL GAINS

Killing a child for the insurance money seems to be more common in fathers than in mothers. (For details of financially-motivated fathers who kill, see the 'Money* for Nothing' chapter.) But occasionally a mother will murder her child for profit, sometimes even repeating this homicidal behaviour again and again. These murders often have dual motives, with the mother enjoying her role as the bereaved victim – or taking a sadistic pleasure from her offspring's last moments – as well as pocketing the cash.

DIANA LUMBRERA

Married at seventeen, Texas-born Diana gave birth to her first child, Melissa, in Lubbock the following year. The already stormy marriage grew even stormier under the stress of dealing with a new baby. Yet Melissa's birth in 1975 was followed by Joanne's in 1976. The teenager regularly took both babies to the doctor, complaining that they were suffering from various symptoms. Medics repeatedly found both babies to be healthy and were baffled by her obsessive behaviour. She also insured her daughters for between $3-5,000 each, naming herself as the beneficiary.

Joanne's death

When Joanne was three months old, Diana took her to the emergency room saying that she'd had convulsions and stopped breathing. The baby was dead on arrival and the doctors attributed the death to a sudden seizure. The ostensibly-grieving mother collected, and soon spent, the insurance money.

Jose's death

The following year, Diana had a son, Jose Lionel, whom she immediately insured. When he was two months old she brought him to the hospital, saying that he'd been having convulsions. Doctors stabilised him that same day – 10 February 1978 – and kept him in for observation. He appeared to thrive, but, after Diana was left alone with him in hospital on the 13th, the baby alarm sounded at 1am, signalling that he was having breathing difficulties. A nurse hurried to the infant's aid, just in time to see Diana rushing from the room.

That same afternoon, Jose seemed fine – yet Diana phoned her husband to say that the baby was dying. Early that evening, the alarm sounded again and another nurse almost catapulted into Diana as she raced into the corridor. Diana looked guilty and turned back towards her son's sickbay, wailing that he was desperately ill. The nurse found that Jose was cyanotic – he had turned blue through lack of oxygen – and, after half an hour of frantic resuscitation attempts, medics pronounced him dead. The official cause of death was Sudden Infant Death Syndrome. The bereaved mother once again collected a few thousand dollars in insurance money and went on a spending spree.

Melissa's death

Diana's firstborn, Melissa, was the next to die. She'd insured the baby from the start, but on 1 October 1978 she purchased additional cover on the little girl. The following day she took her lifeless body to the hospital at Bovina, Texas, claiming that she'd suffered convulsions just like her siblings. Doctors attributed the death to the child choking on her own vomit and Diana Lumbrera received yet another insurance cheque.

The following year she divorced her husband and began a series of affairs, moving from state to state. In 1980 she gave birth to her late daughter's near-namesake, Melinda, fathered by one of her lovers. The baby was now on borrowed time . . .

Murder for fun

It's likely that, though profit had been her original motive, Diana Lumbrera found that she enjoyed murdering little children – or, at least, she enjoyed the drama that such deaths caused for the family and the hospital. There was definitely a Munchausen's-by-proxy element to the homicides.

On 8 October 1980 she took a cousin's six-week-old daughter, Ericka Aleman, out for a drive. But within half an hour she raced into the local emergency room, with the baby dead in her arms, claiming that convulsions had claimed her life. Her explanation was accepted, and Diana returned to her usual role of the distraught mother, often taking Melinda to the doctor to establish a medical history – though there was nothing wrong with the little girl.

Melinda's death

On 17 August 1982, Diana phoned the emergency services to say that the two-year-old had suffered a convulsion and died. The death was attributed to acute heart failure. Again, Diana collected the insurance policy and moved to another state. Fifteen months later she gave birth to another baby, Daniel, by a different man, and took out insurance on the child.

Daniel's murder

On 25 March 1984, Diana took Daniel to her doctor where he was treated for a minor ear infection. Three days later, the weeping mother told paramedics that the little boy was dead. The pathologist listed the death as septicaemia, despite the fact that blood tests taken at the time of his ear infection showed no evidence of this. Diana collected the insurance money and moved to Garden City, Kansas, where she soon found herself a new boyfriend and got pregnant yet again.

Jose Antonio's murder

On 21 February 1986, Diana gave birth to her sixth child, Jose Antonio. The fact that she called two of her sons Jose, and named her daughters Melissa and Melinda, suggests that they were interchangeable to her, pawns in her game rather than individuals with distinct identities.

Before long she was lying to her employer's credit union, saying that the little boy was suffering from leukaemia. Colleagues were sympathetic and her workplace gave her several hundred dollars in sympathy loans to help pay for his treatment. Lumbrera also secured money by pretending that her father had died in a horrific car crash.

Jose Antonio survived for four years and three months before Diana took him to her MD on 30 April 1990, claiming that he was suffering from mysterious convulsions. The doctor could find nothing wrong with the child, but wrote a prescription for antibiotics which would kill off any infection that might be making him feverish. Diana didn't bother to fill the prescription as she was simply creating a medical smokescreen for her decision to kill Jose, having previously insured him for $5,000.

The following day she carried his corpse into the emergency room in Kansas, wailing that he'd collapsed and expired. But this time medics didn't believe that a healthy four-year-old boy had suddenly died of natural causes. They called the police, who began to make background checks in Texas and Kansas, discovering that all six of Lumbrera's offspring – and her cousin's baby daughter – had mysteriously died in her care.

Charges

Belatedly, the authorities realised that the grieving mother was actually a serial-killer-for-profit. She was charged with the deaths of her six children plus that of Ericka Aleman.

The prosecution at Diana's trial in Garden City, Kansas, said that Jose Antonio had been smothered whilst the defence said that he'd died from a viral infection. The jury took less than an hour to find her guilty and she was sentenced to life imprisonment, with the proviso that she would serve at least fifteen years before becoming eligible for parole.

Lumbrera then went on trial in Texas and confessed to Melissa's murder, to avoid the death penalty – whereupon prosecutors dropped the charges for Melinda and Joanna's murders. She was again sentenced to life imprisonment. Lubbock County handed her a third life sentence after she pleaded no contest to Jose Lionel's death. Castro County, which had charged her with Ericka Aleman's murder, waived charges to save on court costs.

In June 1991 Diana Lumbrera began serving her time in a Kansas prison.

JANIE LOU GIBBS

Though she went on to murder three children and a grandson within eighteen months in her native Georgia, Janie's first victim was her husband of almost twenty years – she had been his fifteen-year-old bride. Janie put arsenic in his lunch on 21 January 1965, and he promptly collapsed and died. As the couple were devout Christian fundamentalists and Janie had devoted her life to running a day-care centre, no one suspected foul play. The doctor put the death down to previously-undiagnosed liver disease; the thirty-four-year-old widow collected the insurance money and gave a tenth of it to her church.

Murdering her three children

Almost a year later, Janie started to poison her sixteen-year-old son's meals. He began to have headaches and dizzy spells, eventually dying in agony. Pretending to be prostrate with grief at his funeral, she benefited from the insurance policy she'd taken out on him. Later that same year she murdered her thirteen-year-old son in the exact same way. Again, she gave a tenth of the insurance money to her beloved church. By now the insurance companies were suspicious, but Janie Lou blocked their requests for autopsies on religious grounds. Her

Christian friends still refused to believe that she was a serial killer, convinced that she had merely been unlucky to lose a husband and two sons in such a short space of time.

In August 1967, Janie's nineteen-year-old son Roger and his wife presented her with her first grandson, Raymond. Janie seemed delighted at the prospect of becoming a grandmother and talked at length about the impending birth. The boy was born healthy, yet by September he was dead. Even more strangely, Roger himself died an agonising death during the same time period. Janie's distraught daughter-in-law, inexplicably twice-bereaved, suspected her mother-in-law was responsible and insisted that the authorities carry out autopsies – despite Janie Lou's continuing objections.

The results proved inconclusive so the hospital called in the state crime lab, which found that the pair had been poisoned with arsenic. The other Gibbs bodies were exhumed and fatal levels of arsenic were also found.

At Christmas 1967, the devout Christian was arrested and admitted to murdering her family. She didn't give a motive but the prosecutor noted that she had gained a total of $31,000 from the deaths, a sizeable sum in Georgia during the 1960s. In February 1968 she was found guilty and received five life sentences.

Released

The insurance killer served out the next thirty years in prison and was expected to die there. But she was released on compassionate grounds in 1999, aged sixty-six, suffering from Parkinson's disease.

CHAPTER TEN
MERCY KILLINGS

When Joanne Hill drowned her four-year-old daughter Naomi in her North Wales home, much was made of the fact that the little girl had cerebral palsy. Lawyers noted that Hill was ashamed of the child and had wanted to give her up for adoption but was overruled by her husband, who loved Naomi very much.

For this was in no way a mercy killing. Naomi's disabilities were mild – she needed leg braces to walk and had hearing difficulties – and she was a happy and contented child who loved spending time with her father. She made up stories to entertain him and was described as a chatterbox.

It's likely that Joanne Hill would have struggled to bond with any child, as she had a history of mental problems and depression. After the murder she continued to display bizarre behaviour, going out drink-driving for eight hours with her daughter's corpse in the boot of her car.

At Chester Crown Court, in September 2008, a jury decided that she was not mentally ill at the time that she drowned her daughter and she was sentenced to serve at least fifteen years. But medical experts asserted that she was now suffering from a serious mental illness, and she'd been flanked in court by two nurses and a security guard. The thirty-one-year-old had been in prison on remand but, after the trial, the judge ordered that she be taken to a psychiatric facility.

Women – and men, as a later chapter will delineate – who resort to genuine mercy killings tend to fall into two camps. Some are caring for a terminally-ill child and are desperate to spare them further suffering or indignity. The second group are looking after adult children with multiple disabilities who are evidencing distress. As these women grow old and less able, they fear for the future of their handicapped son or daughter. These are genuine fears, as care in the community can be woefully inadequate.

WENDOLYN MARKCROW

Wendolyn and her architect husband Paul managed to give their son, Patrick, who was born with Down's syndrome, a happy childhood. A high-functioning teenager, he was even able to attend college. The family, which included two other sons, lived in the picturesque village of Long Crendon in Buckinghamshire, England. But in his twenties Patrick developed autism and his behaviour deteriorated markedly.

He became even more unstable in his thirties. After going to bed at night he would sleep for two hours, then wake up screaming – and his screams would continue until breakfast time. The daytime was little better, as he would often shout out the same word again and again. He also began to batter himself about the head, punching himself in his right eye and causing permanent blindness in July 2003. It was very hard for his ageing mother to control him, as by now he weighed sixteen stone.

Wendolyn had respite during the day when Patrick went to a care centre, but this support ended in 2003 due to funding cuts. As the months passed, he became increasingly self-destructive and was evidently deeply distressed. He also hit his parents if they tried to intervene. Wendolyn took him to a doctor who was very sympathetic (during the visit, Patrick punched himself in the face twenty times) and admitted in a report that even controlling the heavily-built thirty-something for a few minutes in the surgery had been impossible, and that he had no idea how Wendolyn coped.

But still social services refused to provide respite care, though she wrote to them again in 2004, noting, "The crisis is not going to go away. I really must have some support very soon." An internal county council email in May of that year acknowledged this, stating that the situation was urgent. Wendolyn and Paul were now in their mid-sixties and ill with exhaustion. Like seventy-two percent of fulltime carers, Wendolyn was also deeply depressed.

On 28 March 2005, thirty-six-year-old Patrick played the same Elton John record over and over again, then repeatedly shouted the word, "Elton!" Half-crazed with lack of sleep, his sixty-seven-year-old mother gave him fourteen sleeping pills and, when he was deeply unconscious, put a plastic bag over his head and suffocated him. Retreating to her garden shed, she slashed her arm and neck with a knife and lay down to die. She was found the following morning by her distraught husband and rushed to hospital.

Everyone who knew her was sympathetic, aware that she'd been sleep-deprived for many years and that the last twenty had been relatively joyless. The villagers even sent her a book of supportive messages and said that they wanted to welcome her back into the community. The tragedy was compounded shortly afterwards when seventy-year-old Paul died of natural causes. Wendolyn, who constituted no danger to the public, was released on bail.

At Oxford Crown Court in November 2005, the sixty-seven-year-old denied murder but admitted manslaughter on the grounds of diminished responsibility. Supported in court by her two surviving sons and other family members, she was given a two-year suspended sentence and walked free.

CATHIE WILKIESON

Following a difficult pregnancy in Hamilton, Ontario, Cathie's son Ryan was ill from the moment that he was born. At eighteen weeks old, he had eye surgery which failed to correct his partial blindness; at two years old, he was diagnosed with cerebral palsy. He was also deaf but, with the use of a special hearing aid, eventually learned how to speak. A few years later, he developed a debilitating bone condition which left him wheelchair-bound.

Despite her son's multiple infirmities, Cathie was only entitled to twelve hours of respite care a week. She enrolled Ryan in high school but they were unable to cope with his special needs, so he had to leave. In autumn 1994 she begged the authorities to fund home care for Ryan, but this was refused.

That same year, she – and the rest of Canada – read about farmer Robert Latimer's mercy killing of his twelve-year-old daughter, Tracy. A quadriplegic who had feeding difficulties and weighed just under three stone, Tracy had the abilities of a three-year-old and was in constant pain. When the authorities said that they were about to permanently confine her to a hospital, her distressed father decided to act. He put his daughter into the cab of his lorry before pumping carbon monoxide into it then sat in the back of the truck, watching, as she became drowsy and died. Afterwards, he told medics that she had died of natural causes, but an autopsy showed that her system was filled with carbon monoxide. He was sentenced to ten years without the possibility of parole.

Cathie clearly identified with the man's plight, and told a friend that she loved Ryan too much to let him die alone; she would have sat in the vehicle with him as it filled with fumes. On 5 December 1994, she did just that. The forty-three-year-old mother and her sixteen-year-old son were found dead a few hours later in a car in his grandparents' garage, alongside a note from Cathie which said she "could not go on any longer and could not leave him behind."

NO CARING FOR THE CARERS

In October 2008, British mother Claire Bates, thirty-seven, spoke movingly to a woman's magazine about the difficulties of being the mother of a severely-disabled child. Her son, Noah, aged five, has a severe form of cerebral palsy and is also a quadriplegic. He is fed directly by a tube into his stomach, will never walk or talk and is virtually blind. He will need daily nappy changes throughout his life. Yet his parents – sleep-deprived and desperate – are only given four hours of respite care a month.

Claire said that she loved Noah very much, but had once asked her father to put him out of his misery. She urged the public not to judge Joanne Hill (whose case is outlined at the start of this chapter) too harshly, writing, "If we have to imprison her, we should also help her. Perhaps we are all to blame for walking by."

CHAPTER ELEVEN

WICKED STEPMOTHERS

Stepfathers are statistically more likely than stepmothers to kill a child, or to systematically abuse it. Nevertheless, there have been many instances of women, acting *in loco parentis*, who are deeply resentful of their partner's child from a previous relationship and subject that child to fatal levels of abuse.

SUMAIRIA PARVEEN

Ironically, Sumairia started off as a victim of violence as she was repeatedly assaulted by her abusive husband. She left the marriage and, in January 2006, began an affair with her cousin, Abid Ikram. They shared a flat in London, being originally from Pakistan. Abid had just won custody of his son, Talha, a particularly beautiful child, whilst Sumairia had her own baby, a daughter whom she adored.

The couple often went out, leaving baby Talha alone. In March, the neglected eleven-month-old was taken into care and given to foster parents, where he thrived. He learned to walk, said his first words and became an active and happy child. But, three months later, a family court decreed that Talha must be given back to his father and stepmother. Sumairia deeply resented this, seeing the baby boy as coming between her and her man.

In the weeks which followed, the couple regularly took the baby to casualty where he was found to have twisted his limbs and fractured three of his ribs. During one visit, his leg was found to be broken and doctors put it in a plaster cast. They believed the couple's explanation that the child had slipped from a chair or fallen down the stairs. But Talha's supposed accident-proneness increased and he was returned to hospital in an increasingly bruised condition. Sumairia just told medical staff that his cast kept slipping off.

During the last twenty days of his life, the toddler was taken to casualty five times and was seen by at least seven different doctors, but none had the chance to compare notes.

Meanwhile his suffering continued, including beatings and burning with a cigarette. He was also left with a broken tibia. One particular injury was inflicted over a series of days, when the flesh behind his left knee was cut open progressively until the bone and tendon were exposed. But the wound which proved fatal was an untreated broken thigh bone which sent marrow deposits circulating around his body. They invaded his lungs, starving his brain of oxygen.

The couple found the seventeen-month-old motionless in his cot on 6 September 2006, and called for an ambulance. Paramedics noted that the baby's father appeared to be genuinely distressed at his son's condition, but his lover remained quite calm. Talha was rushed to Central Middlesex Hospital where he was pronounced dead on arrival. Horrified doctors said that he looked like he'd been in a car crash, extensively bruised and with broken bones.

Questioned by police, the pair denied abusing the toddler. Sumairia Parveen said that she'd loved the boy as if he were her own son, and Abid Ikram said that he'd never hurt his own child. Shortly after the baby's death, Abid helped his lover decamp to Pakistan. He would later be found guilty of perverting the course of justice by helping her to leave the country, knowing that a police investigation was underway.

The couple were arrested and, in August 2007, went on trial at Southwark Crown Court. The court heard that the twenty-four-year-old stepmother had hated the little boy and subjected him to a catalogue of abuse, whilst his thirty-one-year-old father watched and did nothing. On one occasion he beat the baby with a plastic cricket bat at his lover's insistence. They were both cleared of murder but found guilty of 'causing or allowing' the death of Talha Ikram, and were remanded in custody. Under the 'causing or allowing' verdict, the individual who dealt the fatal blow does not have to be identified.

The following month, they were sentenced to nine years in jail. Abid Ikram got a further twelve months for perverting the course of justice. The court recommended that Sumairia Parveen be deported after her release.

TRACEY WRIGHT

Some children are doubly tragic, in that they are failed by their biological parents and later murdered by a stepparent. Lauren Wright suffered this fate at the hands of her stepmother, Tracey Wright.

Lauren was born on 16 July 1993, the product of a brief affair between Jennifer Bennett and Craig Wright, then both resident in Herefordshire. He denied paternity until a blood test proved that he was the father, after which he saw little of his daughter for her first three years. Jennifer didn't want the child and often left her at a nearby pub, where she was fed by locals who took pity on her. On other occasions she phoned Craig and said that she would hit Lauren unless he came round immediately. Social workers were concerned that she was being neglected, and she was placed on Herefordshire social services' child-protection register.

When Lauren was four, Jennifer and her latest boyfriend took her on holiday to Turkey with three of their other children. But Jennifer constantly shouted at Lauren; she ended the little girl's holiday by dumping her at the British consulate and scratching her photo out of her passport, saying that she was no longer her child. Bewildered officials returned the frightened little girl to Britain, where she was met at the airport by Craig and his mother Christine.

· Christine, who was running a pub in Norfolk, gained custody of Lauren in January 1998. She started school there, a friendly child who craved affection and was desperate to please, and she thrived in her grandmother's care. But, in May 1998, Christine's pub failed and she moved house, got a new job and was unable to continue fostering the little girl. Lauren was returned to her father, whom she liked, and went to live with him in Welney. He soon began a relationship with single mother-of-two Tracey Scarff, a playground supervisor. Months later they married and she became Mrs Wright – in name only.

Daily abuse

Tracey Wright resented Lauren from the start, and treated her differently to her own natural son and daughter. On rainy days the three would be seen walking along the road under an umbrella, whilst Lauren walked behind, soaked, carrying all of their bags.

Tracey beat Lauren with a cane, forced her to eat insects and gave her sandwiches filled with pepper. The little girl began to wet the bed and was beaten for this too, being made to stand close to the fire for an hour. As soon as she got home from school, she was sent to her room without food or water. She was regularly humiliated by Tracey, who by now was also humiliating Craig in public.

Lauren's hair began to fall out due to malnutrition as she became pale and thin. On 14 May 2000, a male neighbour made an anonymous phone call to Cambridgeshire social services, explaining that the little girl looked shellshocked and had bruises on her face and neck. That same day, an anonymous female phoned Norfolk social services to report that the child was being abused.

The following day, Lauren was seen by a paediatrician at the local hospital who asked her about her injuries. But the battered child dutifully echoed her stepmother's lies that she was incredibly accident-prone. She said that she'd been knocked over several times by the family Alsatian and had banged herself against a table and fallen down. One doctor was suspicious, as some of the injuries looked to have been caused by a cane or stick. He sent her for a second opinion from another doctor, who believed the playground assistant's account of her stepdaughter's injuries.

In mid-April 2001, another anonymous call was made to Norfolk social services stating that Lauren appeared to have been abused. A week later social services wrote to Tracey Wright, requesting a home visit. Later that month, Herefordshire social services contacted their counterparts in Norfolk to say that they were concerned about the child.

On 2 May, Tracey punched Lauren so viciously in the stomach that part of her digestive system collapsed. She began to vomit copiously and was clearly in agony. She was in no fit state to go to school, so Tracey told her teachers she was ill with gastroenteritis. Though she lied to relatives that the six-year-old had seen a doctor, she did not seek medical help. When Lauren's relatives visited her sickroom and saw her bruises, Tracey said that Lauren had pulled a wardrobe down on top of herself.

On the morning of 8 May, Lauren got up to use the bathroom and her stepmother punched her twice in her already-damaged stomach. The blows were observed by her son, who would later testify in court that he was also punched at times by his mother. Lauren died in bed within minutes, though Tracey Wright didn't discover this until shortly after midday. She ran screaming to relatives, who phoned the emergency services before desperately attempting mouth-to-mouth resuscitation. Paramedics arrived quickly, but rigor mortis had already begun to set in. That night, Tracey and Craig went to the pub together. In the days that followed they were again seen in the pub, where Tracey was laughing and joking but Craig looked subdued.

Court

In September 2001, the couple – she by now aged thirty-one, he thirty-eight – went on trial at Norwich Crown Court, denying cruelty and manslaughter. Craig said that he had been at work, at the pub or out fishing and had rarely seen Lauren in the last few weeks of her life. He claimed that she got up just as he was leaving for work, and was in bed when he came home. But the prosecution alleged that he must have noticed her thinning hair, stick-like arms and legs, and her increasingly withdrawn state.

Prosecutor Graham Parkins QC said, "Tracey Wright treated this child abysmally, physically assaulting her on numerous occasions." He described one instance where Wright had hit the child about the head in the street, knocking her to the pavement. Her corpse had been emaciated and was covered in sixty bruises, nineteen of which were on her shins and had been caused by kicks. The jury heard that, shortly before her death, she had become virtually voiceless and "looked like a poster child for the NSPCC".

Later that month, the pair were found guilty of manslaughter and wilful neglect. Craig Wright, who had failed to intervene whilst his daughter was being starved and beaten to death, was given a three-year sentence. Tracey Wright was sentenced to ten years for manslaughter and five years for neglect, the sentences to run consecutively.

Ironically, Lauren's grave in the village of South Mimms is well-tended in a way that the child herself rarely was.

PART TWO
FATAL FATHERS

CHAPTER TWELVE

SETTLING SCORES

The ending of a marriage or cohabitation – especially one which has produced children – is never easy. But at least the person who chooses to end the relationship has made the positive decision to move on. In contrast, the person who has been ditched can be left with feelings of rage and hate.

Men who have previously been violent towards their partners often continue to terrorise them after a formal separation – indeed, a battered woman is most at risk immediately after she leaves her aggressive spouse. A percentage of these men will get their own back on the woman who has deserted them by killing their offspring. Sometimes, in an act of especial cruelty, they will phone their ex-wife seconds before they kill the children and tell her to listen to their dying cries.

Most of these men take their own lives, or at least attempt to. There are around five hundred and twenty such murder-suicides in America every year. In Britain, fathers kill approximately sixteen children annually, usually following the breakdown of a relationship with their wife or girlfriend. Of children killed by a parent, fifty-three percent are murdered by their fathers and forty-seven percent by their mothers.

DAVID CASS

A car mechanic who worked in Southampton, David Cass went around with a group of friends at least ten years younger. In his late twenties, he was dating girls in their mid-teens. He went out with a teenager called Emma for a month and, when she ended it, threatened to commit suicide.

Shortly after the break-up he began to date Emma's best friend, Kerrie Hughes, who at sixteen was thirteen years his junior. A fantasist, he told her that he owned several houses and had £47,000 in the bank.

A fortnight after they met, she moved in with him at his home in Eastleigh, Hants, and within four months the couple were expecting their first baby. They went on to have two daughters, Ellie and Isobelle. David was an excellent father, changing nappies, giving the children baths and spending time playing with them. Their little faces would light up when he came into the room. Both parents loved the children dearly and took numerous photos of them looking happy, well-dressed and well-fed.

But David was apparently controlling and there were many arguments, culminating in his storming out in late summer 2008. He moved into a caravan close to his workplace and again began to threaten suicide. Kerrie, who still loved him, was alarmed at the thought of him killing himself, but her friend Emma reminded her that he'd made such threats before and hadn't carried them out. It didn't occur to anyone that he would harm the children as he had always been such a devoted dad.

Three weeks after the split, David arrived at Kerrie's house and offered her £250 if she'd have sex with him. She refused. The following day, Saturday 20 September 2008, he was due for the children to stay with him overnight. He arrived as arranged at 2pm and again asked if they could have sex, "for the last time". Kerrie said no.

David then took Ellie, aged three, and Isobelle, aged fourteen months, to his caravan. There, the little girls drew pictures and played with their dolls, teddies and bouncing balls. Only their father knew that they had mere hours to live.

At 5pm on the Sunday, he phoned Kerrie and said that he was about to give the girls their evening meal before bringing them back, so that he and she could bathe them and put them to bed. She could hear the children laughing in the background and all seemed well. But, within the hour, the thirty-three-year-old smothered them to death in the caravan. He phoned his wife again, in tears. This time she couldn't hear any sound from her daughters so she asked him where they were. "They're sleeping," he said. When she protested, "But it's dinner time," he told her they were "sleeping forever". He added that he was going to kill himself, and that soon he'd be sleeping too. David told her he would always love her, and then hung up the phone.

Hoping against hope that it was a cruel joke, Kerrie phoned her mother-in-law but David Cass wasn't there. The twenty-year-old then phoned the emergency services and told them the most likely locations to find her husband and their children, namely his caravan or his workplace. Police raced to the caravan and found both tiny corpses. Breaking into the adjacent garage where Cass worked, they found that he had hanged himself.

Afterwards, his mother said that, though he'd done the wrong thing, he wasn't a monster. He had killed himself rather than lose custody of the children he professed to love. Kerrie said that she would go to his funeral, telling the *Daily Mirror*, "I'll regret it if I don't go. It will be very hard and I can never forgive him for what he did. But we shared a lot together." She also paid tribute to her daughters: "They were the happiest, funniest, prettiest little things a mum could hope for. I feel so lucky to have had them and I will miss them forever."

ROBERT THOMSON

June married Robert Thomson in June 1981, despite her friends begging her not to. She'd later allege that he was controlling from early on in the relationship and that he'd become violent by the following year, when she was pregnant with their first child. The violence apparently included being knocked down stairs, having her eyes blackened and being raped. During the next four years they had two sons and a daughter. The latter, Michelle, was eventually diagnosed as having severe learning difficulties – even in adulthood she would only attain a mental age of five.

June left Robert on four separate occasions during the next two decades, but she always returned to him. Around the turn of the millennium they had a fourth child together who they called Ryan.

Robert remained controlling, insisting that he be paid Michelle's disability allowance and Ryan's child benefit. If he fancied a late-night takeaway, he thought nothing of getting his wife out of bed and sending her out to buy it. By now their oldest son, Shawn, had left Scotland and moved to England as he apparently hated his father. Their second son, Ross, also left but returned after the couple soundproofed his room.

By now the family were living in a cottage in Buckhaven, an old coastal fishing town on the east coast of Fife, where they kept a low profile. Michelle was obviously going to be dependent on the Thomsons for life, but she had a series of carers who looked after her in her own home.

One of the carers alleged that Robert had molested her, and police quizzed him twice about this, though the case didn't go to court. But it was the last straw for June Thomson and, in 2007, she told him that she was leaving him forever and filing for divorce. By now their children were all adults, apart from seven-year-old Ryan. Robert seemed devoted to Ryan and often played football with him. He had also built him a play area behind the house. He similarly spent time with twenty-year-old Ross, often taking him for a game of pool. As such, June Thomson had no qualms about leaving their offspring with him for extended visits, though she wanted them to live with her.

Death threats

But Robert was devastated at the end of their twenty-seven-year marriage and told his brother that he was contemplating suicide. When June moved into a flat, he became increasingly withdrawn.

Later, the fifty-year-old lorry driver and machine operator told workmates that he was worried about paying maintenance – June was seeking a £50,000 settlement plus £250 a month – and feared that he might lose custody of the children. On 2 May 2007, the couple attended a court hearing and she was, as he feared, given custody.

Knowing that he'd lost control, Robert Thomson became increasingly enraged. He apparently told one of Michelle's carers that he was going to kill Michelle and then himself, but the carer didn't take him seriously.

The following day, June was preparing to move into a new flat in Markinch with twenty-five-year-old Michelle and seven-year-old Ryan. She left them both at her former cottage, where her ex-husband and her son Ross were still residing, whilst she got organised. June noted that her husband was very stressed and angry, but she had no reason to believe that he'd harm the children, believing his rage was wholly directed at her. She left and neighbours looked on approvingly as Robert played with his offspring in the garden, kicking a ball around with Ryan and pushing Michelle on her swing.

He took them to Kirkcaldy for a few hours, where they visited a supermarket and a burger bar. When they came back that afternoon, Ryan went to his bedroom to play a computer game and Michelle went to her room to play with her favourite doll.

At about 4pm, Robert Thomson told Ross that he needed further groceries, gave the youth £20 and sent him back to the supermarket in Kirkcaldy which they'd visited earlier. Now that he had the house to himself, he wrote his wife a suicide note which said not to blame herself and that he would take care of the children. He added that there had already been "too much pain, lies and hurt". Towards the end of the note he suggested that she should "move on alone".

Sometime during the next hour, he stabbed Michelle a total of fourteen times and Ryan twelve times. One of the knives broke partway through the second attack and so he switched to another and kept on stabbing. The blood which spattered over the walls and floor of Michelle's pretty pink bedroom testified to the fact that she'd put up a tremendous struggle; though she had the mentality of a small child, she had the strength of a typical twenty-five-year-old woman in her physical prime.

Afterwards, Robert Thomson tucked the children into their separate beds and showered. When Ross returned at 5.45pm, his father greeted him wearing a dressing gown. Ross went out again shortly afterwards to collect his girlfriend and brought her back to the house an hour later, after which they watched a DVD.

Meanwhile, Robert Thomson had gone to the marital bedroom, got into bed and used a large knife to cut his wrists. He also stabbed himself in the stomach. Fifteen minutes later, June Thomson arrived at the house, went up to Ryan's room and saw that he appeared to be fast asleep. She pulled back the bedcovers to find her dead son staring up at her, blood on his abdomen and stab wounds visible in his sides.

Racing to Michelle's room, she found her daughter dead in bed and blood everywhere. She began screaming, "He's killed them!" Ross came downstairs to see what was happening. Going into the double bedroom, they found Robert in bed, bleeding from his injuries. He was taken to hospital in Dunfermline where he was later interviewed and charged. Upon his recovery, he was transferred to Carstairs mental hospital but found to be sane and moved to Perth prison.

Behind closed doors

Journalists attempted to find details of the couple's relationship prior to the tragedy, but they had kept themselves to themselves and rarely socialised. A neighbour who lived some distance away said that they had seemed a normal couple, if very quiet, and that Robert sometimes had a few pints at the local pub or played pool with Ross. He'd appeared to dote on his children. When she'd first heard that the cottage had become a murder scene, she'd assumed that he'd killed June but not his offspring. Other locals echoed this view, saying, "Surely a father wouldn't kill his own bairns?"

Life

Thomson admitted his guilt from the start, which meant that he automatically got a life sentence. This was handed down in September

2008 at Edinburgh High Court. His face flushed and heavily-veined, his hair thinning and his expression bleak, he looked much older than his actual fifty-one years. Judge Lord Menzies told him, "What you have done, and what you have pleaded guilty to, is indescribably awful." June was in court to see justice being done. Afterwards, she talked about the day of the murder, acknowledging, "He must have been planning to punish me by killing them." Later still, she described him as "full of pure evil".

The following month, Robert Thomson was returned to court to hear the extent of his sentence. He was told that he must serve seventeen years before becoming eligible for parole.

An editor's perspective

One of the journalists who covered this Fife case in depth was Jerzy Morkis, a former chairman of the Society of Editors in Scotland and the current editor of the *East Fife Mail*. In November 2008, we spoke about the case and I asked him why local people had made statements such as, "Surely a father wouldn't kill his own bairns?" Why were people in such denial about the nature of this particular crime?

Jerzy, who has thirty years' journalistic experience, replied, "It wasn't a case of people being in denial, the horrors of parents who kill their children or a parent killing the entire family are well enough publicised – the community was aware crimes like this happen. What it wasn't prepared for, and no community would be, is it happening right in your midst. To everyone on the outside of the Thomson family they seem to have been perceived as fitting that term 'normal'. Of course they had their trials and tribulations, but Robert Thomson held down a job with a long-established reputable firm, his wife worked, they both seemed committed to their family, had their own cottage on the edge of town . . . then, suddenly, behind their four walls this happened."

The newspaperman continued: "The fact the father was immediately in police custody after the horror led to what could be described as a *muted disbelief*. Even the subsequent court case, the national media coverage, Mrs Thomson's own thoughts, none of this has really helped the community understand why this happened. It's known *what* happened but there's not a satisfactory explanation of *why*. Robert Thomson isn't saying; perhaps he doesn't even know. June Thomson launched a petition to have the home bulldozed. There has been solid support for that, which perhaps provides an indication of community feeling. To many people, the cottage is a painful and constant reminder of something incomprehensible."

So was this the worst case of a homicidal father that he'd reported on? Jerzy confirmed that it was. "Thankfully, murders remain few and far between in Fife and I've never reported on a filicide case like this. Hopefully, this area will never see another but, of course, since the Thomson case there have been others nationally – the Christopher Foster case in September took familicide into every home. There you had a case where Foster almost tried to erase his family's entire existence – wife, daughter, pets, livestock, property, all destroyed. The Thomson case was different and his victims were deliberately the most vulnerable in his family. And there is something even darker about that. Again, the case will always stick out, not just because of the brutality of the crime, but because there are no clues which help comprehend his act."

I note that Thomson appears to fit into the revenge category of fathers who kill, willing to murder his children in order to hurt his ex-wife. Jerzy replies: "The revenge theory is the closest we do have to an explanation, but there are aspects there that don't provide all the answers. There has been very little real information on the dynamics of the Thomson family, and especially the dynamics between husband and wife. Certainly there is now the perception that Thomson had always to be in control and the break-up of his marriage and family propelled him towards this twisted revenge.

"The fact that his two children suffered such multiple stab wounds undermines the 'cold calculated' theory, but then again, the fact that he moved from one room to another to repeat the attack does add credence to the entire 'premeditated' view. Revenge, rage, frustration, even sacrifice, perhaps? All were there and while we will maybe never be able to understand what was going on in Thomson's head, I think none of us likes to focus too much on the terror Michelle and Ryan will have felt as someone they loved and trusted inflicted such agony on them."

Finally, does he view family killers like Thomson as mad, bad, sad, or a combination? And, judging by his mailbox at the *East Fife Mail*, how do his readers regard such men?

"There's definitely a combination of factors at work; they will vary from one individual to another and as to what the common link is that makes you slaughter your children or family, we'll probably never know. There's a tragic hopelessness to the parents who kill, then take their own lives. These are cruel, bleak incidents. Did Thomson really mean to kill himself, or couldn't? The answer to that brings another chilling factor into this case. As for our mailbox, I don't think we received a single letter. Unlike a death we'd had a short time before, no teachers would speak, no neighbours . . . The community went very quiet, there hasn't been a communal outpouring of grief. There were reports of June Thomson attracting a stalker, there have been many reports and articles in the national media since the case, the petititon to have the house demolished . . . all of this has probably distorted how people feel. In some respects, there hasn't been a time for community reflection, the tragedy is still ongoing."

Sadly, within days of this interview another Scottish-based father, Ashok Kalyanjee, admitted murdering his two sons earlier in 2008, in what also appeared to be a revenge attack.

ASHOK KALYANJEE

Born in India, Ashok relocated to Britain with his parents in 1991, when he was in his late twenties. Later, he worked behind the counter of a post office in Royston, Glasgow, where he appeared to be a lonely man who befriended the local children by giving them sweets. Worried parents eventually complained to his boss, after which Ashok confined himself to offering chocolates to the occasional woman whom he hoped to date. He spent many of his evenings at the local bingo hall, where he would drink eight or nine pints and become visibly depressed.

In March 2001, he married Giselle Ross but insisted that they spend their honeymoon night at his mother's house – despite the fact that she could only speak Punjabi. Throughout their marriage, he returned to his ailing mother's flat most nights for dinner (he was apparently her only source of companionship) and also took his laundry there. He also spent time at a casino and amassed large gambling debts.

Ashok and Giselle had a son, Paul, but the relationship remained strained. In July 2004 they divorced, but they continued to sleep together and their second son, Jay, was born in January 2006. Ashok was enraged when Giselle didn't put his name on the birth certificate, and refused to believe that Jay was his – though a DNA test proved his paternity. But neighbours said that he appeared devoted to both boys and it was clear that they loved spending time with him. Giselle was also an excellent parent, and the boys were happy and well-liked in the community.

But the devout Christian continued to gamble and drink, and appeared to be unravelling. His mood spiralled further downwards when someone crashed into the taxi cab he now drove, and he had to find work as the manager of a call centre instead. He wanted to reconcile with Giselle, complaining to anyone who would listen that he wasn't getting as much access to his sons as he would have liked.

On Saturday 3 May 2008, Ashok took the children – Paul, aged six, and Jay, aged two – to the Campsie Fells, a local beauty spot, for an outing in the car, promising that he would buy them toys and sports gear. But, when they arrived, he parked the car and stabbed them – before slashing their throats and putting their bloodsoaked bodies in the boot.

The forty-six-year-old phoned his ex-wife that lunchtime and promised her, "You'll regret what you did to me in this life." After hanging up, he poured petrol on himself and the car and set it alight, also slashing his own throat. He was discovered close to death, with terrible burns, and rushed to the nearest hospital.

When he recovered, he was transferred to Barlinnie prison. In November 2008, despite not entering a formal guilty plea, he admitted stabbing his two sons to death. Lawyers said that they were awaiting tests which would establish his state of mind and that he would be sentenced the following month. But by then his mental health had further declined and sentencing was deferred.

In January 2009, the child killer was jailed for a minimum of twenty-one years at Paisley High Court, the judge commenting that it would have been twenty-eight if he hadn't pleaded guilty.

BRIAN PHILCOX

Karate expert Brian enjoyed an eighteen-year marriage which only ended when his wife died of cancer. Afterwards, he raised so much money for cancer charities that he was named Man of the Year. He was also chairman of the Federation of English Karate Organisations.

He remarried, but was incensed when his second wife Evelyn – known as Lyn – left him in 2006 after eight years of marriage. Lyn could no longer stand the beatings that he was meting out to her teenage son from her first marriage, Ryan. Increasingly fearful of her martial-artist husband, she moved in with her mother who lived close to the family home. Statistically, this should have decreased her risk of becoming a victim, as violent men are more likely to assault ex-partners who live alone.

But Philcox continued to terrorise his wife, often turning up at her mother's house late at night and banging on the windows. Presumably this frightened the couple's biological children, Amy, aged seven, and Owen, who was only three. This antisocial behaviour aside, Brian was a good father and would regularly play football with the children during access visits. They spent several days a week with him.

The courts fixed a hearing for Monday 16 June 2008 to decide whether or not thirty-seven-year-old Lyn would get the house in Runcorn, Cheshire. As the day approached, Brian's mood darkened and he told a neighbour that he'd lost his wife, was losing his kids and was going to lose his house. He added, "I'd rather burn it down than give it to that bitch." That same week, he phoned Fathers4Justice in a distressed state, asking about the likelihood of his being able to obtain child custody.

On Friday 13th, fifty-two-year-old Philcox collected the couple's children as arranged in his Land Rover. He was supposed to return them the following day. Unknown to anyone at this stage, he had left a hoax bomb in the family home and had sent another to a relative, believed to be his stepson Ryan.

On the Saturday, he took the children on a steam-train ride at Snowdonia. Later that day, he was seen parked off the A470 in Wales, smoking in his vehicle; presumably the children were in the backseat or playing nearby at this time. When he didn't return with Amy and Owen as planned, Lyn phoned the police.

The following morning – it was Father's Day – Philcox phoned her and said, "I'll make the papers, just you see. I've left you a present." He then gassed himself and the children in his Land Rover, which was parked in a lay-by on an unclassified road – a steep track flanked on both sides by heavy foliage – in Conwy Valley, North Wales. All three died of carbon monoxide poisoning. They were found by a traumatised walker at 3pm.

Shortly afterwards, bomb disposal experts blew up a hoax bomb in a controlled explosion at Brian Philcox's marital home. They did the same to the second one, which he'd sent to a relative.

Sadly, the case echoed another murder-suicide in Wales by a vengeful husband, five years before . . .

KEITH YOUNG

Keith, a farm labourer, was twenty-four and living with his common-law wife and their daughter when he met fourteen-year-old Samantha. They met in secret for the next six years until she became pregnant with his child in 1996, whereupon they set up home together in Cheshire.

Over the next few years the couple had four sons, but the

relationship was often stormy and Keith hit Samantha on several occasions. She forgave him and they married in 2001. The violence continued, however, and she left him to move into a council house near the marital home in Weaverham.

Keith was given access to his sons on Wednesdays and every second weekend, but he proved to be such a good father that he was given additional access. Secretly, he wanted to return to the marriage and told his estranged wife in March 2003 that he loved her more than he loved the children and didn't want one without the other. Remembering the times that he'd assaulted her, she sensibly refused to reconcile.

Keith started to make vague threats, stating that if she started divorce proceedings against him, "Things would go with a bang and you would be left wondering what happened." He also told friends that he planned to commit suicide and take the boys with him, but apparently no one took him seriously or warned Samantha. He was enraged when he found out that she'd started a new relationship and become pregnant, realising that he would never win her back.

On 26 March 2003, the thirty-eight-year-old arranged to take his sons – Joshua, aged seven, Thomas, aged six, Callum, aged five, and Daniel, aged three – out in his jeep. In the early hours of the morning, when he still hadn't returned, Samantha phoned his mobile. He answered and immediately snapped, "Save your breath."

She asked where he was and he replied, "You don't need to know." He was actually parked in the Horseshoe Pass, near Llangollen, North Wales, and had the boys in the back of the jeep, dressed in their pyjamas and wrapped in quilts. He also had a petrol lawnmower with its engine running in the jeep.

Samantha asked where the boys were, and he said that they were in the back of the vehicle. He asked her if she could hear the mower's engine and she replied that she could.

Desperate to save her children, Samantha said that she'd abort her pregnancy and reunite with him, but her husband replied, "It's too late. You would have me arrested."

"It's not too late," twenty-eight-year-old Samantha pleaded.

Keith Young replied, "It is too late. Dan's dead." For the three-year-old was first to expire.

Samantha asked to speak to her other children. Keith put seven-year-old Joshua on the phone, told him to say goodbye to his mother and to tell her that he loved her. The petrified seven-year-old did just that.

"Where are you?" Samantha asked for a second time. Keith replied that another of their children had died. Seconds later he said that a third boy had died, and that he himself was feeling sleepy. She then heard his breathing deepen markedly.

The distraught young mother phoned the police, who tracked down the position of her husband's mobile phone and traced the vehicle within two hours. They smashed the windows to reach the boys, but all four children, and their father, had died of carbon monoxide poisoning and could not be revived.

When Brian Philcox gassed his children on Father's Day 2008, Samantha (who now has a daughter) offered to speak to Lyn Philcox in an attempt to comfort her. Samantha said that she had seen psychologists and counsellors but this hadn't helped, the pain never goes away. She also echoed the views of every sane person in the country, when she said, "It doesn't matter what happens between a couple – the children should never be the victims."

CHRISTOPHER TOWNSEND

This father – who designed sets for television programmes, including *Casualty* – fought a bitter battle for guardianship of his son, Charlie Bob, after his marriage broke up. On Wednesday 23 April 2008, he left a court hearing in a rage, aware that he was unlikely to get full custody. He went to his local pub and told friends that the system stank, that it was prejudiced against fathers. They were all aware that he wasn't coping and that the custody fight had taken a lot out of him.

Christopher always looked after his son on Wednesday nights, so that evening he took the six-year-old to his semidetached £320,000 home in Long Ashton, outside Bristol. At 6am, passers-by saw flames coming from the house and alerted the fire brigade. They found that fifty-one-year-old Christopher had hanged himself in the garage and Charlie Bob was dead in an upstairs room.

CHRISTOPHER HAWKINS

Enraged that his ex-wife Valerie had a new boyfriend, Christopher Hawkins, forty-seven, arranged an access visit with his four-year-old son, Ryan, on the day after what would have been his seventeenth wedding anniversary. When his fourteen-year-old daughter, Donna, arrived to collect the little boy, Hawkins locked her in, apologised to her, and then began stabbing her with a carving knife. She collapsed and he told her, "I've got to kill Ryan now." He went to the four-year-old and stabbed him nine times, the blade twice piercing his heart. Meanwhile, a horrifically-injured Donna managed to open the door and crawl into the street.

Paramedics arrived promptly at the house in Slaithwaite, near Huddersfield, to find that Ryan had bled to death. Donna was still alive but had been stabbed in her mouth, chest, abdomen, liver and extremities, a total of thirteen injuries. Her father had also carved a chunk out of her arm. She was rushed to intensive care where her mother took up a vigil at her bedside. Thanks to skilful surgery, she survived. Hawkins' sixteen-year-old daughter, Natalie, was out of the house and so escaped the vengeful attack.

Meanwhile, Hawkins went to the local pub where he'd been manager until his marriage failed, told staff and customers what he'd done, and then took refuge in his local church. Arrested, he admitted stabbing both children, saying that he did it because his wife had started an affair with a work colleague, shortly before leaving him. He later alleged, during his eight-day trial at Leeds Crown Court, that he'd been hearing voices and said that he could no longer remember anything.

But the jury didn't believe his version of events, and the judge (who praised Donna's courage) accused him of crying crocodile tears. On 5 March 2008, he was sentenced to a minimum twenty-one-year term, with another twelve years for the attack on his daughter to run concurrently. As he was led away, he looked up at his daughters in the public gallery and called, "I love you, Donna. I love you, Natalie." His ex-wife later said that Donna would remain psychologically scarred by her ordeal at her father's hands.

SHAHAJAN KABIR

Facing deportation from Britain back to his native Bangladesh because he had been refused political asylum – he had already overstayed his visa by eight years – Kabir failed to snatch his ten-month-old baby son in Carlisle town centre during the autumn of 2003. The forty-year-old, who was estranged from the baby's twenty-year-old mother, Lorna Martin, then decided that if he couldn't have baby Hassan, no one could.

Taking a knife from the curry house where he worked in Carlisle, he followed Lorna, her mother Pauline and Hassan in his pushchair into a branch of Greggs' bakery on 21 October 2003. Smiling, Kabir bent down and cut three times at his son's throat, slitting it from ear to ear before he was disarmed by a passerby. Lorna and her mother were also wounded by the illegal immigrant.

In court, Kabir claimed to be suffering from depression and said that his life was over now that his son was dead. He was sentenced to a minimum of thirteen years, but this was later increased to sixteen years by the Appeals Court, which took into account how traumatised various members of the public had been at witnessing the baby's death.

As the following cases show, American fathers are just as likely to seek revenge on their ex-wives by murdering their children – a crime which seems to be slightly on the increase ...

MICHAEL JOSEPH PASSARO

Passaro's first wife died when she was hit and killed by a car whilst attempting to assist others at the scene of an accident. He remarried, but his second marriage failed. Working by day and taking nursing classes at night, thirty-six-year-old Passaro brooded on his failed relationship and blamed it on Karen, his ex-wife.

To get back at her, he decided to burn himself and their two-year-old daughter, Maggie, to death. He wrote a suicide note to Karen on 23 November 1998, saying that he hoped that she would "live in pain" for the rest of her life, then strapped his daughter into his van outside her Myrtle Beach, South Carolina home. But, when he was badly injured, Michael Passaro's life-force kicked in and he jumped from the vehicle. Tragically, his toddler daughter had already expired due to her horrific burns.

In 2000, a now-recovered Passaro pleaded guilty to murder and arson, and was sentenced to death. He later waived his appeals, saying that he wanted to die, as life imprisonment equalled a death sentence to him. But his wishes were ignored by anti-death-penalty campaigners who petitioned to save his life.

Passaro remained steadfast in his desire to die, and was executed by lethal injection on 13 September 2002.

PATRICK GLEESON

Embittered by the break-up with his partner Edna Smith, unemployed Patrick Gleeson went to court and asked for his child maintenance payments to be reduced, claiming that he had financial problems. He returned to court complaining that his ex was preventing him from seeing the children as often as he wanted. He later applied to the court for full custody.

On 22 November 2002, he had an access visit in which he took his children – Ashley, five, and her three-year-old brother Joshua – out for a burger. He was supposed to return them in the evening, but phoned and asked Edna if he could keep them for another three days. Reluctant to make him angry, as he had a violent temper, she agreed to this. She had no idea that he'd bought a .25 Beretta handgun in Chicago a few weeks before.

Gleeson took the children to the house in Illinois which he shared with his girlfriend, Dena Fuglseth. Sometime during the next couple of days, he shot her through the head, leaving her body behind the basement trapdoor. He also shot both of his children through the head with the same weapon. Their blood was later found on a mattress in Dena's home, so he may well have killed them as they slept.

For reasons that have never been made clear, he put his offspring's corpses in his van and dumped them in the Des Plaines River before driving down to Florida. Meanwhile, Edna had reported that Patrick hadn't returned the children. The police went to Dena's house and found her dead. A huge manhunt was launched and the crime was featured on *America's Most Wanted*. Police feared a violent showdown, but a passing motorist reported the location of Gleeson's vehicle to the authorities. He was found sleeping in his van and surrendered peacefully.

He later made a statement saying that he loved Dena and that they would "be together someday in heaven". He had similar hopes for a supernatural reunion with his children, writing Edna a letter which said, "tonight they sleep with angels, safe, secure and protected from you." He wrote another five pages of vitriol to the desolate Edna, saying that the dispute over visitation rights had hurt him and the children but that she would "never lay another hand on Ashley or Josh."

Charged with three counts of murder, using a firearm and kidnapping, he was given three life sentences and is destined to die in prison.

CHAPTER THIRTEEN
TEMPORARY INSANITY

Occasionally a parent will murder a child during a psychotic episode, a temporary break with reality. Though psychotics often believe that their children are possessed, they don't fit into the 'heaven can't wait' category as they were not religious zealots to start with.

ALBERTO IZAGA

Millionaire businessman Alberto Izaga was devoted to his wife, Ligla, and two-year-old daughter, Yanire. The Spanish-born executive worked in London for insurance giant Swiss Re and the family lived in a luxurious Thames-side apartment with views of the Houses of Parliament. Well-liked at work and beloved by his relatives, he told colleagues that his little daughter was "the most precious treasure on Earth".

During an American holiday with his wife, however, Mr Izaga was clearly under stress. The couple went to a cinema in New York, but the only seats available were for *Bug* – a horror film with religious imagery in which cockroaches crawl under people's skin. It was an unfortunate choice of viewing for someone already feeling anxious and pressurised, and may have reminded him of his religious instruction at a Jesuit university.

A few weeks later, during a trip to Geneva in late May 2007, he couldn't sleep for three nights and colleagues noted that he was constantly on edge. Yet, rather than trying to relax, he went to hear a motivational speaker who talked about leaving his family for considerable periods of time and pushing himself to achieve his goals. Though he was already a high-flyer, with a degree in law and business studies and a top executive position, Alberto Izaga was profoundly affected by this rhetoric. The next evening, back in London, he went out for a meal with his wife – but, as they approached the restaurant, he began talking to himself and gesticulating wildly.

The couple returned home and, at 4.30am, the thirty-six-year-old sat up in bed and began punching the pillow. He started to talk about the motivational speech, and to ramble about the Jesuits and about the film *Bug*. He also said that his firm was part of a secret sect which was trying to take over the financial world. He was sweating profusely and, at one stage, broke down in tears. Ligla phoned a friend for help, who became an aural witness to Alberto Izaga's psychotic breakdown. He was screaming, in his native Spanish, "Bitch, die, you bastard, die! I've killed the daughter. She's disappeared now. It's finished. It's over." At this stage, Yanire was still asleep in her cot.

Murder

The child awoke at 8am and her father lifted her from her crib. She began to cry and he started to shake her. He first hit his wife on the back, then turned his psychotic rage on Yanire, saying, "I know what I have to do. I have to kill her."

Then he began screaming. "God doesn't exist! The universe doesn't exist! Humanity doesn't exist!" He proceeded to kick and punch the daughter whom he adored, after which he repeatedly battered her head into the floor. "I just want to sleep!" he screamed. "It's the only thing I want to do." Continuing the attack, he shouted, "She doesn't die, she doesn't die!" Ligla tried to protect Yanire, but her husband continued pummelling her.

Hearing screams coming from the apartment, concerned neighbours alerted the police. They arrived to find Ligla in a state of shock and Alberto cradling his severely-injured daughter, who was covered in blood. Arrested, he called the police by the name of the owner of Swiss Re then chanted the words 'Big Ben' for ten minutes.

Yanire was rushed to hospital with a fractured skull but died two days later from brain damage, on 5 June 2007. Ligla was so distraught at her daughter's death and her husband's breakdown that she was hospitalised for some time. Meanwhile, Izaga was sent to a mental hospital where he was diagnosed as seriously mentally ill. He told psychiatrists that he, his wife and daughter were all possessed by the Devil. The experts agreed that he'd suffered the rapid onset of an acute psychosis.

At the Old Bailey in January 2008, his wife stood by him, explaining, "Alberto was simply not himself. He loved us. It is impossible to believe this has happened." Judge Richard Hone told the unfortunate man, "No sentence I can impose on you can be greater than the one you will impose on yourself. This is a truly agonising case." He was found not guilty of murder due to insanity, and sent to a mental hospital from which he will be released when he finally recovers. His wife visits him every day and has begged him not to give up on life.

JOHN HOGAN

Depression ran in Hogan's family – both of his brothers had committed suicide. But he was a devoted father, whose wife Natasha would later claim that he was obsessed by the children, who he would always put before anyone else.

In 2005 he set up his own tiling business in Bradley Stoke, near Bristol, and was working incredibly long hours. The couple were seeing little of each other and the marriage became increasingly unstable. Neighbours later said that, on two occasions, John physically threw Natasha out of the house late at night and they heard her crying in the garden, begging to be let back in.

Understandably, she began to consider divorce and started to secretly research the process on the internet. In the hope of improving their relationship, the couple agreed to book a holiday to Crete – but, a week before they were due to leave, John found out that Natasha was thinking of leaving him. He was both shocked and enraged.

The couple went to Crete as planned, but the relationship remained volatile. On the fourth day of the holiday, Natasha said that she might go and stay with her mother when they returned to Britain. John began to shout at her, asking what the point of the holiday was if she was already planning to leave. He said that he would never allow her to get the house in a divorce settlement, but, if she did, he would burn it to the ground. That night, he told the receptionist that the family were leaving on the next available flight. Storming up to their room, he started to pack their suitcases. Noticing that they were so badly packed that they wouldn't close, Natasha began to unpack them again.

John continued to shout at her with a crazed look in his eyes. Natasha begged him to stop for the sake of the children, who were both in the room. Liam, aged six, couldn't stop crying; like all children, he was devastated by parental arguments.

Suddenly everything went quiet. When Natasha looked around, all three were gone. She could hear a woman at ground level, screaming.

Realising that John must have jumped over the balcony with the children, a drop of fifty feet, she phoned reception and told them to get an ambulance, then raced downstairs. She could see Mia, aged two, being lifted up. The toddler was looking around and seemed relatively unharmed. She had suffered a broken arm, but would make a full recovery. Liam, in contrast, was lying in a heap and it was obvious that his legs were broken. Then he stopped breathing and his mother began to give him artificial resuscitation, aided by a medic. But he would be pronounced dead at the hospital.

Hogan was knocked unconscious by the fall, but revived, sustaining a broken arm, broken leg and chest injuries. Filled with remorse, he once again tried to commit suicide in custody.

In August 2006, Natasha was granted a divorce.

On 21 January 2008, John Hogan's trial started in Greece. He denied planning to kill his children, and the court was told that he'd suffered an "earthquake of a psychosis". The judge concluded that Hogan had been so deranged by the failure of his marriage that he was not responsible for his murderous actions. He was found not guilty by reason of insanity and admitted to a Greek psychiatric facility.

In March 2008, a Bristol inquest returned a verdict of unlawful killing. Police handed over their files to the Crown Prosecution Service to determine if he should stand trial when he returned to the UK. In September of that same year, Ogan issued a statement about the moments when he'd grabbed his children and jumped, claiming, "these five to ten seconds of insanity were not John Hogan."

Natasha, who had by now remarried and moved to Australia with her surviving child, urged the CPS to prosecute. She insisted that justice had not been done. But, in late September 2008, they said that there was no case to answer as no new evidence had come forward.

In November of that year, two High Court judges granted a full judicial review after Hogan's barrister argued that the UK coroner, when returning the verdict of unlawful killing, had failed to take Hogan's state of mind into account.

In May 2009, the High Court quashed an inquest verdict of unlawful killing and he was cleared of murdering Liam. As this book was about to go to press, John Hogan was due to be released from a psychiatric facility in Crete.

CHAPTER FOURTEEN

LASHING OUT

Children are particularly at risk from fathers who beat their wives and from those with a criminal record for violence. Men who abuse their pets are also more likely to abuse their families. Sometimes neighbours manage to flag up the abuse before it reaches homicidal proportions – seven thousand abused youngsters were helped in Britain in 2008, because concerned neighbours contacted the National Society for the Prevention of Cruelty to Children to report their fears.

WILLIAM JENNINGS

Most physically-abusive fathers who commit murder are caught comparatively quickly, either because the child's battered body is found or because a witness to the cruelty – often the child's mother or a sibling – comes forward. But William Jennings got away with homicide for twenty-six years.

In December 1962, twenty-four-year-old Jennings was looking after his three-year-old son, Stephen, and two of Stephen's pre-school siblings whilst his wife, Eileen, took their new baby to the local clinic. But when Stephen wet the bed his father punched or kicked him, fracturing his ribs and quickly causing his death.

Jennings took his son's corpse, wrapped in a sack, to a railway embankment about three quarters of a mile from his home in Cleckheaton, West Yorkshire, and buried it under a pile of stones. To his relief, heavy snow quickly covered the burial site. When Eileen returned from the clinic, he told her that Stephen had been playing outside and had disappeared. He repeated this story to the police. A huge search was mounted but it was hampered by the snow-covered ground, which took two months to thaw, and searchers failed to uncover the child's body. Later, a wall partially collapsed over the makeshift burial site. Jennings told everyone that the boy must have been taken by travellers, though many suspected that he'd played a part in his young son's disappearance as he was known to possess a mercurial temper.

Eventually his marriage failed, and Jennings moved to Wolverhampton to remarry. Chillingly, for a man who now knew that he couldn't control his temper, he fathered another two children. He must have thought that his homicidal attack would never come to light.

Years later, on 7 April 1988, a Jack Russell terrier unearthed a small human skull on an embankment. Its owner, who by a sad coincidence had taken part in the original search for the missing boy, immediately fetched the police. A search revealed the rest of the child's skeleton and forensics established that these were the remains of Stephen Jennings, who had died as a result of a severe beating which fractured his ribs.

Arrested shortly after, his father soon admitted the murder, explaining how he'd knocked the three-year-old through the banister as a punishment for soiling himself and Stephen had fallen down the stairs. He said that the child had lived for a few minutes, and that he'd performed the kiss of life. But a medical expert at his trial said that the three-year-old must have died immediately because his injuries were so severe.

At Leeds Crown Court on 23 May 1988, Jennings pleaded guilty to manslaughter and was given life imprisonment. A subsequent appeal failed.

A confused rationale

Hard-hitting fathers like William Jennings deliberately hurt their children in the belief that they are building character, though repeated violence actually has the opposite effect – making children likely to soil themselves, experience nightmares and become either intolerably clingy or excessively withdrawn. But, in a few cases, the father may be a sadist who deliberately tortures – and sometimes sexually assaults – his progeny.

ANDREW RANDALL

Jessica Randall was born in 2005, and for the first seven weeks of her life her sadistic, thirty-three-year-old father tortured and sexually abused her. Incredibly, she was seen by thirty health workers in her native Kettering, none of whom took the decision to remove the baby from his care. When Jessica was fifty-four days old her father battered her to death, her injuries including broken ribs and a fractured skull. Andrew Randall was jailed for life at Northampton Crown Court in March 2007.

PATRICK BOURGEOIS

Patrick Bourgeois and Michelle DuMond had a son together whom they called PJ (short for Patrick Junior), but the relationship swiftly deteriorated and Patrick left the area, taking the toddler from Lewistown, Pennsylvania to Columbus, Ohio, to live with him. He made the move with his girlfriend, mother-of-two Tracy Lynn Bratton, who left her own children behind with relatives.

PJ was a quiet and friendly child, but he suffered hugely at his father's hands, being frequently beaten and bitten. Tracy also bit the little boy. They refused to leave water by PJ's bedside, so if he woke up feeling thirsty he would drink from the toilet bowl. As a punishment for this, the couple sometimes tied him up overnight.

On 27 February 1996, shortly after returning from a visit to his mother, the three-year-old refused to eat the eggs that he'd been given for his evening meal. Enraged, Patrick and Tracy dragged him around the kitchen by his ears, leaving them bruised and swollen. Patrick also bit him in the side, leaving strong teeth indentations in the boy's flesh, and hit him about the head. Thereafter, they tied his wrists behind his back and bound his legs tightly together, putting him to bed lying on his back.

PJ suffered such severe head trauma that his brain started to bleed. The blood ran down his throat and, as he was heavily bound, he couldn't roll onto his side or stomach. Blood would later be found in his lungs, airway, stomach and bowels.

Bitemarks

The following day, the emergency services received a call that a little boy was having difficulty breathing. But when they arrived at Bourgeois' trailer, no one answered their increasingly desperate knocks. They could hear a couple arguing and, when Tracy and Patrick eventually opened the door, saw that the floor had been very recently washed.

PJ was lying lifeless on the floor with blood coming out of his nose and mouth. His thirty-four-pound body was a mass of bruises. His injuries were so bad that one of the paramedics who drove him to the hospital – a man who had seen more than his share of horrors – went home that night in tears. An autopsy determined that the toddler had been battered and had choked to death on his own blood.

When interviewed by police, Patrick said that PJ had tried to bite him on the finger so he'd bitten him back. The police officer hid his shock that a grown man could bite a three-year-old boy as a punishment. He asked why PJ was bleeding, and Patrick said that he'd backhanded the boy during a little tiff. (PJ's injuries showed that he'd been hit repeatedly about the head.)

Police searched the mobile home and found blood spatters on the bottom of the fridge and the foot of the cabinets, which the couple had overlooked when cleaning the three-year-old's blood from the kitchen floor. Detectives asked why tape residue was found on PJ's wrists and legs, and they admitted taping him before putting him to bed – the discarded tape was found in the couple's rubbish bin. Tracy also admitted to biting the boy. Both were sent to prison for involuntary manslaughter, and sentenced to seven to twenty-five years.

For the next five months, a jailed Patrick Bourgeois fought for the right to bury the son he'd killed in Columbus, Ohio. His mother protested that she wanted the body returned to Lewistown, Pennsylvania. Meanwhile the autopsied corpse remained in the mortuary. Eventually, Franklin County Court decided on his burial place.

No justice

From prison, the couple continued to argue about who had done what to the unfortunate child. Yet, after a mere three years and two months, before she was even eligible for her first parole hearing, Tracy Bratton was released on the orders of Judge Nodine Miller who granted her what is known as 'supershock probation'. Judge Miller said that the torture and tying-up of PJ had been, "fraught with ignorance, immaturity and inexperience more than malevolence," and claimed, "Bratton is unlikely to commit another offence. The public does not need to be protected from Bratton." She added that Tracy Bratton's children from a previous relationship, aged seven and nine, were living with her relatives in Pennsylvania, but as they were in ill health it was best that Tracy regained custody. The public were appalled at the thought of this sadistic woman being in charge of other youngsters, or anyone vulnerable.

Not to be outdone, Patrick Bourgeois' lawyers also petitioned for his early release and, after serving a mere three years and ten months, he was set free. Ordering his release, Judge Miller said, "These particular circumstances were so abhorrent, it is hard to conceive of such a replay in Bourgeois' lifetime." (In other words, Patrick Bourgeois' excessive cruelty towards his son earned him an early release.) The judge said that PJ had been "difficult" and "misbehaving" on the night he died, as if refusing to eat his dinner was a sufficient justification to beat him to death.

BILL BAGNESKI

Most violent fathers are removed from the home after killing one of their children, but Bill Bagneski has the dubious distinction of murdering two of his offspring in separate incidents.

A military man and a strict disciplinarian, thirty-four-year-old Bill Bagneski was stationed at Hinesville, Georgia, in August 1989, when he beat his nine-month-old daughter Amy about the face. A neighbour noted the baby's injuries and insisted on driving them to the emergency room. As medics treated the infant's injuries, Bagneski shouted at her to stop crying – abusive parents often imagine that childhood distress is an act put on to provoke them, and that such displays are under a baby's conscious control.

Unsurprisingly, doctors didn't believe Bagneski's story that the nine-month-old had jumped off of the sofa and landed face down, so, upon discharge from hospital, she was taken into foster care. Two months later she was returned to Bagneski and his wife Robyn but, fortunately, Robyn divorced him shortly afterwards and took custody of their child.

In 1997 Bagneski moved back to his native Green Bay, Wisconsin, and married again, this time to a woman called Kelly. Two years later the couple had a son, Joel. On 2 November 1999 Kelly went to work, leaving her husband asleep on the understanding that he would babysit when he awoke. He claimed that he slept through the alarm and woke up to find the baby dead – which would be attributed to Sudden Infant Death Syndrome, as there were no visible injuries.

In 2001, Kelly and Bill had a daughter to whom they gave the name Kelby, just one letter away from her mother's name. Later that same year, Bill was babysitting and phoned medics to say that the baby wasn't breathing. Paramedics found her unconscious and rushed her to hospital, where she died. Bagneski told the police that the infant had been behaving difficultly as per usual, and had suddenly stopped breathing as she played in the lounge.

But a post-mortem showed that her death was due to swelling on the brain and retinal haemorrhages. The case was handed over to the FBI.

Meanwhile, Kelly – who taught parenting classes at a local college – opted to become pregnant again, convinced that her husband was innocent. The day after the Bagneskis' second daughter was born, the authorities took her into care.

The FBI ruled that Kelby's death had not been accidental; with hindsight, Joel's death was also deemed to have been a result of abuse, and so Bill Bagneski was charged with two counts of first-degree intentional homicide. Shortly before his trial, he pleaded no contest to reduced charges of first-degree reckless homicide, and was sentenced to between twenty-seven and forty years. Incredibly, his second wife maintained that he would never knowingly harm their children and said that she'd stand by her man.

CHAPTER FIFTEEN
MONEY FOR NOTHING

Loving parents often describe their children as priceless – but sociopathic parents think nothing of insuring their offspring and murdering them for financial gain. There's often a dual motive in these cases, with the father wanting to fund a more hedonistic lifestyle and resenting the time that his wife spends with the children. Or, if she's an ex-wife, he may be motivated by both the desire for money and revenge.

SHANE GOODE
On the eve of Michael Shane Goode's sixteenth birthday in 1977 – he liked to be known by his middle name of Shane – his ten-year-old stepsister died, having spent six weeks in hospital due to a horrific car accident. This wasn't the only tragedy to befall the Goodes, as, many years later, one of his stepbrothers would hang himself following a failed marriage.

Though handsome and slimly built, Shane had little self-esteem. His first marriage in 1981 to his high-school sweetheart ended in divorce after six years when he hit her so hard that he perforated her eardrum. Their daughter Tiffany was three at the time. The following year he met a bookkeeper called Annette (who had a daughter from a previous marriage) and convinced her that his first wife had been difficult and therefore to blame for the break-up of the relationship. Annette and Shane soon married, but none of his family attended the Pasadena, Texas, ceremony, though they lived nearby.

From the onset of the marriage, Shane was moody, controlling and incredibly jealous of Annette's friends. He was a postal carrier by day, but spent his weekends with the National Guard, the USA's domestic civil defence army. He told other members he was prepared to die for his country, and that he knew how to kill people and get away with it.

Shane was always short of money and so arranged for his brother-in-law Steven (Annette's brother) to steal his sports car and sell it. No one else in the family knew anything about this. Shane netted insurance money of almost $14,000, enough to pay off his debts, and for a few weeks he seemed more relaxed and amicable. Then he returned to being his usual changeable self.

Fatherhood

Annette became pregnant early in the marriage; Shane persuaded her to have an abortion as he wasn't ready to be a father for a second time. But the marriage remained volatile, and he left her to set up home alone. However, the couple occasionally reconciled when they were feeling lonely and Annette got pregnant yet again. He begged her to have another abortion, as he was already struggling to pay maintenance for his existing daughter, Tiffany, but she refused. Enraged, he walked out on her shouting that he wanted nothing to do with the impending birth.

The baby was born on 27 August 1991, christened Katherine Renee Goode, though she would always be known by her middle name. By now Annette had realised that her life was better without Shane, and she didn't initially tell him about his second daughter but she did file for divorce.

As part of the divorce petition, Annette's attorney requested that Shane pay maintenance for baby Renee. Shane resented the request and retorted that the little girl wasn't his. He became even more embittered when the courts insisted that he take a paternity test. His rage built when the DNA test proved that he *was* the father and he was ordered to pay child support. He was worried that he'd have to sell his beloved pickup truck to afford the maintenance payments, but fortunately his father agreed to lend him $5,000.

When Renee was eighteen months old, Shane took out a life insurance policy on her for $50,000 and one for the same amount on his older daughter, Tiffany. He didn't tell Annette about this. When his girlfriend, Sunny, who he was living with, overheard an answering machine message from the insurance company and questioned him, he admitted he was thinking of taking out medical insurance on the little girl. Sunny understandably wondered why he'd insure a child that he had never seen.

Shane now decided that he wanted to have contact visits with his daughter, though he admitted to his girlfriend that it was more to annoy his ex-wife than to form a relationship with his eighteen-month-old child. The law was on his side, so Annette reluctantly gave him access.

Over the next few months he took out his mood swings and resentment at having to pay maintenance on the little girl. She would return from a visit looking upset and would show no interest in her toys for the next few hours, sitting and staring into space. When she was two years old and unsettled during a sleepover at his home, he showed no empathy and spanked her for getting out of bed.

Meanwhile, Shane's first wife was becoming increasingly perturbed at the way he was treating their eight-year-old, Tiffany. She told her mother that her father had dressed her up in adult clothing and makeup and taken her to a nightclub where they had danced together. When confronted, Shane made light of the incident.

But, increasingly dissatisfied with his relationship, Shane brooded over his life and ran up a huge telephone bill by calling sex chat lines. He knew that he'd have to pay maintenance cheques for Renee for another sixteen years whilst his debts mounted. However, if she died on the other hand . . .

Murder

On 22 January 1994, he invited his firstborn daughter Tiffany, Michelle (Annette's twelve-year-old daughter from her first marriage) and two-

and-a-half-year-old Renee to a slumber party at his parents' house. The following morning, Michelle found the toddler lying motionless under her sleeping bag with liquid seeping from her mouth. She had been dead for several hours, as rigor mortis had already begun to set in. Police arrived to find Shane rocking his dead daughter in his arms, but they noticed that he wasn't tearful and his subsequent statement was similarly emotionless. His girlfriend, Sunny, was so troubled by his callousness that she would later testify for the prosecution.

An autopsy showed lung congestion and bloody froth, suggestive of asphyxiation. But the pathologist's report said that the manner of death was undetermined, and Renee's body was released for burial.

After the funeral, Annette and her mother continued to protest to the authorities that Shane had murdered the little girl. He was still awaiting the insurance money because the coroner hadn't yet completed the paperwork, which can often take months.

A female detective investigated Shane Goode and became convinced that he was guilty. She persuaded the authorities to exhume Renee and, during the second autopsy, the pathologist cut through the muscles and removed the diaphragm so that he could examine the back of the chest wall. This revealed haemorrhaging, which must have been caused by extreme force applied to the toddler's abdomen for at least five minutes. In other words, she had been squeezed to death.

Trial

At Shane Goode's trial, the defence said that Renee had died from Sudden Infant Death Syndrome (SIDS) and that the $50,000 insurance policy which Shane had taken out on her life was to have been used for her college education. The prosecution countered that the second autopsy showed trauma to the child and therefore she hadn't been a SIDS victim. The doctor who had performed the second autopsy used a life-sized doll to demonstrate how Renee Goode had been squeezed to death. Brain death would have occurred in approximately five minutes, though it might have been ten minutes or more before cardiac arrest.

Annette took the stand, telling how, after her daughter's death, she'd asked Shane if he had additional insurance on the two-and-a-half-year-old. He denied it. But he did admit to a small insurance policy that he'd taken out at work which she already knew about.

Shane Goode took the stand, looking and sounding confident. He said that his second wife and Sunny, who had both testified against him, were bitter that their relationships had broken down, that this was their motivation for painting him as money-obsessed and uncaring. But he had to admit that he'd had debts which he was desperate to pay off at the time Renee died – outstanding household bills, car payments, loan repayments, child maintenance arrears and divorce attorneys' fees.

He spoke emotionlessly of how Michelle had told him that Renee wasn't moving, describing picking the child up and noticing that she was cold and stiff with purplish discolouration on one side of her face.

The jury were out for three hours and then returned with a guilty verdict. Goode remained impassive, even when Annette read out a victim-impact statement describing their daughter as bright, cheerful, lovable, energetic and affectionate, a girl who "could have been anything: a teacher, doctor, lawyer, even an astronaut".

Confession

The child killer began serving his life sentence in an Amarillo jail and appeared to adjust quickly to prison life. A year and a half after the murder, he wrote a letter to Annette confessing his guilt. He said that, though he hadn't carried out the murder in the way that the court described it, he had killed her and that it was a cowardly and selfish thing to do. He wrote, somewhat elliptically, that he had convinced himself the murder was the only way out. But he played down the financial motive, saying that he'd acted out of bitterness at the ending of their relationship. He added that he'd since found religion and that his God had forgiven him.

STEPHEN VAN DER SLUYS

Raised as a Jehovah's Witness, Stephen married another Witness in September 1974, when he was twenty-two. His bride, Jane, was only eighteen and completely devoted to him. The couple started their married life living with relatives in Syracuse, New York. Though the new husband boasted that he could play football at a professional level, he mainly lived off welfare. (This is unusual amongst Jehovah's Witnesses, who prefer to support each other rather than seek state help.) He loved expensive clothes and flashy cars, but made no attempt to work for them. Such leech-like behaviour is one of the signs of a psychopath.

Heath's death

Eight months after their wedding, the Van Der Sluys' son, Heath, was born a healthy, happy baby. Stephen seemed attached to his son but complained about how much time Jane spent with the infant, claiming that they didn't have fun as a couple anymore. And yet, early the following year, he got Jane pregnant again.

Three weeks before Heath's first birthday – an anniversary which Jehovah's Witnesses don't celebrate – Stephen took out an insurance policy on his firstborn for $10,000. It was a surprising move for a man who was always pleading poverty.

On 8 October 1976, Jane, by now almost nine months pregnant with their second child, went to the obstetrician to keep a routine appointment, leaving Stephen alone in the house to look after the sixteen-month-old. The little boy was playing contentedly in the lounge when Jane left.

Shortly afterwards, Stephen phoned the Syracuse police to say that his son was choking. They arrived to find Heath unconscious on the couch; although they performed artificial resuscitation – as did the ambulance crew who followed them – the little boy died.

The remarkably calm father told police that he'd put Heath down for a nap at midday, then had decided to put a coin in the piggy bank in the baby's room. But he realised belatedly that dropping the quarter into the slot might wake him, so he put the coin next to the diaper pail instead. Heath, he continued, must have awoken, picked up the coin and swallowed it, choking to death.

The baby was examined, found to be clean and well-nourished, and the couple's home was immaculate. As there were no signs of child abuse, an autopsy was deemed unnecessary and 'coin lodged in throat' was the official cause of death. Shortly afterwards, Stephen received $10,000 from the insurance company.

Heather's death

Twelve days after Heath's untimely death, a distraught Jane gave birth to a daughter whom they'd decided, months before, to call Heather. (It would be interesting to know if Stephen chose the names. Some psychologists believe that parents who choose names beginning with the same letter for their children are opting for a style of false bonding – in the way that insecure couples wear matching outfits, or get identical tattoos.)

Jane's days were immediately taken up with the new baby and with grieving for the loss of Heath. But Stephen seemed more interested in spending the insurance money, buying himself a brand new Pontiac and designer clothes. Stephen's father remarried, so the couple moved out of his home and into an upstairs flat in Syracuse. Their lives continued to revolve around the local Jehovah's Witness Kingdom Hall.

Shortly before Heather turned six weeks, Stephen Van Der Sluys took out a $10,000 insurance policy on her. A month later, he woke Jane up in the middle of the night, holding Heather and screaming that the child wasn't breathing. Thankfully, Jane reacted quickly; she used her fingers to check that Heather's airway wasn't obstructed, whereupon the infant vomited. Jane then breathed air into her mouth. Paramedics arrived swiftly and further revived the child; she was back to normal shortly after reaching the local hospital, though they kept her in for four days and carried out various tests, all of which showed that she was perfectly healthy and progressing well.

Later that week, Jane got her hair cut short and hated it. She mused aloud about whether she should go out and buy a pair of hair tongs to add some curl to her new style. Stephen encouraged her to go, despite the fact that it was snowing heavily. He commented that she'd hardly been anywhere since the birth and offered to look after little Heather. Jane took the car, and was back home with her purchase in less than an hour.

On her return she checked on Heather, who was lying in her crib, only to find that the baby was dead. She became hysterical, and Stephen looked suitably distraught. This time an autopsy was performed, but no cause of death was discovered, so the pathologist wrote Sudden Infant Death Syndrome on the death certificate. Again, Stephen Van Der Sluys collected the insurance money and went on a spending spree.

Vickie's murder

Jane's father suspected that money-mad Stephen was now a double murderer. He feared for the fate of his future grandchildren, so he asked them to move in with him and his wife in Mechanicville, near the state capital of Albany, inviting Stephen to join the family industrial-cleaning firm. Stephen proved to be a poor employee but a fertile son-in-law and, on 14 October 1977, the Van Der Sluys had their third child. They called the little girl Vickie Lynn. She was extensively tested in hospital and pronounced fit and well.

Jane's parents made sure that Stephen was never alone with baby Vickie, though their vigilance made for a somewhat claustrophobic lifestyle. The two couples worked together, lived together and worshipped together at the Kingdom Hall. Stephen seemed devoted to his daughter, and had the family take numerous photographs of him with Vickie. But he showed no interest in providing for her, mainly living off a mixture of insurance payouts and welfare cheques.

On 6 December 1978, he took out a policy on his own life and Jane's, and insisted also on having the fourteen-month-old insured for $30,000.

The following month, Jane's father needed help to clean the Kingdom Hall and Jane volunteered. By now Vickie was a robust little girl, and they had no qualms about leaving her with her apparently-devoted father. But when Jane returned from the church at midnight, the child was dead in her crib. Stephen said that she'd been acting strangely, was breathing noisily and had asked for a glass of water. He'd given her the drink and then laid her down to sleep.

Though most cases of Sudden Infant Death Syndrome occur between one and six months, and Vickie was fifteen months old, the pathologist wrote SIDS on the death certificate.

By March of that year, Stephen had cashed the insurance cheque and bought himself yet another car, a limited edition Trans Am costing $15,000. He also bought himself a designer suit and an expensive coat, plus a fur coat for Jane. The couple moved to Oklahoma where Stephen planned to learn welding, but he showed no aptitude for his new trade and within eighteen months they returned, broke as usual, to New York.

The ones that got away

In April 1981, Jane gave birth to their fourth child, Shane, but refused to let Stephen insure him, saying that she didn't want to tempt fate. So Stephen made money by claiming on his insurance policies, citing a mental disability and telling a psychiatrist that he was clinically depressed because his first three children had died.

Shane and his sister Jennifer, born in March 1983, would live because their father had no financial incentive to murder them. They were also hooked up to a baby monitor that would have sounded the moment that their breathing stopped.

Statutory rape

Outwardly, Stephen Van Der Sluys' life was all about his religion and his family, but inwardly he lusted for hedonism and excitement. At Christmas 1984 he and Jane arranged to informally foster another

Jehovah's Witness, a sixteen-year-old girl from a troubled background. By now, the Van Der Sluys were living in Ontario County and were stalwarts at the local Kingdom Hall. Everyone was impressed that they were willing to take on a teenager – but, almost immediately, Stephen began to clandestinely have sex with her.

Within two months the girl returned to her family, but she was already expecting his baby. When she told Stephen he went to her father and admitted that he'd impregnated the teenager. Hoping for damage limitation, he wept and talked about the loss of his first three children to SIDS, painting himself as a victim rather than a predator. He also admitted that his long-suffering wife was due to give birth in the same month as the sixteen-year-old.

The teen's father went to the police and, in April 1985, they arrested the father-from-hell for having sex with a minor. (She was below the age of consent in Ontario County.) That July, he pleaded guilty to thirty-six counts of statutory rape and sodomy.

Admission

Police had long suspected that he'd had something to do with the deaths of his first three children, and now they pressed him to make a full admission. Much to their surprise, he began to falteringly tell them partial truths. He swore that he hadn't harmed his firstborn, Heath – though detectives were convinced that he had – but admitted that he'd been holding his secondborn, Heather, when he suddenly became convinced that she was about to expire. After rambling and sobbing, he added, "I felt that she should die." He'd put her on her stomach in the crib (a baby should always be laid down to sleep on its back – but this wasn't the advice given in the 1970s), and put her face into the pillow. His wife had returned to find her dead.

He made a similar rambling statement about Vickie's death, saying that she'd looked at him as if to say, "Help me," and had started crying. He'd put his hand over her mouth for about a minute but she was still wailing inconsolably. He told police that he could tell she was going to expire and so he lay her on her stomach in the crib, placing her face into the pillow, before she duly died.

Van Der Sluys said that he'd killed both girls, but that he hadn't planned to, and added that he'd done it to get more love from Jane, not for the insurance money. But investigators were convinced that cash was his main motive. After all, he'd gone on huge spending sprees when the cheques arrived, rather than spending time with his desolate wife.

Exhumations

The authorities exhumed all three children, but Heath and Heather's corpses were too decomposed to offer any clues. Fortunately, a suspicious local undertaker had carefully embalmed the third baby, Vickie, convinced that one day she'd be dug up and autopsied. He'd done a remarkable job of preserving the fifteen-month-old; pathologists cut her open to find lung lesions consistent with smothering.

Van Der Sluys refused to incriminate himself in Heath's death, so he was only charged with Heather and Vickie's homicides. Whilst he was in custody, his teenage victim gave birth to his illegitimate daughter and, five days later, his wife gave birth to his sixth child, a boy. Her religion had taught her to be a dutiful and compliant wife, so she was standing by Stephen. The police felt that she was living in a world of her own.

Sentenced for Vickie's murder

But in summer 1986, aware that Vickie's autopsy suggested foul play, Stephen Van Der Sluys pleaded guilty to manslaughter one, which carried a sentence of eight to twenty-five years. It allowed him to convince himself that the death hadn't been premeditated, that he'd merely suffered a sudden brainstorm and done the wrong thing.

Sentenced for Heather's murder

When it came to Heather's murder, Stephen opted to be tried by a judge rather than a jury. The trial opened on 23 September 1986 at Onondaga County Courthouse in Syracuse.

The prosecution claimed that SIDS was a hollow term, meaning not a cause of death but the *absence* of a cause of death. They said that smothering could easily be mistaken for Sudden Infant Death Syndrome. An expert witness testified that pathologists often put down SIDS on the death certificate rather than carry out a full autopsy, and said that the insurance on these children was a strong motive for bringing about their untimely deaths.

In turn, the defence suggested that chemicals in the home – everything from carpet shampoo to perm lotion – could have killed Heather, or that she might have succumbed to a bad cold.

In summary, the prosecution said, "This is killing for greed and it's a killing because of inadequacy." They saw the defendant as an inadequate because he'd resented the time that his wife spent with the children, and had wanted her to himself at whatever cost

Five days later, the judge found Stephen Van Der Sluys guilty of murder. He was sentenced to twenty-five years to life. A few weeks later, his wife finally admitted to herself that he was guilty of the murders and filed for divorce.

Van Der Sluys is currently housed at Attica prison, and will become eligible for parole in 2019.

RONALD CLARK O'BRYAN

In the aforementioned cases, the children died relatively quickly from suffocation. O'Bryan, however, poisoned his son and watched him die an agonising death.

Ronald O'Bryan, a married man with two children, ran up large debts and secretly decided to insure and kill one or both of them. He took out $40,000 insurance policies on eight-year-old Timothy and five-year-old Elizabeth in 1974, but did not tell his wife. In the same timeframe, he boasted to his fellow employees in Texas that his money problems would soon be over, and asked one of them where he could obtain potassium cyanide.

Once he'd secured some of the deadly poison, the thirty-year-old bought five Pixy Stix – large plastic tubes filled with sherbet which were popular at the time in America. He carefully opened the tubes, mixed cyanide into the sherbet and tightly resealed them. Hiding the sweets in a bag, he accompanied his wife and children to a friend's house in Pasadena for Halloween. He hadn't been the best father in the world, so his wife was pleasantly surprised when he offered to take their children and those of a friend to trick-and-treat around the neighbourhood.

Before long, every child had a basket filled with candy and O'Bryan had given out all of the poisoned Pixy Stix, making sure that his son had one. By poisoning strangers as well as his own offspring, he planned to make it look like a random act by a mad person in the neighbourhood.

Back at the friends' house, all the children sat down at the table to enjoy their sweets, but O'Bryan was horrified to see his friend's son reaching for Timothy's Pixy Stix. He knocked it out of the boy's hand, explaining that it was for his son.

By mid-evening, when they returned to their home in Deer Park, Timothy still hadn't touched the lethal candy, so his father suggested he try some before going to bed. The eight-year-old obediently took a swallow of the usually-sweet powder, but said that it tasted bitter. He went to bed but almost immediately got up again, telling his father that he had stomach pains. Murmuring that this was nothing to worry about, O'Bryan urged him to lie down, but, seconds later, Timothy rushed to the bathroom and vomited. He screamed in agony and his mother, a nurse, insisted that they phone the emergency services. By the time they got to the hospital, Timothy was dead.

Police soon ascertained that the Pixy Stix had been poisoned and asked O'Bryan where Timothy had got it. He replied that a stranger had opened his door a crack and handed out five of the Stix, and that he'd distributed them around the neighbourhood. Detectives quickly alerted everyone who had been trick or treating, and located the other candies; one eleven-year-old boy had fallen asleep whilst clutching his, thankfully unable to prise off the top, and Timothy's five-year-old sister, Elizabeth, hadn't yet started hers.

But within days O'Bryan was in the frame, when an insurance agent told police that he'd recently taken out policies on his children. Detectives also found out that he'd asked a chemist about the use of poisons. Even more damningly, cyanide mixed with sherbet had been found on a knife in his home – presumably the knife which he'd used to cut open the Pixy Stix and stir the poison into the original contents. He was arrested, still loudly proclaiming his innocence. But his wife testified against him at his trial, and it took the jury only an hour to find him guilty. He was sentenced to death.

For almost ten years, the killer – who was now nicknamed the Candyman – lived on Huntsville's Death Row. But, on 31 March 1984, his luck finally ran out and he went to the death chamber, having apparently enjoyed a last meal of pizza. He made a final statement, saying, "What is about to transpire in a few moments is wrong . . . I pray and ask God's forgiveness for all of us respectively as human beings." His death by lethal injection was much more humane than that of his son.

CHAPTER SIXTEEN
FAMILY KILLERS

Men who kill their entire families tend to fit roughly into two categories, though traits found within these categories – such as the need to exert control – can overlap.

There's the man with an inflated sense of his own importance who sets himself up as the breadwinner, often adhering to a 'no wife of mine will ever work' ethic. He refuses to confide his problems to his spouse or relatives, even when he's sacked, demoted or facing bankruptcy.

Such men often live over-romanticised family lives and are desperate to present a united front to in-laws and outsiders, sometimes today even setting up a website to publicly portray their happiness. Ironically, as the relationship becomes stale, they often take a mistress or use prostitutes.

When the idealised picture that they have created breaks down because their deception becomes apparent, or because of external pressures, the man becomes depressed and despairing. His solution is to murder his spouse and offspring, sometimes even killing his parents or parents-in-law. Thereafter, he may turn the gun on himself. (The murder weapon is often a firearm, though other popular methods of slaying family members include suffocation or smothering, followed by a hanging suicide.)

The second category is that of the controlling father who becomes incensed when his wife or children make lifestyle choices which he disapproves of. In frustration, he annihilates his spouse and offspring.

These murders are often familicide-suicides, but, if he goes on the run, he invariably remarries and creates another family which he controls in an equally unhealthy way.

There is one familicide – mainly perpetrated by fathers – every six to eight weeks in the UK.

CHRISTOPHER FOSTER

Outwardly, Christopher had it all – a loving wife and daughter and a palatial mansion, Osbaston House in Maesbrook, Shropshire. He had made his fortune by selling pipe-insulation technology to the oil industry, but had latterly incurred heavy losses. In October 2007, his company went into liquidation with debts of £1.8 million. Christopher owed over £800,000 to the tax man, but he didn't tell his family about his increasing money problems and they continued to enjoy a luxurious lifestyle. That same month, he was issued with a High Court order which prevented him from selling his house.

By May of the following year, he was accused by a judge of stripping assets from his company to thwart his creditors. The judge also branded him as untrustworthy.

Foster knew that the bailiffs were due to arrive on Tuesday 26 August, that his family would lose their home and stables and he'd no longer be able to send his daughter to her private school.

On the 25th, the fifty-year-old tycoon, accompanied by his forty-nine-year-old wife Jill and fifteen-year-old daughter Kirstie, attended a neighbour's barbeque. Everyone acted normally and posed happily for a photograph, though Christopher drank steadily throughout the festivities. Shortly after midnight they left their neighbour's house and walked home. Jill went to bed and Kirstie went to her room and logged onto an internet chatroom, where she began sending messages to her many friends.

Meanwhile, Christopher went to the cellar and loaded his shotgun. His image was captured on CCTV, and would later help detectives piece together what had happened: In the early hours of the morning, he crept up to the top floor and went into Kirstie's room, where he shot her through the head as she slept. (Earlier reports stated that she was chatting online before midnight when she was murdered, but later evidence suggest she was killed between 1am and 4am when fast asleep.) He then went downstairs to the bedroom where his wife lay sleeping and killed her in the exact same way.

The businessman also shot the family's three horses and four dogs before driving a horse trailer in front of the driveway's security gates and puncturing its tyres, knowing that this would block access for the emergency services. He ran a network of pipes through his house and to his outbuildings, using them to flood his house with oil. Returning to the marital bedroom, he set the oil alight. As the blaze took hold, he put the shotgun to his head and fired. It was now around 4:45am.

Five minutes later, a neighbour was awakened by the sound of the petrol tanks in Christopher Foster's four cars – which included a Porsche and a Land Rover – exploding. The fire brigade arrived to find that the £1.2-million mansion was an impenetrable inferno; it was three days before Christopher and Jill's bodies were recovered from the skeletal framework, and four days before Kirstie's body was found, the remains so badly charred that they had to be identified from dental records.

Friends and relatives of the family later confirmed that the Fosters were a close-knit trio, and expressed their shock at the double murder and suicide.

NEIL ENTWISTLE

Neil and his brother Russell grew up in a working-class family in Worksop, Nottinghamshire. His mother, Yvonne, was a part-time school-dinner lady, his father Clifford a miner who later became a Bassetlaw district councillor. Yvonne was protective of her sons and would play football in the garden with them when they were teenagers, rather than risk them getting into trouble on the streets.

Neil was a quiet boy who did well at school and went on to York University to study electrical engineering and business management, where he showed a natural aptitude for computers. He also enjoyed outdoor sports and joined the university rowing team. It was there, in 1999, that he met Rachel Elizabeth Souza, an exchange student from America, studying English Literature, who became the team's coxswain. They fell in love and he seemed to overcome his natural shyness, telling everyone that he was going to spend the rest of his life with her.

Psychologists would later speculate that he suffered from Narcissistic Personality Disorder, where a person has an inflated sense of their own importance and a desperate need for love and attention. They tend to idealise love, are preoccupied with fantasies of success and wealth and react inappropriately to criticism from others.

Marriage

Just over a year after they met Rachel had to return to her prestigious Catholic college, Holy Cross, USA, to complete her degree. But the couple kept in touch by phone and email, and, after she graduated in 2001, she returned to England for a teacher-training course. The following year, Neil graduated with a Masters in electrical engineering and began to work as an IT consultant for a defence contractor. Colleagues found him to be mild-mannered and unfailingly polite. Though the couple couldn't see each other as often as they wanted due to work and studying commitments, she referred to him as her knight in shining armour and Neil spoke of her in equally glowing terms.

In 2003, he posted a message on the Friends Reunited website saying that he was soon to marry the most wonderful woman in the world. That same year, he established a website which offered to help customers set up their own internet pornography businesses, a service for which he charged £2000. Meanwhile, Rachel began to teach English and drama at St Augustine's High School in Redditch, where she was a popular member of staff.

In August the couple married in Massachusetts, holding their reception at a re-enactment village which mirrors life in the seventeenth century. They honeymooned in the Mediterranean, posting photographs on their website – www.rachelandneil.org – of their luxurious cruise. (After the murders the website was removed.)

When their honeymoon ended, they returned to England and to their respective jobs, renting a cottage in the Midlands. Neil kept his day job but spent some of his spare time setting up two more websites, namely www.deephotsex.com (offering photographs of young women, often in fetish poses) and www.bigpenismanual.com (which offered penis-enlargement techniques). He made money from both sites and also sold software on eBay with a good rating, though this would later change.

Though he had a talent for computer design, he sometimes suffered from low self-esteem, telling Rachel that his working-class accent was holding him back and that he'd never make a success of his life when he sounded like a miner's son. But he seemed genuinely pleased when Rachel became pregnant with his first child.

Fatherhood

On 9 April 2005 she gave birth to a seven-pound baby, Lilian Rose. The couple were delighted with the new arrival and posted numerous photographs on their family website, signing them with the words, "love, the happy family." Rachel phoned her mother so often with news of their grandchild that the bills were huge.

As the months passed she missed her mother and stepfather more and more, and so the couple decided to relocate to America. Neil resigned from his company, telling them that it was due to domestic reasons. In September, they flew to Massachusetts with six-month-old Lilian and moved in with Rachel's family in their large, hospitable home. Rachel posted a photo of Neil and Lilian on the website with the caption, "I love my Daddy." The couple wept with happiness as they had the baby baptised into their Catholic faith.

Rachel was very close to her mother and stepfather (her father had died when she was nine) and they were delighted to have their granddaughter on the premises, but life was more difficult for Neil as he couldn't find employment. He gained weight and seemed envious of Rachel's bond with her parents, admitting to them that his own family ties were not as close. He also told them that his firm back in England was paying him $10,000 a month for secret military operations, but they noticed that he financed everything with credit cards. He explained this away by saying that his money was tied up in offshore accounts, but that he'd soon have access to it. Rachel was also short of cash, having run up student loans which totalled £18,000.

Increasing debt

Shortly before Christmas 2005, Neil Entwistle took out a month's subscription to a swingers' website, posting that he was an Englishman who had heard that American women were good in bed. And on 4 January 2006 he emailed a female swinger to say that he was in a relationship but "would like a bit more fun in the bedroom". There was obviously trouble in Paradise.

By now, Entwistle's attempts to make money through various internet get-rich-quick schemes were failing, and he continued to sell software on eBay but no longer sent the goods. As a result, on 9 January, he was banned from selling on the site. Some of the items for sale were listed under Rachel's name so she too came under fire, with one irate customer posting the comment, "Rachel Entwistle is a lying bitch."

On 12 January, the couple moved to a luxurious, rented four-bedroom colonial home in Hopkinton, a forty-five-minute drive away from Rachel's family. The house had three bathrooms and an eight-person Jacuzzi. Neil Entwistle paid a two-month deposit plus a month's rent with valid cheques, and said that he hoped to buy the house once his offshore accounts were moved to the US. He also kitted out the house with expensive upmarket furniture and leased a white BMW, both on credit. But the money that he'd made from his get-rich-quick schemes was running out and he knew that he'd never be able to pay the bills.

Until now he'd been something of a fantasist, always able to convince himself that his next idea would result in serious wealth, but now he was listed on various sites that warned customers of internet scams and he'd maxed out on most of his credit cards. Rachel must also have been aware that he was letting people down, as he'd used her email account and she'd received hate mail from dissatisfied customers.

Four days after they moved in, Rachel had used one of their joint credit cards but it was refused through lack of funds. It's believed that the couple had a serious argument. Rachel went to bed early and Neil accessed a porn site, doubtless bringing himself to orgasm in order to relax. That same night, someone using his 'ent' username asked a search engine to list the best ways to kill someone and also typed in the search criteria, 'how to kill with a knife'. The following afternoon, the same account was used to search for 'knife in neck kill' and 'quick suicide method'. In the same timeframe, Neil sent a photograph of himself, leaning back in a chair and clutching his erection, to an adult sex site.

On the 18th, Rachel questioned Neil about an interview that he was going for, and he angrily reassured her he would get the job and make lots of money. In reality, it had fallen through and he had no other prospects. That night he again trawled the internet for sex, looking at pornography in a bid to distract himself from thinking about his debts. How could he admit to his wife and in-laws that he wanted more than a conventional marriage could offer and that he was verging on bankruptcy? His parents-in-law had treated him like a son and believed that he was completely devoted to their beloved daughter and grandchild, and that he could financially support his little family.

On the evening of Thursday 19 January 2006, Rachel spoke to her mother briefly on the phone, telling her that she was still busy unpacking items for the new house and preparing for a forthcoming dinner party. That same day, either she or Neil took yet another photo of a beaming Lilian. But, on the Friday, Rachel failed to answer her mother's calls, as she and baby Lilian were dead.

The murders

When friends whom the couple had invited around for dinner arrived at the house on Saturday night, they couldn't get an answer and called the police. The television was on downstairs and the radio was playing in the baby's bedroom. The couple's basset hound, Sally, was in a crate without food though she had a bowl of water. (The friends walked and fed the animal before returning her to the lounge.) The couple's BMW was also missing from the garage, but Rachel's mobile phone was in the house, filled with messages from worried family and friends.

Police noticed linen crumpled on top of the couple's bed, but they didn't investigate further. If they had done so they would have found the corpses of Rachel and Lilian Rose lying beneath. Satisfied that no foul play had taken place, they locked up the house – which, unusually, had all of the shutters down – and left.

The following day, Rachel's friends and family made a public plea for them to return, as there was still no sign of the family and the dog was sounding increasingly distressed. This time, when officers entered the house they could smell decomposition and traced it to the master bedroom. Gingerly lifting a corner of the quilt, they saw a foot.

Early reports said that the mother and baby had been beaten about the face, but no further information has emerged about this so it's possible that decomposition was initially mistaken for bruising. Both twenty-seven-year-old Rachel and nine-month-old Lilian appeared to have been shot whilst sleeping, one bullet going through Rachel's forehead whilst the other entered Lilian's stomach, causing massive internal injuries and passing through her body to lodge in Rachel's chest. Rachel had died instantly but the baby had lived for a few minutes, curled into her mother's breast. The weapon was a Colt .22 calibre revolver. This was one of the guns which Rachel Entwistle's stepfather owned and had taught Neil how to shoot.

The couple's BMW was missing but later found at Logan International Airport, Boston. Investigators found that Neil Entwistle had driven it there and boarded a plane to England at 8:15am on

21 January. Arriving in London, he rented a car and drove for eight hundred miles with breaks, eventually spending the night in a hotel in his home town of Worksop. On Sunday 23, he arrived at his parents' house.

Neil Entwistle's story

On Monday at 11:30am, Neil's father, Clifford Entwistle, phoned Rachel's stepfather, Joseph Matterazzo, and said that Neil had called him to explain that something had happened to Rachel and the baby. "What did he tell you?" Joe asked guardedly.

Cliff said that Neil had gone out for twenty minutes on the morning of Friday 21 and returned to find his family murdered in the bedroom. He'd called the police then driven to Matterazzo's house, but found it empty, became confused and took a flight back to England. Cliff added that he didn't know where Neil currently was.

Joe hung up on him in disgust, but moments later the phone rang again. This time Neil was on the line. He insisted that he'd gone out, come back and found them "like that", and didn't know what had happened. Joe once again hung up and phoned the state police. The following day, they declared Neil Entwistle a 'person of interest' to the enquiry. They had by now autopsied the bodies and only then became aware that Rachel had been shot in the head, as the bullet hole was small and hidden by her hair.

Neil now spoke on the phone to a detective, saying that he'd come back from a shopping trip to find that his family had been shot. This was of interest to investigators as the cause of death hadn't been apparent when they found the bodies. It was only when they moved Lilian away from her mother that they saw the entry wound in Rachel's chest, and it was only when Rachel was autopsied that they found that she'd also been shot above her hairline. Upon finding the bodies, Neil continued, he'd decided to commit suicide and had grabbed a kitchen knife, but then put it back – fearing that stabbing himself to death would hurt too much.

He then claimed he drove to his in-laws' place, planning to shoot himself with one of his father-in-law's guns. But the couple were out at work and he no longer had his key, so he left and took a plane to England to be with his parents. (Detectives knew this was a lie as they'd found keys to his in-laws' house in his BMW.)

For the rest of the week he remained behind closed doors with his parents. By now, the double murder had become international news and reporters were camped outside the Entwistles' immaculately-painted home. When he briefly left the house on 31 January he was watched by Worksop police, as American detectives had asked them to keep an eye on him.

Meanwhile, Massachusetts detectives continued to investigate the deaths of his wife and daughter. Remembering that he'd mentioned Joseph Matterazzo's guns, they sent them for forensic tests and found Rachel's DNA on the muzzle of the .22 calibre Colt, suggesting that she had been shot from eighteen inches away, so close that tiny droplets of blood and cerebral matter had spattered onto the gun's muzzle. Rachel had never handled the gun, but Joe had taught Neil to shoot with it.

Seven weeks after she was baptised, Lilian Rose and her mother were buried. Neil Entwistle did not return to the States to attend the double funeral, though he went back to the place where he'd met Rachel for the first time and spent the day there. "Never ask why God allowed this to happen," the priest said, before telling mourners that their deity wasn't to blame.

Though he must have known that his arrest was pending, Neil Entwistle remained obsessed with money. On 7 February, he phoned the landlord of the murder house and asked for his deposit back. On the 8th a US judge signed off a warrant for his arrest.

Arrest

On 9 February 2006, Neil Entwistle went to London for the day with a friend and got on the tube, the numbers of various escort agencies in his pocket. When he heard that detectives were waiting for him on the platform, he asked his friend if there was any way that he could avoid them. There wasn't. Shortly before midday Scotland Yard arrested him. In his pocket they found notes about his life story and how he intended to sell it to the highest-bidding newspaper. He wrote that he had so much material that they could serialise it over an entire week. After spending a night in a British jail, he then said that he did not want to fight extradition and was duly returned to Massachusetts, where he was remanded in custody.

In jail awaiting trial, he lost weight but told guards that he'd needed to lose a few pounds in the first place. He was given access to the prison psychologist but soon said that he didn't want further psychological help. In a letter to his parents he appeared to be suicidal, saying that this might be the last missive he ever wrote to them and that he had nothing to look forward to. He added that his last wish was to be cremated and have his ashes sprinkled on Rachel and Lilian's grave.

Entwistle was moved to the medical unit for his own protection where, ironically, he was attacked by a paranoid schizophrenic. Though kicked and bruised, he sustained no lasting injuries. After three weeks, the staff declared that he wasn't suicidal and he was returned to his lonely prison cell.

Trial

On 6 June 2008 his trial began in Woburn, outside Boston. He was charged with the double murder plus illegal possession of a firearm and ammunition. Despite the evidence, he pleaded not guilty. In court he would not meet his in-laws' gaze, though he smiled at his parents and brother who sat in the front row of the public gallery. Clifford and Yvonne Entwistle wept as they heard of the pornographic websites which he'd contacted and when they saw photographs of the baby's bloodstained clothing. Neil Entwistle also wept briefly at this point.

The prosecution said that, faced with mounting debts and an unsatisfactory sex life, he had killed his wife and baby with his father-in-law's Colt .22, returned the gun to his in-laws' house whilst they were at work then fled to England, driving around aimlessly for hours – perhaps trying to concoct a plan – before arriving at his parents' house.

The defence countered that Rachel, whilst suffering from post-natal depression, had shot Lilian, the bullet going on to enter her own body. She had then shot herself in the head. Allegedly making the grim discovery after returning from a four-hour shopping trip, Neil had returned the gun to her stepfather's house in order to hide the truth and preserve her honour. (Their religion had persuaded them that suicide was morally wrong.) Gunshot residue had been found on both of Rachel's hands and on a pillow, but not on things which Neil had been known to touch.

She rather than he, said the defence, could have been the person making searches online using words like 'euthanasia' and 'suicide'. But they couldn't reasonably explain why Neil Entwistle had immediately left the country after discovering the deaths.

Neil said that he'd gone into a trance after finding the bodies, but computer records showed that he'd gone online an hour and a half after Rachel and Lilian were believed to have been killed. The defence said that it was to check his email, whilst the prosecution alleged that it was to look at internet porn.

By now Entwistle had changed the part of his story which said that his in-laws were out and he was unable to gain access to leave them a note about what had happened. He now said, through his lawyer, that he had entered the house and returned the gun to avoid Rachel's memory being tarnished with the supposed stigma of suicide.

A fortnight later the jury went out to deliberate their verdict. They decided that Neil's interest in internet swinging sites wasn't a motive for the murders, believing them to be mostly fantasy. But they took the possibility of Rachel's suicide seriously and a juror of the same height held her right arm at different lengths to simulate shooting herself through her hairline. She and the other jurors agreed that, if Rachel shot herself in the head, she'd have gun-burn marks all over her face.

(She'd also presumably be finding it hard to concentrate, having inadvertently shot herself in the torso whilst shooting Lilian.)

On 25 June, after two days of deliberation, they found the twenty-nine-year-old guilty of both murders. Entwistle closed his eyes momentarily when he heard the verdict but was otherwise emotionless.

Further investigation

After the verdict was handed down, true-crime readers posted on various blogs, questioning why gunshot residues had been found on Rachel's hands but not on things which Neil had touched within hours of the shooting – such as his BMW's steering wheel and his father-in-law's keys. To understand more about this aspect of the case I interviewed Paul Millen, who has over thirty years' experience in the scientific investigation of crime. He runs the forensic firm Paul Millen Associates (www.paulmillen.co.uk) and has authored the book *Crime Scene Investigator*.

Paul told me, "Gunshot residues are very delicate. When we examine a suspect we usually tape (with sticky tabs) hands (upper folds and creases), the face and comb the hair (any facial and head).

"Gunshot residue (GSRs), also known as firearm discharge residues (FDRs), are in fact primer residues from the percussion cap of the ammunition. This is the chemical which goes 'bang' and forces the bullet or shot out of the weapon. They form a cloud which falls on items in the immediate proximity.

"The residue consists of spherical (molten) particles containing a mixture of lead, barium and antimony. They are only found in this combination in FDRs. They are delicate and will fall off exposed skin within three or fours hours. They remain longer on hair as it acts as a kind of net."

Paul continued: "FDRs are found in very small amounts only. They are found usually using a scanning electron microscope, and a scientist will report that they have found them even if they find only a few (or in some cases even one) particles, such is the rarity of the elements. Finding more indicates a great probability of close contact and quick sampling.

"The particles remain longer on hair and clothing. Washing the skin or hair and washing clothes will remove most if not all traces. So sampling or recovering clothing early and before washing is essential.

"Looking for blood or tissue in the muzzle of a weapon is an important search to indicate the weapon's close proximity to the victim, along with powder burns (concentration of residues) on the victim's skin."

This puts the conspiracy theories to rest: Entwistle had simply showered away the gunshot residues before leaving the house.

A life sentence

The day after being found guilty, Neil Entwistle was sentenced. The jury rejected the option offered by the judge of a fifteen-year sentence followed by the possibility of parole. Instead, he was given two life sentences for the murders plus an additional ten years for firearms offences, as he didn't have a licence to carry a gun. The judge also decreed that he must never be allowed to profit from writing a book about the case. Entwistle looked surprised at the judge's decree.

He will spend the rest of his life within the bleak walls of Cedar Junction prison, near Boston. A maximum-security jail which houses some of America's most feared inmates, it has a suicide rate that is three times the national average.

KENNETH SEGUIN

Sadly, the same area of Massachusetts was the scene of a similar familicide fourteen years earlier, when a supposedly perfect father murdered his wife and both of his children before trying to blame the killings on two other men.

Kenneth Seguin was raised in Hopkington, near Boston, where Neil and Rachel Entwistle would eventually rent their luxurious colonial home. He would later allege that he was sexually abused twice during his childhood by one of his uncles, a Roman Catholic priest.

Kenneth, who was good-looking, married the equally attractive Mary Ann (known to her friends as Polly) in 1981. By the mid-1980s they had two equally beautiful children – their son, Daniel, followed two years later by a daughter, Amy. They lived in Holliston, near his childhood town of Hopkington.

The computer executive appeared devoted to his family, often enjoying time at a holiday cottage with them at Cape Cod and coaching Daniel's soccer league. Neighbours referred to them as looking like characters out of a Norman Rockwell painting. (Rockwell was the twentieth-century American artist who produced sketches of loving couples and doting parents, his cosy Americana finding fame on the covers of the *Saturday Evening Post*.) Mary Ann enjoyed her aerobics classes and Kenneth raised money for a Roman Catholic mission. But, in a bid to enjoy an upscale suburban lifestyle, he also spent way beyond his means.

By 1990 serious cracks were appearing in the marriage. The couple argued constantly over work and money, but only their closest friends knew of this as they still presented a united front to the community. Mary Ann threatened to leave Kenneth and he contemplated suicide.

The following year his attempts at building a dream home for the family fell through, leaving him with even more debt. In the same timeframe he faced mounting pressures at work and was prescribed Prozac, though he only took a few tablets before storing it away in the medicine chest. He also saw a stress-management counsellor.

In the autumn of 1991 Kenneth's father-in-law died, contributing to the increasingly low mood. The couple's arguments escalated over the next few months until he again felt suicidal. If Mary Ann left him and took the children with her, as he feared, then everyone would know that their perfect family life had been a mirage . . .

Three murders

On 28 April 1992 Kenneth Seguin took a razor from his office, concealing it (and possibly also a knife) in his trouser pocket before he took the children to a soccer game. Afterwards he gave them juice cartons, laced with over-the-counter sleeping pills, to drink.

Parking outside a phone booth he used it to call his wife, who was out at a cosmetics party. Seguin left a perfectly reasonable-sounding message on the answering machine. He said that the kids had persuaded him to take them on an impromptu drive to the Cape, and that she shouldn't worry, sounding normal, even slightly upbeat. It's possible that at this stage Kenneth Seguin was planning to kill himself after murdering the children. Suicidal people often cheer up, knowing that their problems are about to end.

The thirty-four-year-old father drove his increasingly-drowsy five-year-old daughter and seven-year-old son to Franklin, near Hopkington. When they lost consciousness he slit their throats, slashing so ferociously at Daniel's neck that he almost severed his head. He also cut the children's wrists so deeply that Amy's hands were almost hanging off. Finally, the previously-devoted family man dumped their bodies into a Franklin pond and cleaned up the inside of his vehicle before returning home.

Seguin let himself quietly into the house and entered the master bedroom where his wife slept. He'd later say that he lay down beside her for two or three hours before killing her, but no one can verify this statement. What's certain is that – sometime between 10pm and 8am – he battered the thirty-four-year-old's head with an axe as she slept.

Afterwards, the computer executive went downstairs and poured himself a glass of orange juice, before writing a list of chores which he had to accomplish. This included helping the priest whom he would later accuse of molesting him; afterwards, he intended to paint his mother-in-law's house. When the coast was clear, Seguin wrapped his wife's nightdress-clad corpse in bed linen and towels and drove to the Sudbury River in Hopkington State Park, where he threw the body in.

A convenient amnesia

Within hours, Mary Ann's body was seen floating in the river – and eight hours later, one mile away, two canoeists found Kenneth Seguin wandering around a wooded area with cuts to his body, wrists and neck. They called the emergency services, who arrived to find him lying on his side. He was rushed to hospital, where he was patched up before being interviewed by police.

Seguin told them that two men had broken into his home, battered his wife with an axe, drugged his children and dumped his wife's body at an unknown location. They'd driven him to the woods before slashing him with a knife.

Police immediately began a massive search for the couple's children, though after searching the home and both family vehicles and finding blood traces they feared the worst. Suspicion turned on the computer programmer when it became obvious that his wounds were self-inflicted, and they found his message on the answering machine saying that he'd taken the children to the Cape.

Two days later, Kenneth hobbled into court and pleaded not guilty to his wife's murder, though the assistant district attorney insisted he'd be answering a charge of murder in the first degree. His wrists, neck and one foot were bandaged and he had stitches to a wound at his temple. His shirt was torn and he was sporting a new beard. The prisoner ignored journalists' questions as to what had happened to Daniel and Amy, though he had previously told his lawyer that he didn't know where they were.

A court-appointed psychiatrist said that Seguin showed no signs of mental illness, though he claimed to have memory gaps (killers often have such convenient amnesia) and suicidal thoughts. His lawyer asked for him to be moved to a mental hospital for observation, but the judge refused this and also denied the killer bail.

Seguin told his lawyer that he missed his wife and that he was fearful for the future of his son and daughter. After the arraignment he was returned to Middlesex County Jail.

Meanwhile, the search for the missing children continued. Hundreds of searchers and tracker dogs combed Hopkington State Park and the adjacent reservoir, whilst helicopters hovered overhead. The following day divers pulled Daniel and Amy's virtually bloodless bodies from the sludge at the bottom of the pond, and Seguin was indicted for their murders too.

Trial

During Kenneth Seguin's trial in early 1993, at Middlesex County Superior Court, his attorney said that he had suffered a psychotic episode during which he killed his children and wife. The defence also suggested that his use of Prozac might have caused suicidal ideation. (But the drug would have had to be remarkably long-lasting, as Seguin hadn't taken it in the past eighteen months.)

Seguin had by now retracted the 'two bad men did it' story. He now claimed that he killed his family and tried to kill himself as he believed they would be "reunited in heaven". He also claimed that the alleged sexual abuse in childhood by a priest had affected his mind, whilst the defence noted that he had 'only' struck his wife once with the axe, suggesting that he hadn't wanted to cause her pain. He'd also drugged Amy and Daniel before slashing them and had apparently cut deeply to ensure that they died quickly. The defence also claimed his self-inflicted wounds were a serious suicide attempt.

The prosecution countered that Seguin had phoned his wife en route to taking the children to their deaths, and that the message he left for her on their answering machine showed no signs of disordered thinking. He had taken the drugged juice and murder weapons with him to kill Daniel and Amy, carefully disposing of their corpses and cleaning up afterwards. He had then gone on to kill his wife, covertly removing her body from the house and quietly disposing of it. He had also faked his own assault and been in a lucid state when discovered, yet had lied to the police about having no clue as to his family's whereabouts.

On 7 February 1993, the jury found him guilty of second-degree murder. They said afterwards that they had rejected a verdict of first-degree murder, because they recognised that severe stress and depression had left him mentally impaired – but they also believed that he'd known his actions were wrong and that he wasn't insane.

The judge sentenced him to life, with the possibility of parole after thirty years. He stared woodenly at the floor as the sentence was handed down, but said nothing. His lawyers appealed on a technicality, but his sentence was upheld.

That December, Kenneth Seguin was stabbed by another prisoner at Walpole Maximum State Prison, but the wound was not fatal. He went on to run the prisoner's union, a position he still holds to this day.

CHRISTIAN MICHAEL LONGO

Christian's mother and father separated when he was three, after which he and his two-year-old brother lived with their mother. She later married a fellow Roman Catholic, Joe Longo, who loved the boys dearly and became their legal guardian.

When Chris – as he preferred to be known – was ten, his mother became a Jehovah's Witness and took him and his younger brother to five meetings a week, with further religious study at home in Indianapolis. Soon he was ministering to other children and, from age eleven, gave Bible readings at the church. The school holidays were similarly given over to religion and were spent going from door to door, trying to convert strangers to his mother's beliefs.

The Witnesses preached that anyone who didn't share their creed was 'worldly' and that the faithful shouldn't socialise with them, so Chris missed out on parties and sleepovers with his school friends. He was also banned from partaking in after-school sports, as anything which took him away from his spiritual life was considered to be bad.

Chris was bright and his teachers told him that he had untapped potential, but his faith told him that the world was about to end so there was little purpose in further education. By the time that the Longos moved to Louisville, Kentucky, he was getting Cs and Ds in his subjects, despite having a high IQ. The family then moved to Ypsilanti in Michigan where, at sixteen, he left school and took a series of menial jobs.

At eighteen Chris asked his parents if he could go on his first ever date, as he found himself attracted to twenty-five-year-old MaryJane Baker, a fellow Jehovah's Witness who worked for a paediatrician. But his parents said that he was too immature to court a woman and couldn't date whilst he lived under their roof.

Determined to forge a life for himself, Chris moved into a flat with two other Witnesses, though he struggled to pay his share of the rent from his photography-shop assistant's wages. He and MaryJane quickly became inseparable, though she was understandably troubled when he stole money from his employer to buy her an engagement ring.

Their religion forbade sex before marriage so they opted for a short engagement, marrying on 13 March 1993. Chris had just turned nineteen whilst MaryJane was almost twenty-six.

After their honeymoon in Jamaica, generously paid for by Chris's parents, the couple rented an apartment in Ypsilanti. MaryJane was a natural introvert whilst Chris was extroverted, so he sometimes felt stifled by the relationship. Taking a better-paid job as a field manager with Publications Circulation Fulfilment, he spent freely on computers and photography equipment and bought his wife expensive designer clothes.

A father of three

In the summer of 1996, MaryJane became pregnant. Both parents-to-be were delighted, and Chris set up a website to celebrate the pregnancy. The couple even hired an artist to decorate the nursery. Chris attended the birth on 28 February 1997 and proudly brought home Zachery, his firstborn son.

MaryJane was almost thirty when Zachery was born and her biological clock was ticking. Chris also wanted a second child, and so was delighted when Sadie was born on 30 April 1998. He'd been travelling a lot in his job but apparently gave it up so that he wouldn't miss landmark family moments, such as his child's first steps.

He took a sales job with a lower salary, which meant that his evenings were free and he was able to spend more time at Kingdom Hall. The Jehovah's Witnesses were so pleased with his commitment that they considered making him a congregational elder, and his fellow worshippers were impressed that he seemed so devoted to his young family.

But the father-of-two was struggling to pay the bills, and, with MaryJane's blessing, booked a vasectomy – but before he could have the operation, he found that she was pregnant again.

Their daughter Madison was born prematurely on 19 October 1999 and spent a month in hospital, when Chris understandably did very little work at his commission-based job. Yet he continued to spend freely and soon maxed out on his fourteen credit cards. Keen to give friends the impression that he was a high flyer and that money was plentiful, he was deeply humiliated when his wife's car was repossessed.

Theft

Determined to succeed, he left his sales job and set up his own company, cleaning newly-built homes for the construction industry. Convinced that he would soon be a rich man, he promised to buy the home-based MaryJane a minivan. He worked incredibly long hours, and was successful on paper, but the construction companies were slow payers and he soon had serious cash-flow problems which he hid from his wife. In order to look successful, he stole a minivan worth $34,000 by taking it for a test drive (he gave the car dealer a fake driving licence) and never brought it back. He repainted the van, changed the number plate and gave it to MaryJane as a gift, later falsifying emails which looked as if they had come from the van's finance company. This was the second time that he had resorted to crime in order to look good to his family and fellow Witnesses. Sadly, it was a pattern which he would repeat with ultimately fatal results.

A joyless life

Shortly after stealing the minivan, Chris had an affair with a married Jehovah's Witness and sent her emails, saying that his life had been joyless before she came along and that he would always love her. MaryJane found the emails and went to the elders, who barred Chris from some church activities. At twenty-six, the age when most men are only thinking about settling down, he was already supporting a wife, three small children and the family pet, a beautiful husky dog called Kyra. His business was failing fast but he couldn't bring himself to file for bankruptcy.

Desperate for a quick financial fix, he deposited counterfeit cheques totalling $17,000 in his account and initially got away with it. But, instead of using the money to pay outstanding bills and save a nest egg for the future, he bought himself a second-hand motor boat and jet skis. He was emotionally still a boy, in need of instant gratification, who was trying to lead a mature man's life.

When he went to deposit yet another forged cheque he was arrested and charged. MaryJane was shocked at this latest deceit but agreed to stand by him. Both Longos hoped against hope that word of his crime wouldn't leak out.

On 21 September 2000 Chris went to court and was given eighty hours of community service, also ordered to pay more than $30,000 to the company that he'd defrauded. He took the sentence calmly, but was shaken when details were reported in the local newspaper. How things looked were more important to Longo than how things actually were. When the Jehovah's Witness elders read about his crimes he was promptly 'disfellowshipped', which meant that he could still attend services but that no one was allowed to speak or make eye contact with him. He was even shunned by his Jehovah's Witness parents. It was a devastating blow for a man who needed to be loved and admired, so he decided to stay away from the Kingdom Hall.

His wife remained devout, she and the children attending services without him. Meanwhile, the couple fielded numerous phone calls about their increasing debts.

In January 2001, Chris forged his father's signature on a credit-card application and used the card to buy scuba equipment and diving lessons. Again, these were bizarre choices, as by now his company had failed and he owed his parents over $100,000. He also owed back wages to his employees, all of whom were fellow Witnesses.

By May he couldn't stand being ostracised any longer, and persuaded MaryJane to move with him and the children from their home in Ypsilanti to a warehouse in Toledo, Ohio, an hour's drive away. They told no one of the move in a bid to outwit the police and their creditors.

Further crimes

Temporarily unemployed, Chris Longo made money by stealing goods and selling them, and by pawning his diving equipment. He also continued to forge cheques. When the police impounded his stolen van and boat, he went on the run with his family in a rental truck. Cruelly, he released their dog, Kyra, on a piece of wasteland. (Animals which are abandoned in this way suffer terribly.) When Zachery asked what had happened to his beloved pet, he said that the dog was on holiday just like they were and was staying with a kindly farmer. The four-year-old accepted this. But MaryJane was soon worn down by trying to keep the children happy as they missed their pet, were often hungry and no longer had a stable routine.

Eventually they reached Yachats, a little hamlet on the West Coast, and rented a holiday chalet there. By now, Chris was so broke that he had to pawn their television set in order to buy food. But he didn't have enough money to pay the rent for the chalet for more than a few days, so the family went on the road again.

The Longos drove on to Newport, Oregon, where by washing windows Chris raised enough for a room at a travel lodge. With five of them cramped in one small motel room, the family survived on noodles and cereal.

Chris's lack of education made it difficult for him to find well-paying work, so he took a part-time job at a coffee shop in the hope that someone else would leave and he'd be given more hours. He refused to walk to work, believing that arriving in his truck gave him status, but when he ran out of money for petrol he simply filled up his vehicle at a garage then drove off. Meanwhile, MaryJane and the children spent most of their days at the children's section of the local library.

In December 2001 Chris moved his family into a much more expensive condominium hotel in Newport, despite the fact that one month's rent equalled one month's salary. He knew that he'd never be able to pay the second month's rent, but spent a few days living in relative luxury, even inviting another couple whom they'd recently befriended over for a meal.

As a single man he might have enjoyed such *bonhomie* on a regular basis – but, with four other mouths to feed, his life would remain cumbersome. A rational adult would have claimed welfare benefits or simply jumped ship, but he had been brought up to believe that the man of the house had to appear strong and capable, to be the provider. To leave his family would make him seem weak and immoral, but if *they* appeared to have deserted *him* he would be viewed sympathetically . . .

Four murders

During the third week of December 2001, Chris Longo told his co-workers that his wife had left him and gone to Michigan, taking the children with her. He appeared to be coping well with his unexpected freedom, arriving at a Christmas party at a local restaurant in a brand new car which he'd stolen hours earlier from a showroom. He laughed and joked with other revellers and they assumed that he was putting on a brave face. He would also begin to make use of a nearby gym.

On the 19th, his four-year-old son Zachery's body was washed up on the shore: it had been weighed down with a pillowcase containing a rock but had slipped free. There was no identification on the body. Three days later, three-year-old Sadie's body was discovered by divers with a pillowcase tied around her ankle. She too had been weighed down with a rock.

As he worked out at the gym, Chris Longo heard the news that two unidentified children's bodies had been found in local waters. For a man who apparently believed that his offspring were in Michigan with his wife, he had a sudden inexplicable urge to leave town and drove to San Francisco, sleeping in the stolen car and later spending two nights at a youth hostel, though he kept a low profile for such an extroverted man.

A woman who had babysat for the Longos and had seen artist's sketches of the children on television sadly identified the two bodies, as police began searching for the rest of the family, fearing the worst.

The search ended on 27 December, when divers found a large suitcase in the water close to the Longos' condominium. It contained the nude body of MaryJane Longo, who had been battered about the head and strangled. A second weighted suitcase contained the corpse of two-year-old Madison, who had been murdered in the same way. Most spouses and children who become homicide victims are killed by a member of their family, so police were now very keen to locate Christian Michael Longo, who had abruptly left his job at the coffee shop.

Identity theft

On 27 December, unaware that his wife and youngest child's corpses had also been found, Chris Longo took a flight to Dallas and another on to Mexico. Broke as per usual, he used a stolen credit card to pay for both flights. Arriving in Cancun, Mexico, he took the identity of journalist Michael Finkel as he'd previously enjoyed the man's features in everything from *National Geographic* to *Skiing* magazine. (Finkel would later write an absorbing book, *True Story*, about this identity theft and his later correspondence with Longo.) On 11 January 2002, Christian Michael Longo was placed on the FBI's Most Wanted List.

Meanwhile, he socialised in the sun with other tourists and found that many of the female holidaymakers were attracted to him. By his second week in Cancun he started dating a German photographer and they became lovers. He told her that he was divorced but had never had children; he also claimed to be Michael Finkel, in the region to research travel articles. Together they went hiking and scuba diving and visited a monkey sanctuary.

But by now Longo's photograph had appeared all around the world, and a tour guide told the FBI's fugitive program in Mexico City that the family killer was living in Cancun. On 13 January he was arrested without incident in his modest cabin. The following morning he boarded a plane to Houston, handcuffed to an FBI officer. The officer would later allege that he asked Longo why he'd killed his children and that he'd replied, "I sent them to a better place."

He was flown from Houston to the Lincoln County Jail, where detectives questioned him about the murders. Longo wept copiously but did not admit to being the killer. He said that he wasn't yet "right with God", and so hadn't attempted to join them by committing suicide. He also explained that Witnesses believe that people are only sleeping in the grave, that everyone will be resurrected someday by Jehovah and, if they pass a test, will be sent to Paradise.

Detectives noted that he referred to MaryJane as "the wife", objectifying her rather than using her name. And in letters to journalist Michael Finkel he wrote of his wife and children in the third person, noting that "a much loved family was suddenly no more". (Criminals often do this to disassociate their violent acts from themselves, saying, "She was hit by a bottle," rather than the more honest, "I hit her with a bottle.") Still sociable, he made friends with the men in the neighbouring cells on the maximum security wing, a Wiccan and a Seventh Day Adventist. He also read prolifically.

For the first time ever he had time to contemplate his life, writing to Finkel: "I'm grateful for the holding pattern that my life is in now. If I wasn't in here, there'd be much more to stress about."

A psychologist hired by the defence found that Longo had a narcissistic personality disorder, that he had an above-average need for love and attention and tended to present everything in a positive light.

He desperately needed the approval and admiration of others and was preoccupied with daydreams of unlimited success. Ironically, MaryJane had cherished, approved of and admired him, yet he'd killed the very thing he loved . . .

Court

Initially, at his arraignment, Longo's attorneys said that he was 'standing mute'. This essentially meant that, whilst he hadn't stated that he wasn't guilty, it would allow him the option of later changing his plea to not guilty by reason of insanity. But, at a plea hearing in early 2003, he said that he was not guilty of the murders of Zachery and Sadie but guilty of the murders of MaryJane and baby Madison.

The trial for the murders of Zachery and Sadie began on 10 March 2003 in Oregon. The prosecution alleged that Longo had murdered his wife, and then all three children, disposing of MaryJane and baby Madison's body in Yaquina Bay, adjacent to his condominium. Unfortunately for Longo he had broken a pipe on the dock with one of the weighted suitcases, causing a continuous water spray which made it easy for the authorities to identify the dumping site.

Putting the other two children in his vehicle, the prosecution alleged, he drove for fifteen minutes until he reached Lint Slough Bridge where he dropped them into the water. At 4:30am a lorry driver saw a man resembling Longo parked on the bridge and asked if he needed help, but the man replied that he was fine.

Prosecutors also noted that, six months before his family died, Chris Longo had downloaded an instruction book on murder from the internet. He also owned a book on changing your identity and had obituaries of dead men that he'd cut from newspapers, plus details of their social security numbers which he'd obtained by fraudulent means.

A few days before the murders he'd started to dispose of the family's photograph albums, which suggested premeditation. After the murders he'd thrown out five rubbish bags filled with his family's clothes, shoes, scrapbooks and mementoes. Within a few hours, the man who'd claimed that marriage and fatherhood were everything had transformed himself into a carefree bachelor.

He'd also told an acquaintance that MaryJane had been having an affair for years and had left him for another man. (No one who knew her well believed this defamatory statement – she was devoted to Chris and saw marriage as a lifelong commitment.) The acquaintance had believed Longo's version of events and had pitied him, until Zachery's body was fished from its watery grave.

The court was shown photographs of the four corpses. MaryJane's injuries were particularly shocking, her face and neck bruised purple, her body forced into a suitcase. Michael Finkel, who attended the trial, later wrote, "It was the graphic images of MaryJane that eliminated any notion I'd had that the killings were somehow motivated by love or compassion. MaryJane's murder was clearly a violent and frenzied act." Longo wept when Zachery's body was described as being "in amazing condition", despite the time that it had spent in the water.

The defence had a difficult case, given that Chris had already admitted to murdering MaryJane and baby Madison. Noting that no blood had been found in the Longos' condominium, the alleged murder site, they let the defendant take the stand.

The defendant's tale

Longo spoke at length about his childhood, his relationship with MaryJane and his employment history. He talked of their last journey together, how they'd even pawned her engagement ring to survive. He'd felt ashamed at having to take a part-time job in a coffee shop because he believed that he had the potential to be a journalist or an entrepreneur, so he'd told his co-workers that he was from a wealthy family, ran an online business and was merely working in Starbucks to get life experience. In reality, he and his family were living in a $20-a-night room in a Travel Inn, subsisting on noodles and cereal.

Longo said that he'd bought a book about changing one's identity because he was wanted by the police and needed a new name to apply for a job with prospects, so that he'd apparently have a clean record when employers ran background checks. He also said that he'd downloaded a book about hitmen in order to glean some content for a website about forbidden knowledge which he'd launched. But after a mere eight people had paid the $12 membership fee, he'd had to shut down the enterprise and go on the road.

Longo admitted that, by Sunday 16 December 2001, the family had been in the condominium for two and a half weeks but still hadn't paid any rent. He'd lied to MaryJane, saying that he'd been promoted and that his salary increase was covering all the bills – but in reality he knew that they were going to be evicted the following morning, and had no money to rent anywhere else.

According to Longo, he told MaryJane the truth in the early hours of the morning, admitting to various frauds and thefts. He said that she'd slapped him and he'd left the marital bedroom, going to sleep with the two older children in the lounge. The following day she'd driven him to work and picked him up again at night. He said that she'd been acting oddly and that, when they returned to the condominium, she had become hysterical. It was then that he'd noticed Madison was dead.

Longo continued on the witness stand with his unlikely version of events. He said that he'd shaken his wife a few times, hitting her head against the wall, as he tried to establish the whereabouts of his other two children. He also alleged that she'd said, "They're in the water," whereupon he'd choked her to death.

Longo said he'd crushed her body into a suitcase and began to do the same with Madison, claiming he then realised that the little girl was unconscious but breathing. Believing that she was too far gone to be saved, he had squeezed her throat until she expired, and then put her in a second case. He carried both cases outside to the docks and dropped them into the bay, then threw all of the children's clothes and photo albums in a dumpster. He said that he'd had no idea what had happened to Zachery and Sadie until he was arrested in Mexico.

It's unclear how Longo thought that this ridiculous story would bolster his defence. MaryJane had been an exemplary mother who was breastfeeding Madison and had bonded completely with the baby. She was so devoted to her little ones that she even took them with her when she picked Chris up from his work at night, rather than leaving them alone for a few minutes in the motel. She had not been disfellowshipped from the Kingdom Hall, and so various family members would have accommodated her and the children if she'd chosen to end her marriage to a pathological liar.

Guilty

The prosecution understandably had a field day. Why hadn't he phoned for an ambulance for Madison when he realised that she was still breathing? Why had he driven to a dumpster with the family's possessions rather than search for his other two children? Why had he stolen a car and gone to a party rather than spend time mourning for his offspring, and why had he fled to Mexico when the first of the bodies was found? Longo gave vapid answers to every question, and it didn't escape the spectators' notice that he finished giving his evidence on April Fool's Day.

The jury, comprising four men and eight women, took a mere four hours to find him guilty of murdering Zachery and Sadie. He had already admitted to murdering MaryJane and Madison.

The penalty phase included a plea from the defence to let Longo live. They noted that he'd never previously been violent and could serve a useful life in prison – but the image of the four dead bodies and the element of premeditation must have been uppermost in the jury's mind. On 16 April 2003, after four days' deliberation, they returned a death sentence.

Afterwards, Chris wrote to Michael Finkel, admitting that he'd murdered his entire family. He said that he'd deliberately blackened MaryJane's name on the stand because he knew that no one would believe him and that the jury would sentence him to death, bringing justice for her family.

In his latest version of events he said that he'd come home to find his wife suffocating Madison, that he'd strangled both of them and thrown them into the bay, then put his two remaining children in his vehicle where they'd soon gone to sleep. He'd found that he couldn't bear to tell them what had happened to their mother and little sister, and so he parked on the Lint Slough Bridge, weighed them down with rocks and dropped them into the water. Zachery had remained asleep, but Sadie had opened her eyes and screamed.

It's possible that both children were indeed still alive when they entered the river. Zachery's autopsy report stated that the cause of death was consistent with drowning, as silt from the river had been found in his airway. But it was equally possible that the silt had washed into his airway as he lay dead on the river bed.

Currently on Oregon's Death Row, Chris Longo spends his days exercising, watching television and reading. He also does janitorial duties for the prison. He has many female penpals, several of whom have proposed marriage, as well as various male penpals who apparently felt a bond with him after watching televised excerpts from his trial. As Oregon executes few of its condemned prisoners, he may well die of old age.

JEAN-CLAUDE ROMAND

Jean-Claude was born in 1954 to Anne-Marie and Aime Romand, a housewife and forester respectively, in Clairvaux, France. His mother suffered from ill health and subsequently had two ectopic pregnancies where the foetus developed outside the uterus. The couple were deeply religious and didn't want to talk about pregnancy in front of their young son, so he feared the worst when his mother was hospitalised and believed that she was going to die. When she returned home, he promised himself that he would be the perfect son who would never give her any cause for alarm.

And for the rest of his childhood he succeeded, being unfailingly polite and always smiling. Deep down though, he was desperately lonely but only told his boyhood fears to his dog.

Sent to boarding school, he was bullied and pretended to be ill in order to be sent home. He spent the rest of the year living with his introverted parents and rarely saw anyone else. Though he had a high IQ and was a voracious reader, he wanted to be a forester like his father because he loved the woods.

But when he went to university at Lyon, he saw that forestry wasn't a respected career and so switched to medicine. Psychologists later wondered if he did so to understand his mother's illness. But he was also attracted to his distant cousin, Florence, who was studying medicine at Lyon.

Depression

Jean-Claude's parents thought that Florence was ideal. She, too, was a Catholic, an old-fashioned girl who liked baking cakes for church fetes. Though she wasn't particularly enamoured of him, he joined her social circle and courted her until their first act of lovemaking when he was twenty-one.

Immediately afterwards, Florence said that she only wanted to be friends and broke off the relationship. Jean-Claude hid his feelings as usual, but the strain took its toll as he slept in and missed one of his second-year exams. Shortly after this he left his friends at a nightclub and returned, blood-spattered and bruised, telling them that he'd been abducted by several men and beaten up. In truth, he'd inflicted the injuries on himself to get attention, to feel more alive.

Failing at his studies, Jean-Claude could no longer pretend that all was well, spiralling into a deep depression where he shut himself away in the apartment that his parents had rented for him. He no longer went to university, cleaned the flat or socialised, and he lived exclusively off tinned food. Eventually one of his friends visited, whereupon Jean-Claude lied and said that he had cancer. In retrospect, both this and the previous lie about being beaten up were a form of Munchausen's syndrome, where sufferers invent or cause symptoms in order to receive attention and care. (The syndrome is more common in men, though Munchausen's-by-proxy, where the sufferer harms their own child or another person in their care, is much more common in women.)

Jean-Claude's friend tidied up the flat and cooked for him, as the young man's cancer apparently went into remission. He soon returned to his studies at university.

But, unknown to his friend, Jean-Claude never again sat an end-of-term exam. He went to lectures and read books in the library, even helping Florence (who sympathised with his various illnesses) with her studying. And he lived off the money that his parents gladly gave their student son. Yet each year, when the exams came around, he sent in fake medical certificates explaining that he was ill and had to remain at home for the duration of the exam period. He then re-enrolled the following year.

Florence failed her exams and switched to pharmacology, making it easier for him to lie about his ostensibly excellent qualifications. She wasn't surprised when he told her that he'd landed a good job as a research scientist at the World Health Organisation in Geneva, and was trying to find a cure for heart disease. Impressed by his dedication to his career, she married him and they relocated to Ferney-Voltaire in France, a manageable drive away from Jean-Claude's supposed workplace just over the border in Switzerland.

A good father

On 14 May 1985 the Romands had their first child, Caroline. Almost two years later, on 2 February 1987, they had their son Antoine.

Jean-Claude adored his young family and played with them endlessly, also taking numerous photographs. They loved him too. As they matured, he drove them to school every day and at weekends he took them skiing or to child-friendly restaurants.

In turn, the children wrote proudly in their essays that Daddy was a doctor – but this remained a lie. For every day, after taking the children to school, the bogus medic would drive to a service station and sit there, reading magazines and scientific journals and drinking tea. Several times a month he drove to the World Health Organisation, his ostensible workplace, and went in on a visitor's pass. There he would use the bank, post office and facilities so that he came home with WHO stamps. He also brought home the organisation's free literature and left it lying around the house. When Florence wanted to call him, she simply used his answering service and it beeped him, whereupon he'd call her right back.

Bizarrely, he funded himself and his family by continuing to draw on his parents' bank account (and by spending money which he and Florence had banked from the sale of an apartment) just as he had as a student in Lyon. Even more bizarrely, they never questioned why a high-earning WHO scientist had to drain their financial resources month after month. Jean-Claude must have been incredibly selfish – after all, he could have taken a job in a nearby town, so providing for his wife and children whilst still maintaining his doctor myth.

Fraud

Eventually, of course, his parents' money ran out – but luckily this coincided with a relative asking him to help invest a sizeable sum of money. Jean-Claude took the money and began to live off it. He told other relatives about the connections he had to high finance and they too gladly invested in his lucrative-sounding schemes.

A potential mistress

Bored and increasingly dissatisfied with his life, Jean-Claude began to court the ex-wife of one of his friends. She soon asked him to invest her life savings. After all, he seemed plausible, taking her to upmarket restaurants and buying her expensive gifts. He quickly became besotted with her – just as he had initially been with Florence – and would phone her several times a day. At first the attraction was mutual, but

Jean-Claude must have been an indifferent or peculiar lover, for, after they had sex for the first time, she told him that they could only be friends. She had no idea that she was echoing Florence's words of many years before.

Lonely and longing for something new, the unemployed family man continued to see her in a platonic capacity. But the deception was getting too much for him and, one day, he phoned a doctor friend to say that he was having a coronary. The doctor examined him, diagnosed a panic attack and prepared to leave. Desperate for attention, Jean-Claude admitted the affair (though he possibly kept quiet about its brevity) and lied that he had cancer, a story which had won him sympathy in the past.

The deception deepens

By now his life was becoming increasingly fraught. His investors had begun to ask for their money back, but of course he'd spent it. And one of the mothers at the Romand children's school asked Florence why her family had never attended the lavish World Health Organisation Christmas party, one of the highlights of the year. She explained that Jean-Claude didn't like to spoil the children, but the excuse must have sounded lame even to her. Then the school reported that they'd tried to contact Jean-Claude at the WHO, but couldn't find him listed in the international register.

Florence questioned her husband about these inconsistencies in his life and he made excuses, then claimed again that he had cancer. He 'withdrew' from work and lay at home in a deep depression, but revived slightly when asked to sit on the parents-teachers committee. Suddenly he had status again. He voted to demote an adulterous teacher, a majority viewpoint, then did an abrupt U-turn and campaigned for the teacher's reinstatement, saying that the man's sex life should be a private affair. Some of the other parents were visibly angry at Jean-Claude Romand's newfound liberalism and he shrank from them, apparently fearing physical violence.

Ironically, those who most fear violence are often the ones who inflict it as they project their own aggression onto others. Now the bogus doctor hatched a plan to rid himself of his entire family and his one-time lover, so that he could start again.

Familicide

At dawn on Saturday 9 January 1993, he battered in his wife's skull as she lay sleeping. Later, he got the children up for breakfast as usual and fed them, telling them not to wake Mummy. After they'd eaten, he took his five-year-old daughter upstairs and shot her as she lay on her stomach on the bed. Moments later he called to his seven-year-old son, and shot him too.

Jean-Claude Romand drove to his parents' house and had lunch, before promising his father that he'd fix a defective heating valve in the bedroom. As they examined the valve, he shot the old man twice in the back. Returning to the lounge, he shot his mother in the front. He also shot their pet Labrador, despite being an animal lover, as he believed that his parents would want it with them in their afterlife.

The five-times killer went on to keep a prearranged date to take mass in church with his mistress, after which he drove her to a quiet location and sprayed her with teargas before using a stun gun on her. She pleaded for her life and he relented, sobbing and telling her that he was terminally ill. Unaware that he'd already killed his extended family, she told him that if he sought psychiatric help she wouldn't go to the police.

Fire

Jean-Claude returned to the house where his dead wife and children lay, and passed the time recording programmes on the VCR. At 3am he prepared to fake his own attempted suicide, doubtless hoping that he could plead insanity and serve a short period in a psychiatric facility. He took twenty barbiturates which were ten years past their sell-by date and set the attic on fire, knowing that the street cleaners were nearby at this time and would see the flames from far away.

When the smoke began to get dense, he opened the window of the room he was in. Unfortunately for him he then lost consciousness, fell back into the room and was badly burned.

Jean-Claude Romand spent the next few days in a coma, with his religious friends praying that he would die rather than revive to find that his wife and children had died in this awful accident. But, when his murdered parents were found, the authorities began to realise that Dr Romand was not what he seemed.

When the family man regained consciousness, he told the police that a shadowy figure had attacked him and must have set the fire. The stranger must also have killed his parents. "You don't kill your mother and father. It's God's second commandment," he said. But the police were able to prove that he'd bought the gun which fired the lethal shots at his mother, father, their dog and his children. Florence had apparently been bludgeoned to death with the household's rolling pin. Realising that the evidence was stacked against him, he admitted the murders, saying that he believed his wife and children were in Heaven and had forgiven him.

Jean-Claude Romand was sentenced to life imprisonment, with a recommendation that he serve at least twenty-two years. He will be eligible for parole in 2015, when he is aged sixty-one.

MOHAMMED RIAZ

Whilst the likes of Neil Entwistle, Christian Longo and Jean-Claude Romand killed in order to escape from financial pressures and return to a more carefree bachelorhood, UK-based Mohammed Riaz chose to take his own life, and that of his family, rather than let them become Westernised. As such, he fits into the controlling category of family killers.

Riaz was a traditional Muslim who grew up in the North West Frontier Province of Pakistan and had little formal education. He had an arranged marriage to an Anglo-Pakistani woman called Caneze, who had been born in the UK but educated in Pakistan, returning to the UK in her mid-teens. She was also a Muslim. The couple lived in Accrington, Lancashire in England.

Caneze spoke perfect English, whilst Mohammed knew only a few words. She was better educated than he and did voluntary work for a child-improvement centre, working with schools and mosques. She was also an interpreter for the local authority and was regarded as an extrovert pillar of the community. In contrast, Mohammed was a quiet and retiring man who worked at a plastic bag-manufacturing factory in Blackburn.

Mohammed wanted his daughters to be raised as traditional Muslims, whilst his wife took a more relaxed approach. She would buy their children Western clothes; enraged, he would destroy outfit after outfit. He insisted that his daughters wouldn't go to college when they grew up and that they'd have arranged marriages.

In 2003, Caneze's traditionalist father died and she became even more liberal. Tensions in the marriage continued to build as she became a diversity adviser to Accrington Stanley football club. Mohammed's stress intensified when their teenage son, Adam, was admitted to hospital with bone cancer and the prognosis was poor.

On 31 October 2006, Caneze and the couple's four daughters – Sayrah, aged sixteen, Sophia, aged fifteen, Alicia, aged ten, and Hannah, aged three – enjoyed a Halloween party at their end-of-terrace home. It's likely that Mohammed regarded this as a final affront to his religion. He waited until the early hours of the morning, when the family were asleep, then locked the house from the inside and poured two cans of petrol outside the room where his wife and three-year-old daughter slept. After lighting the fuel, he went into another room to die.

His wife and all four daughters burned to death in the resultant inferno, though Mohammed Riaz lived for two days in the specialist burns unit at a Manchester hospital before succumbing to his injuries. Adam, whose cancer was by now terminal, was let out of hospital to attend the funeral of his family but died six weeks later. Friends, family and the police later paid tribute to Caneze and her children, and local people of various ethnicities and religions wept openly at the funeral.

CHRISTOPHER MICHAEL BENOIT

Benoit is one of the few family killers who does not fit into the idealised or controlling pattern. Instead, steroid abuse and brain damage caused increasing rage and paranoia, and he killed his family before taking his own life.

Born to a French-Canadian couple in Montreal in 1967, he was a small but athletic child. When he was still at primary school, he saw a similarly small-built wrestler, the Dynamite Kid, performing impressive feats on television. From then on the little boy was determined to become like his wrestling hero, and even shaved his head in order to copy the man. He begged his father, Michael, to buy him a set of weights and his father obliged for his twelfth Christmas. Thereafter, Chris spent little time with his parents or siblings, obsessively lifting weights instead in his mirrored room.

That same year the family moved to Edmonton, where Chris alienated schoolfriend after schoolfriend who doubled as his training partners – for none of them could keep up with his obsessive weightlifting schedule. Completely focused on his ambition, he had no time for partying or for girls.

He spent hours at Edmonton wrestling shows, carrying the wrestler's bags, sweeping the ring and testing the ropes. Most of the wrestlers thought that the tiny thirteen-year-old was only nine or ten and they were gruffly kind to him, appreciating his humble manner and deferential speech.

Chris Benoit may have been little but his ambitions were large. By fourteen he was wearing three or four t-shirts at a time to add bulk to his frame, and by his mid-teens he was using steroids, which at that time were not recognised as having serious side effects.

At sixteen he left school and became a full-time wrestler, a profession which would often take him to the limits of his endurance. Veteran wrestlers and trainers took sadistic pleasure in physically and psychologically breaking rookies such as Benoit, and he was repeatedly beaten and urinated on. His food and drink were sometimes laced with large quantities of laxatives by other wrestlers, bored with the amount of time they spent on the road en route to the next gig.

Chris moved to Japan to further his wrestling ambitions, though the Japanese training was even more brutal than that which he'd endured back home in Canada. He also perfected his craft in Mexico and Europe, marrying a woman called Martina who he met in Germany. The marriage produced two children and, though it later broke up, Martina said that he was a mild-mannered and loving man.

Chris was also a good friend to various veteran wrestlers but he was uncharacteristically sadistic towards rookies, doing to them the type of things which had been done to him.

A second marriage

By mid-1997, Chris had become close to wrestling manager Nancy Sullivan. A beautiful woman, she had previously played the submissive role in the ring where her wrestler-husband would lead her around on a leash. But the marriage had descended into mutual violence, and she sought solace in Chris's steroid-enhanced arms.

On 25 February 2000 she gave birth to their son, whom they called Daniel. Chris put frequent updates about – and photographs of – the infant on his website, and said that being a father was "awesome". That same year, he won a coveted world wrestling title and, in November, he and Nancy wed. From the onset – perhaps trying to compensate for the fact that he was geographically estranged from his first two children – he was a devoted dad.

The following year, he shattered two discs in his neck during a wrestling match and had major surgery. When doctors told him that he'd be unable to wrestle for a year, he became hysterical and suffered a complete emotional collapse. Despite their warnings he began training as soon as he got home, taking massive doses of painkillers in order to cope.

During this year away from the ring, his relationship with Nancy deteriorated markedly. He became addicted to the painkillers and continued to take them after he returned to work, enacting routines which included being thrown around the ring and jumped on by his opponents. He also insisted on making a diving head-butt from the ropes during every wrestling match, despite the fact that it often left him concussed and medics warned him he was doing irreparable damage to his brain. Sensible wrestlers faked many of the more dangerous moves, but Chris thought that he was short-changing the fans if he wasn't genuinely bloodied and bruised by the end of every contest, and would continue to wrestle even when concussed. He continued to take huge doses of steroids and became aggressive towards his wife, when they were behind closed doors at their luxurious home in a gated community.

A dysfunctional household

By 2003 Nancy had filed for divorce, citing his cruelty. That same year she also took out a restraining order, alleging domestic violence. She told friends that Benoit would fly into terrible rages and throw the furniture about, that she feared for her safety. But she later withdrew both petitions, determined to make their marriage work. A cannabis user for many years, she was by now imbibing large quantities of alcohol and prescription tranquillisers.

In 2004 Chris won another title and was said to be at the top of his game. The mayor of his hometown even declared a Chris Benoit Day to celebrate the local-man-made-good. To outsiders, Chris was still the committed family man, buying his son a series of action figures and enrolling him in a church nursery.

Nancy was also a devoted parent and would bring the little boy to wrestling matches, dressed in a formal suit and bow tie. At the end of the match, his blood-stained father would cuddle him and kiss his cheek. The affection was mutual and Daniel even attempted to copy his father's exercise regime.

But, the following year, Chris's wrestler friend Eddie Guerrero, aged thirty-eight, died of steroid abuse. Chris began to unravel. A lapsed

Catholic, he now returned to his childhood beliefs. He wrote letter after letter to his dead friend in his diary, writing that he and born-again Christian Eddie would be "together in Heaven". Ominously, he added, "I will be with you soon." In the same timeframe, he added antidepressants to the already potent mix of 'roids and painkillers that he was on. In February 2006, another of his steroid-using wrestling associates died at age forty. That same year, Benoit had shoulder surgery but remained in constant pain.

Paranoid

In spring 2007 the Benoits toured Britain. Externally all was well, but there were rumours that Chris had been giving Daniel, who was small for his age, injections of human-growth hormone and that this was understandably causing marital disagreements. Nancy also confided to a friend that the steroids which Chris was taking in large doses were making him increasingly paranoid. He had become convinced that Daniel was going to be kidnapped and insisted that his school keep the classroom locked. He also thought that he was being followed, and told his chauffeur to constantly vary his routes home. And he bought Rottweilers to patrol the grounds of his house, regarding them as attack dogs rather than pets.

It was increasingly clear that the lights were still on, but there was no one home. Acquaintances noticed that the wrestler would often stare into space, unable to focus on the conversation. In the ring he sometimes barked out one-word orders, instead of acting out the prearranged script.

In early June 2007, Nancy bought Chris a silver crucifix on a chain. But she must have doubted that divine intervention would work, as she also hid his steroids. Completely addicted, Benoit simply went to his doctor and got more. During the second week of June he took out a life-insurance policy, naming his first wife and the two children from that marriage as beneficiaries. When Nancy demanded that he add her name and Daniel's, he refused. The fight which followed was violent.

Afterwards, Nancy confided to a friend that she was thinking about filing for divorce. She was by now taking so many painkillers that she and Benoit must have been in a permanently drug-addled haze.

On Friday 22 June, Chris and Daniel enjoyed a barbeque in the garden. That evening, a female from the Benoit residence (who police would later assume was Nancy) phoned directory enquiries and asked for the number of the local police department. A few minutes later, Nancy left two normal-sounding messages on a neighbour's answering machine.

Shortly afterwards, Chris tied Nancy up in one of the upstairs rooms. Some writers would later wonder if she'd thought that they were about to have bondage sex, as she was only wearing a towel and there were no signs of a struggle. But this is speculation as, by then, the drugs had made Chris impotent. What's certain is that, after binding Nancy's wrists and ankles with duct tape, he knelt on her back, wound a television cable around her neck and strangled her to death. Fetching one of his treasured bibles, he left it lying by her side.

Benoit spent the night in the house and, on the following day, crept into Daniel's room and used a wrestling hold to suffocate the sleeping seven-year-old. He placed a bible at his son's side and then spent some time on the internet, researching the prophet Elijah who had allegedly resurrected a dead boy.

Later that morning, Chris phoned the airport and changed that day's flight to a later one which would still give him time to wrestle in a Texas tournament. He also phoned a friend and explained that he'd no longer be able to meet him before the match. He sounded stressed, so a further mutual friend called to ask if everything was alright, whereupon Benoit said that his wife and son were ill.

He didn't take a plane to Texas, but instead remained in the house with the corpses for the remainder of Saturday and all day Sunday, during which time he destroyed his diaries and other personal effects. He also tore up photos which Nancy had taken of her earlier domestic-abuse injuries – he was apparently attempting to sanitise his life before the murders, yet made no attempt to hide or destroy his steroids and large stack of non-prescription medicines.

When wrestling officials phoned to ask why he hadn't turned up, Chris Benoit repeated the lie that his family were ill and vomiting blood. He sounded normal during these phone calls but he had always been good at hiding his feelings. Indeed, he had only broken down twice in public, both times when talking of his wrestling friend Eddie's premature death.

In the early hours of Monday morning, Benoit sent several texts to a friend, saying that the side door of the garage was open and his Rottweilers were in the pool area. Satisfied that the dogs would soon be found, he went to his home gym and committed suicide by hanging himself from his weights machine.

After his death, journalists found that a doctor had been supplying the desperate wrestler with ten months worth of steroids on a monthly basis, and an autopsy showed that he had ten times the normal level of testosterone in his system when he died. His brain was so badly damaged through repeated injury that it resembled that of a man more than twice his age.

Sadly, Benoit was an accident waiting to happen. He'd been warned again and again to stop doing specific aerobatics, to start faking injuries rather than engaging in lunatic stunts which broke bones and caused permanent brain damage. With his million-dollar house, money in the bank and an appreciative fanbase, he could easily have moved sideways into another aspect of the wrestling business or the keep-fit industry. As Matthew Randazzo, his posthumous biographer, put it, "Child killer Chris Benoit is no victim – the voluntary choice to pursue a pro-wrestling career is fundamentally too stupid, irresponsible and silly ever to allow for victimhood."

CHAPTER SEVENTEEN
IN THE NAME OF HONOUR

For most rational adults, making a baby means creating a unique person who grows up to have free will and to make their own decisions. But some extreme traditionalist families refuse to let their daughters date – far less marry – the partner of their choice. If the girl insists on living her own life they are prepared to murder her, often by a particularly violent method. There were thirty such honour killings discovered in Britain between 2005 and 2007, but there are undoubtedly more cases which remain undiscovered as the killer's family and community often conspire to cover up the homicide.

MAHMOD MAHMOD

A Kurd living in London, the quirkily-named Mahmod Mahmod believed that his twenty-year-old daughter, Banaz, had brought disgrace on the family by leaving her unhappy marriage to an Iraqi Kurd, arranged for her when she was seventeen. Her father beat her and called her a whore for becoming Westernised. His rage increased when she fell in love with an Iranian Kurd, Rhamat Suleimani. The couple were deeply in love but received death threats from Banaz's relatives.

Banaz was badly beaten up by strangers, and was convinced that her father and his brother, her uncle Ari, were behind this attempted murder. Speaking from her hospital bed, she warned that both men wanted to kill her. Her boyfriend took mobile-phone footage of her statement, which would later be shown in court.

Mahmod Mahmod, fifty-two, and his brother Ari, fifty, knew that the police would soon be closing in. On 24 January 2006, they arranged for several young men from the Kurdish community to murder Banaz at her home in Mitcham, Surrey. She was kicked, punched and raped during an ordeal which lasted two and a half hours, after which the men garrotted her to death.

Her boyfriend fearfully reported her missing. If he hadn't, then perhaps her disappearance would never have come to light. Meanwhile, someone stuffed Banaz's broken body into a suitcase and took it to Birmingham, where it was buried in a back garden. It would be found, badly decomposed, in April of that year.

Details of the twenty-year-old's agonising last hours came to light when one of her killers, thirty-year-old Mohamad Hama, visited a friend in prison. Police secretly taped the conversation and heard Hama laughing as he described stamping on her neck to force her soul from her body. He said that Banaz's uncle had supervised her ordeal.

At the Old Bailey trial, Banaz's sister, Berkhai, said that if she hadn't escaped from her father's house she would have suffered the same fate. Mahmod Mahmod was sentenced to life imprisonment in July 2007 for his daughter's murder, with the mandate that he serve a minimum of twenty years. His brother Ari was given a twenty-three-year minimum sentence.

ABDALLA YONES

Yones, a refugee from Iraqi Kurdistan, lived in London with his family as a volunteer worker at the Patriotic Union of Kurdistan. He wanted his children to marry fellow Muslims and may have been considering an arranged marriage for his teenage daughter, Heshu.

Heshu suffered terribly at her father's hands, as he beat her for wearing makeup and for going to friends' houses after school. Planning to run away, she wrote him a letter which said, "Bye Dad, sorry I was so much trouble. Me and you will probably never understand each other. But I'm sorry I wasn't what you wanted . . ." She added, "for an older man you have a good strong punch and kick. I hope you enjoyed testing your strength on me."

At sixteen, she fell in love with a Lebanese Christian boy at school and enjoyed a sexual relationship with him. But someone sent an anonymous letter to her father, saying that she was behaving like a prostitute. He had wanted to marry her off to a cousin in Kurdistan, but now realised that this was not an option as she was no longer a virgin. Yones decided that his family's honour was at stake, and that Heshu had to die.

On 12 October 2002 his wife went out, taking their twelve-year-old son with her. Terrified at being alone with her violent father, Heshu locked herself in the bathroom but Abdalla Yones battered down the door. The forty-eight-year-old stabbed her eleven times and cut her throat, leaving her to bleed to death. In an apparent murder-suicide, he sliced at his own throat before throwing himself from the third-floor balcony of the family's flat in Acton, west London.

But Yones survived, though he spent the next four months in hospital. He maintained that he and his daughter had been attacked by members of al-Qaeda, but detectives had read Heshu's letter and knew how often he had brutalised her. A week before his trial began, he admitted that he'd made up the story about Islamic terrorists and had stabbed the teenager to death. Yones was sentenced to life imprisonment at the Old Bailey in September 2003.

Afterwards, Andy Baker, the head of the Metropolitan Police's serious crime directorate, said, "There is no honour in killing another human being."

ABDEL NASSER IBRAHIM

In an unusual variation on the honour-killing motive – a kind of pre-emptive strike – this father attempted to murder all seven of his daughters because he was enraged that he had no sons.

An Islamic traditionalist, he refused to let the girls attend school. In October 2004, he had an argument with his wife of eighteen years over her supposed failure to provide a boy child. (In reality, it's the man's sperm which determines a baby's gender.) Upset and afraid of his rage, she left their home in Sohag, near Cairo, and went to stay at her parents' house.

Hours later, the forty-seven-year-old Egyptian, who was a mosque prayer-caller in Tima, fetched two knives and stabbed his sleeping daughters repeatedly. Their screams pierced the dawn air and awoke the alarmed neighbours. Some time later, the neighbours called the police. They arrived to find Ibrahim had murdered Samar, aged fifteen, Isra, aged ten, Fatima, aged eight, and Zeinab, aged seven. The other three girls recovered from their wounds.

Arrested and asked to explain his actions, Ibrahim said that he had feared his daughters would grow up to become promiscuous. His sentence was not reported in the British press.

ALI ABDEL-OADER

Incredibly, some so-called honour killers still get away with murder. Ali Abdel-Oader, an Iraqi with links to the police and the Basra government, went berserk when he found out that his seventeen-year-old daughter, Rand, had grown close to a Christian British soldier. She told her best friend that he was called Paul, and that he referred to her as his princess. She had met him through voluntary work that she was doing in Basra, and he had vowed to take her back to London with him.

But her father was so enraged when he found out about their five-month romance that he beat her to death, repeatedly kicking her and stamping on her throat. He was questioned by Iraqi police for two hours, then released without charge. Afterwards, Sergeant Ali Jabbar made a statement to the media, saying, "Not much can be done when we have an honour killing. You are in a Muslim society."

CHAPTER EIGHTEEN
HEAVEN CAN'T WAIT

Religious zealots often see themselves as superior to non-believers. They also tend to put religious law (or their own version of it) before the law of the land. The late Ray Wyre, an expert in treating sex offenders, noted that the born-again Christian was the bane of his existence. He also treated many members of the clergy who were particularly active paedophiles.

The following case is particularly heinous, as this self-styled preacher killed his children rather than let them live independently.

MARCUS DELON WESSON

Raised by devout Seventh Day Adventist parents, Marcus' childhood revolved around daily Bible readings, evening and weekend church attendance and choir singing. Friends would later describe him as a black Jesus. His mother beat him – and his three siblings – with a switch when he angered her. He was also beaten by his sadistic, bisexual father, who later had an affair with a teenage male relative.

As he matured, Marcus incorporated his religious father's bisexuality into his own belief system, writing that God and His first creation, Adam, equalled a form of spiritual homosexual union.

In his twenties he began an affair with an older woman and had a child with her, but soon switched his attentions to her fourteen-year-old daughter, Elizabeth. He married Elizabeth in 1974, when she was fifteen and expecting his child. He was twenty-seven. At this stage he worked for a bank but soon quit, and the couple spent the rest of their married life together on welfare benefits.

They had their first son in 1974 and continued to procreate until they'd had eleven children, one of whom died at six months of meningitis and another being stillborn. Marcus parented his nine surviving offspring as he'd been parented, subjecting them to daily prayer meetings which could last for several hours. He said that they were being home-schooled but, as the couple had little formal education, this amounted to little more than reading the Bible. He beat them when they couldn't make sense of his teachings and, as the girls became teenagers, he repeatedly sexually abused them in the name of love.

Incest

Wesson began to create an extended family by impregnating his own daughters, telling them that they had to "have babies for the Lord". Kiana gave birth to two of his children, whilst Sebhrenah gave birth to one. Brandi was also raped by Marcus from the age of fifteen, but did not get pregnant by him. However, three of his nieces had children by him, their sexual abuse beginning at ages twelve to fourteen. His wife knew that he was incestuously fathering children, but merely told him to have sex with the girls when she was out.

The ever-increasing family moved around California. As the older girls grew to womanhood, Marcus allowed them to have jobs in fast-food outlets but beat them if he saw them speaking to male co-workers, reminding them they had to remain faithful to him. He reminded them how "the family that prays together stays together", and that they would lose sight of the Lord if they ever left the Wessons' increasingly-cramped Fresno home.

As he aged, Marcus' views became even more deluded. He decided that he wanted to create a Christian-vampire race and called one of his babies Jeva, the first two letters of Jesus and the first two letters of vampire. He noted how both vampires and Jesus were (in their separate mythologies) resurrected from the grave, and bought mahogany coffins on top of which the children had to sleep. He told his grownup children that, if they were ever approached by social services, they must kill the younger children before turning the gun on themselves – in that way, they would be reunited in Heaven. He also sent his thousand-page religious tract to a New York publishing house, but they rejected it as incomprehensible.

Both of Wesson's nieces fled from his strict control in 2003. However, on 12 March 2004 they heard that Marcus was being evicted and would be moving out of state, so they determined to return and collect their children. But the ensuing row became so heated that one of the women phoned the police.

Marcus blocked the door and then fled to the back room, when the police told him they were phoning a child protection agency. His wife entered the room a few minutes later and exited screaming, "They're all gone!" A SWAT team arrived and kept imploring Marcus to give himself up, claiming somewhat optimistically that he wasn't in trouble. An hour later he walked out of the house, his clothes covered in blood.

Officers handcuffed him, and then entered the back bedroom to find nine young women, children and babies lying dead. They had been shot through the eyes with a .22-calibre handgun which was found to be free of fingerprints. The little ones – a one-year-old boy, a boy and a girl both aged eighteen months, a four-year-old boy, a six-year-old girl, a seven-year-old girl and a seven-year-old boy – had been shot first. Marcus' older children – twenty-five-year-old Sebhrenah and seventeen-year-old Lise – had died approximately an hour later, also of gunshot wounds.

Afterwards, Marcus' mother described him as "a brilliant, God-fearing child" and said that she hoped he'd spend his time in jail reading his Bible. His wife said that she'd like to thank the community for "all your prayers".

Trial

On 25 March 2004 at Fresno County Court, Marcus Wesson pleaded not guilty to nine murder counts and fourteen sex charges. A year later his trial began. The defence said that twenty-five-year-old Sebhrenah's gunshot wound was consistent with suicide, that she had killed her siblings and cousins before turning the gun on herself. The murder weapon had been found under her body, and she had often said that she wanted to die and go to Heaven.

Marcus' wife took the stand and said that she'd have done anything to protect her children – but some of the survivors bravely described what they'd been through, the beatings and the mockery inflicted by their father, whilst their mother, Elizabeth, merely hurried into the other room. Elizabeth had also walked in on Marcus having sex with his daughters and nieces, and had known about Marcus' plan for a murder-suicide pact.

After ten days, the jury found him guilty of nine counts of murder – although he may not have pulled the trigger, they believed that he'd brainwashed his adult children into becoming murderers. He was also found guilty of various sex crimes, ranging from forced oral copulation to rape. Wesson wept as the verdict was read out.

Afterwards, several of his family made religious statements, with one daughter proclaiming, "God loves us all." Though her all-seeing God hadn't intervened to stop all seven children being shot through the head, she was sure that He'd put things right later, on Judgement Day.

The judge decided that Marcus Wesson's judgement day should come sooner, and handed down a death sentence. He was taken to San Quentin State Prison, where he remains on Death Row.

CHAPTER NINETEEN

MEN WHO KILL THEIR PREGNANT WIVES

Pregnancy – particularly a first pregnancy – is frightening for many couples. She may fear losing control of her body, as her belly swells and she's subject to morning sickness and ongoing exhaustion. He may fear that the impending baby will take over their lives, and that they will lose the freedom and closeness they once enjoyed. It's a legitimate concern, as studies have shown that a couple's happiness is unlikely to return to its pre-baby levels until the children have left home.

But the woman has at least made a positive choice to go through with the pregnancy, whereas the man has no option. Some men who fear fatherhood will cope by walking away from their pregnant wives, whilst others remain and hide their distress. Others still lash out – domestic violence often begins during the couple's first pregnancy.

But a tiny percentage of men, often those who have presented themselves as perfect husbands, choose to kill their pregnant spouse and make it look as if the homicide was the act of a stranger. In this way, he can continue to present himself to his wife's parents as the perfect son-in-law – and to his workmates and friends he's a bereaved husband, rather than the no-good who walked out on his pregnant wife.

MARK DOUGLAS HACKING

Mark and Lori Hacking, both from devout Mormon families, were high-school sweethearts in their native Salt Lake City, after which Mark went to Canada to spend a year as a missionary. His religion forbade alcohol, smoking, caffeine, masturbation or watching adult movies – a joyless regime for a teenage boy. Whilst on his mission, Mark was only supposed to read religious books and listen to religious music. He also had to preach to others for hours every day and night. But Mark was at heart a party animal, and, after a few weeks, he began to hang out with girls and have a few beers; he also took up smoking. When this was discovered, he was sent home early in disgrace.

It's likely that Mark lied to Lori about why he'd been sent home, as the pair of them went on to study at the University of Utah together. She graduated with a business degree and got a top job as a brokerage sales assistant in a Wells Fargo bank. Mark, in contrast, became increasingly obsessed with playing computer games and dropped out of his psychology course. But he kept quiet about this, desperate to appear as successful as his paediatrician father who was well-liked in the community. His six siblings also did well in their chosen careers. Later, Lori found out about Mark's deception, but he explained it away by saying that the work he did in a hospital laboratory to fund his studies left him too tired to take seminars. In reality, he had struggled to understand the academic work.

They couple married in the local Mormon temple in 1999, vowing that the marriage would be for eternity. Mark also re-enrolled at university. He was the ideal husband, often preparing candlelit dinners for his wife, writing her love letters and doing DIY chores for her many friends. He told everyone that she was the love of his life, and her parents were delighted that she had such a thoughtful spouse.

But, by 2002, Mark had dropped out of university again. As before, he didn't tell anyone. Instead, he would come home from his job at the laboratory, spread out his medical books and write lengthy essays. He also spent hours at home wearing his medical scrubs. He and Lori were regular churchgoers, and he convinced all of their fellow Mormons that he was going to be a doctor and also knew a great deal about psychology. But the lies took their toll; he had bad panic attacks and suffered from insomnia, also becoming very accident prone.

In 2004 it was time for his class to graduate, and Mark duly sent out all of the invitations. He kept up the deception, hiring a cap and gown and having photos taken in which he held his supposed diploma. On the day of the ceremony he pretended that he'd come down with a vomiting bug and was too ill to attend. Lori and her parents were sympathetic, not suspecting for a moment that he hadn't finished his pre-med course.

Still continuing his deception, Hacking got his wife to help him fill in applications for medical schools, which he never posted. He pretended that he'd been granted interviews and travelled around the country, supposedly impressing his interviewers. After much travel, he told her that he'd been accepted at the University of North Carolina's Medical School in Chapel Hill. Lori joyfully visited the city with him and picked out an apartment, telling everyone that they were moving away.

In June 2004, twenty-seven-year-old Lori, who had stopped taking the pill, missed a period and happily confided in Mark and her friends that she was pregnant. It meant that she'd be giving up work, but she didn't realise that her earnings were crucial to their survival – after all, twenty-eight-year-old Mark had told her that he'd been given a sizeable loan to fund his studies and that he'd eventually be a doctor, earning a considerable salary.

On 17 July 2004, she phoned the financial aid office of North Carolina's medical school with a query about her husband's loan and was horrified to hear that he wasn't enrolled there. She confronted him. He said that his admission papers must have gotten lost in the post, or within the university's internal mailing system. But it was one lie too many. Lori shouted at him, calling him a liar and saying that they couldn't go on like this. It was a natural reaction but it enraged Mark Hacking, who had been raised to see the Mormon man as head of his household and his wife as the submissive follower.

Mark knew that he was on borrowed time. Lori and all of their friends and family expected him to become a mature breadwinner, supporting all three of the family. In truth, he had the maturity of a small boy and could only earn a lab assistant's modest wage. But, if Lori disappeared, he could move to a new area alone and become a different person, without disappointing everyone who believed in him . . .

Murder

Early on the morning of 19 July, he loaded his rifle and shot five-weeks-pregnant Lori through the head whilst she slept. (Her cat was so traumatised by what it saw and heard that it hid in a space beneath the floorboards for several days.) She was wearing her sacred garments, which Mormons believe will protect the wearer from harm. Mark re-dressed her in her running clothes – so that it would look as if she had gone for her usual early morning jog – and stripped the bed of her pillow, which was saturated in her blood. He then enjoyed a cigarette, the first that he'd ever been able to smoke in his own home.

Soon after the murder, Hacking drove Lori's car to Memory Grove Car Park and left it there. When he returned to their apartment, he wrapped her body in a blanket and hid her, the blood-soaked mattress and pillows in a nearby skip, knowing that the contents would be sent to a landfill site later that day. At 10am he phoned Lori's work to say that she hadn't returned from her run in the park, and that he feared for her safety. He told her friends the same thing and they immediately went out to look for her.

But, instead of joining in the search, Mark drove to a nearby bed store and bought a mattress and pillows. He remade the bed before phoning the police.

Within hours, it was clear that the police didn't believe his version of events. They found out that he wasn't enrolled at a North Carolina medical school, despite the fact that he and Lori had packed most of their belongings and were ready to move there. They also discovered the receipt for the mattress and pillows, and found that he'd bought them after phoning Lori's friends to report her missing. It was only a matter of time before he was arrested and charged.

Faked insanity

Hoping that he could put forward an insanity defence, Mark Hacking drank several pints of beer and went to a hotel car park where he took an overdose of barbiturates. He stripped naked, put his sandals back on and began running around the park, screaming inanities. His alarmed family booked him into the psychiatric unit of the hospital where he'd worked for the past few years. Once there, he claimed to have forgotten his name.

Mark's family visited him and promised that they would love him no matter what he had done. Relieved, he told his brothers that he had shot his pregnant wife during an argument and put her corpse in a dumpster, and that it was presumably now buried at the landfill site.

Religious communities often close ranks when one of their members commits a heinous crime, but Mark's brothers did the right thing and went to the authorities. Mark was duly arrested and kept on suicide watch in prison.

For week after week police officers searched the disease-ridden landfill site, a disgusting task for which they deserve much credit. Then, on the thirtieth day, they found the twenty-seven-year-old's decomposing remains. In life she had weighed a hundred and ten pounds, but in death only thirty pounds remained. A detective recognised her luxurious brown hair, but she was formally identified through dental records.

The find sent shock waves through the Mormon community, as the faithful believe that their men and women choose their marriage partners during a previous pre-earthly life and that marriage is sealed "for time and eternity". They also believed that Mark, when he died, would go to the lowest level of everlasting life, the Mormon Terrestrial Kingdom. But what then would happen to Lori who, as a good married Mormon, would normally enter the higher level, the Celestial Kingdom, but could only do so with her husband – unmarried women being unable to enter this Paradise?

Further controversy

There was further confusion, as prosecutors had hoped to charge Hacking for a double homicide. Utah's governing body believes that a foetus suffers in the same way as its mother during her murder, but pro-choice groups pointed out that a five-week foetus has no nervous system and cannot feel pain. The point became moot after Lori's body was found, as her womb and its contents had been crushed by bulldozers. It was impossible to confirm the pregnancy.

On 14 April 2005, Mark Hacking wept as he pleaded guilty to murdering his wife, saying that she was the best thing that had ever happened to him. On 6 June 2005 he was sentenced to six years to life, with the judge stating that he was likely to serve a long sentence for such a coldblooded crime. He soon started writing his version of the murder, which he planned to send to his family and to Lori's. He also wrote to his mother-in-law, admitting that he'd known that Lori was pregnant when he shot her dead.

CHARLES STUART

To casual observers, Charles (who urged his friends to call him Chuck) and Carol Stuart had an enviable marriage. She was attractive and extroverted, a tax attorney for a publishing company. He was more introverted, the manager of a respected Boston department store which specialised in selling fur coats to wealthy Bostonians. His salary was more than double Carol's and together they earned $175,000 a year – an impressive sum in the mid-1980s. In his spare time Charles taught baseball and basketball to children and raised money for charity, just as his father had before him. He was comfortable around young people, but being a sports hero to local kids is completely different to having a child of your own.

Carol was well-educated whilst Charles had never been to college, though he sometimes lied and said that he'd enjoyed a football scholarship. The former altar boy tried to compensate for his lack of qualifications by buying designer clothes and jewellery and getting top-of-the-range haircuts. But he didn't spend all of his money on himself, giving his parents $200 a month as they were in failing health.

Carol had been Charles' first serious girlfriend – they met in 1979 and married in 1985 – and, by 1988, he felt that he'd missed out by not playing the field when he was younger. He began to flirt with a female colleague and bought her jewellery. He also talked about using his superior cooking skills to open his own restaurant. The Stuarts sometimes argued in the evenings about domestic trivia, and Charles always played the role of peacemaker by sending flowers to Carol's workplace the following day.

By the time that Carol Stuart approached thirty, her biological clock was ticking. In spring 1989 she announced gleefully that she was pregnant. Charles later told a friend that he'd asked her to have an abortion, but that she refused as she desperately wanted a baby. The new arrival was due on Charles' thirtieth birthday and, when friends and family congratulated him, he pretended to be pleased.

But inwardly he was terrified. He was tiring of the marriage, and the fact that Carol was giving up work would make it difficult for him to become a restaurateur. Yet their religion, Catholicism, frowned on divorce. And if he left his pregnant wife he'd be seen as the bad guy, whereas if she died . . .

The hit

The couple grew further apart as the weeks passed. She understandably became more and more focused on the impending baby, giving up alcohol and caffeine and kitting out the nursery. Brooding, Charles spent more time down at the bar with his friends.

In September 1989, he asked his brother Michael if he knew anyone who would be willing to take a life. Michael thought that he was just talking nonsense and rebuffed him. The following month he was more specific, asking an old friend to kill Carol. The friend thought he was joking and also refused. But, later that month, Charles persuaded another of his brothers, Matthew, to help him in what he said was an insurance scam.

On 23 October Charles was driving Carol back from a birthing class at a Boston hospital when he pulled over. Then he either shot his heavily-pregnant wife or else had someone else shoot her. It's unlikely that his own bullet wound was self-inflicted, however, as it hit him low on his right-hand side.

His brother Matthew drew up as prearranged. Charles handed him a parcel to get rid of. Matthew drove away and opened it to find that it contained Carol's jewellery, her purse and a gun. He threw the parcel into the Pines River after taking the engagement ring.

Charles had planned that he would just have a minor wound to his foot, whereas Carol's injuries would be fatal. But it seems that his hand – or the gunman's hand – twitched before the trigger was pulled, so when paramedics arrived he was gravely wounded and Carol was still alive.

The couple were rushed to hospital where surgeons performed an emergency caesarean on a dying Carol. The seven-month foetus – whom she had planned to call Christopher – was alive, but weighed only three pounds and had been starved of oxygen for thirty minutes. A priest was called in to baptise him, but the premature child clung to life.

Carol died the next day. Meanwhile, Charles remained in intensive care, with bladder, liver, stomach and intestinal damage necessitating a temporary colostomy. He talked briefly to police, describing his assailant as a black man who had forced them at gunpoint to drive to a rough area of Boston. He had asked for Charles' wallet, which contained a police badge. Apparently thinking that they were undercover officers, the stranger had then shot them and fled. An armed robber called Willie Bennett – who had an IQ of 62, in the mentally-defective range – was arrested, and police were later accused of having intimidated his cellmates into saying that he'd confessed.

Charles was too ill to attend his wife's funeral on 28 October, but he scribbled a note that a friend read out at the ceremony, saying,

"God has called you to his hands . . . to bring you away from the cruelty and violence that fill this world."

On 9 November, the Stuarts' seventeen-day-old baby died. He was buried on the 20th, but Charles was still too ill to attend the private ceremony. Three weeks later he was released from hospital, and collected $82,000 on an insurance policy which his wife's employer had taken out on her. He also applied to collect on another policy worth $100,000. (Journalists would later suggest that Charles Stuart killed his wife for the insurance money. But he was a high earner, and the amount he was due to receive wasn't even enough to pay off their mortgage. He killed to win his freedom, the opportunity to date like a single man and the chance to start again.)

Only on 24 December – when Matthew Stuart's girlfriend Janet went to the police and told them that Matthew and Charles were involved in Carol's death – did his story start to be regarded as unreliable. On 3 January Matthew went to the District Attorney's office, telling them that Willie Bennett was innocent and that he himself was involved.

Charles Stuart knew that his arrest was imminent and that he'd be going to jail for a very long time. Aware that police were probably watching his house, he booked into a motel and asked for a 4:30am alarm call. When it arrived, he dressed casually in a parka and jeans, drove his car to the Tobin Bridge and jumped into the Mystic River. He left a note in his car saying that he couldn't stand being a suspect any longer – though he did not admit to the murder. Conspiracy theorists immediately suggested that he'd been murdered, noting that he'd bought snacks in a store a few hours before his death and had been chatty and cheerful. But this is consistent with suicide, as the person concerned knows that their worries will soon be over for good.

ANDREW HUNTER

This Scottish killer probably murdered his first wife and definitely killed his pregnant second wife. He may also have killed one or more prostitutes.

A difficult start

Andrew's mother died three weeks after his birth and he was abandoned by his father. He was raised by an aunt in Paisley, Scotland, in what was later described as an unremarkable childhood.

As a youth, he joined the Salvation Army and eventually became involved with another Salvationist, Christine, who was eleven years his senior. She mothered him and encouraged his ambition to become a social worker. They married in 1973.

But, by 1976, Hunter was looking for more excitement and had an affair with a man whom he picked up in a sauna. He would remain actively bisexual throughout his life.

In 1977 the Salvation Army sent the twenty-six-year-old to do voluntary work at their citadel in Dundee. At first Christine remained in Glasgow, but, when her husband found employment as an unqualified social worker at a Dundee children's home, she joined him. They later had a son.

Outwardly, their married life was highly respectable. Andrew continued to work in various orphanages during the day and studied for a social-work degree at night. The couple remained committed Salvationists. But Hunter was seducing vulnerable young women whom he met through his work and was also a heavy user of prostitutes.

On 20 March 1979, a man answering Andrew Hunter's description – in his late twenties, slim, pale, with sideburns and a moustache – picked up eighteen-year-old prostitute Carol Lannen, then drove her to Templeton Woods, stripped and strangled her. Her body was found the following day and her clothes were later discovered eighty miles away, on the banks of the River Don. Hunter would later also drive many miles to dispose of his second wife's car . . .

In October 1984, the thirty-three-year-old met a respectable young woman called Lynda Cairns, who lived with a doctor in the house across the road. She too was a social worker and, as her common-law marriage to the doctor had faded to friendship, she and Andrew

Hunter started an affair. When Christine found out she insisted that he end the liaison, which he reluctantly did.

But the couple soon resumed their affair and, the following summer, Andrew left Christine and moved in with Lynda. He had ongoing access to his son, often taking the boy to the cinema. But Lynda wanted marriage and children, and it would be five years before he could obtain a divorce . . .

The first death

On 14 December 1984, Andrew went to Christine's neighbour, saying that he was attempting to return their son after an access visit but his wife wouldn't open the door. He added that her car was in the driveway with the lights on; he could hear music playing in the house and he was very concerned. He phoned Christine from the neighbour's house but she didn't answer, so he went and borrowed a spare key from a friend.

Andrew and his eleven-year-old son let themselves into the house and found Christine swinging from the rafters, a television cable tightly knotted around her neck. She had been dead for several hours.

At the time everyone assumed that she must have committed suicide, though it was against her religion. They were also surprised that a caring mother would let her young son find her body, but they rationalised that she must have been suffering from depression and that this had affected her judgement. Everyone felt pity for the bereaved husband and son.

Further violence

But Andrew Hunter was essentially a control freak. Now that he was getting close to marrying Lynda, he showed his true colours and began to treat her badly. He even hit her in front of witnesses when she suggested that he needn't attend Christine's funeral. On a later occasion he struck her in the face with an umbrella; during yet another argument, he twisted her arm so brutally that she had to go to hospital. In February 1985 the violence escalated and she went to the police.

Still, the couple continued their love-hate relationship – although, unknown to Lynda, Andrew had a brief affair with another young woman, also a social worker, as he had a voracious appetite for sex.

Yet he too was troubled during this time and sought psychiatric treatment for depression. It's clear that Lynda was also distressed, as she began to rely on sleeping tablets and accidentally overdosed one night, after which she was hospitalised for a week.

Sadly, she listened to her heart rather than her head and decided to marry Andrew Hunter. On 1 November 1986 she walked up the aisle with him and vowed, "till death us do part." A man who loved to be the centre of attention, he carried his bible and wore full Highland dress. They honeymooned in Israel before returning to their Carnoustie (near Dundee) home, where, Andrew boasted to acquaintances, they had sex every single day.

But, by early 1987, he needed further sexual adventures and resumed his gay affair with the man he'd met in the sauna ten years earlier. He also resumed his frequent sex sessions with prostitutes.

Lynda's murder

In August 1987, Lynda found out that she was pregnant. She was delighted to be carrying her first child, but Andrew was secretly appalled at the news. He already had a son, who Lynda had become stepmother to, and definitely didn't want another. To make matters worse, Lynda began to suffer from morning sickness and felt equally off-colour throughout the day, so she no longer wanted sex.

On 13 August the couple argued yet again. Lynda said that she wanted to go to her parents' house, some thirty miles away, until she felt better. Andrew offered to drive her – and her fourteen-year-old terrier, Shep – there in her car.

As they drove, it's likely that Andrew Hunter mulled over his options. Even if Lynda stayed with her parents permanently, he'd have to support their child until it was eighteen. It was maintenance money that he'd rather spend on other women or, indeed, men. He'd also have to spend time with the new baby, or face the disapproval of his fellow Salvationists – time that he'd rather spend with prostitutes.

Parking in Melville Woods, he reached for Shep's lead and looped it around his pregnant wife's throat, tightening it until she strangled to death. After carrying her body deeper into the woods, he hurried back to the car.

Hunter knew that Lynda went everywhere with her dog, so he could hardly bring the terrier home with him. After driving a few miles he parked and removed Shep's collar, before letting the dog out of the car. Driving on to Carnoustie, he parked the Vauxhall Cavalier several miles from the house then took the bus to Dundee, where he handed in an essay which formed part of his social-work course.

When Lynda's sister arrived to visit her in the afternoon, he said that they'd had a minor argument and that she'd gone to visit her parents. He seemed entirely at ease with the situation, even taking the other woman for a round of crazy golf. That night he went to a works-related party until 11pm, when a colleague dropped him off outside his home.

Establishing an alibi

By midnight, Hunter had left his house again and walked to the part of Carnoustie where he'd hidden his wife's car. Donning a blonde wig so that he resembled her, he drove across the Forth Bridge, though he had to stop briefly to change a tyre. After driving for three hundred miles, he parked the car on a double yellow line in Manchester and made his way home by train. He figured that police would find the car and assume that Lynda had left him, and had perhaps been carjacked. To establish an alibi he bought his son a pair of trainers in Dundee that lunchtime, knowing that the receipt would give the date and time.

That night, at 7pm, he reported his wife's disappearance to the police. They soon discovered her vehicle and were baffled as to why a pregnant woman with a career would suddenly leave Scotland for England. They questioned the deserted husband several times, commenting on how disinterested he seemed in his wife and unborn child's disappearance, but the social worker glibly replied that he had trained himself never to show emotion.

Detectives were sure that Lynda Hunter was dead but, in the absence of a body, found it difficult to take their enquiries further – especially as Andrew apparently had an alibi, having been at his colleague's party till 11pm and shopping in Dundee at 1:06pm the following day.

Convinced that he was in the clear, Hunter resumed having sex with his favourite call girls – even sleeping with one of his vulnerable clients, a heroin-addicted prostitute aged twenty-two.

Crimewatch

Fortunately, the police were able to feature Lynda's disappearance in a televised *Crimewatch* reconstruction. Callers phoned in to say that they'd seen a distressed-looking Lynda in her car near Fernie Castle. The man driving the car matched Andrew Hunter's description. Even more tellingly, a dog matching Shep's description had been found wandering about in the St Michael's area and had been put down as a stray.

Police now mounted a search of St Michael's Woods. Andrew joined in, safe in the knowledge that he'd dumped Lynda's corpse in Melville Woods, several miles away.

But time was running out for the social worker. On 11 February 1988 a man walking his dog found Lynda's badly-decomposed corpse, the lead which had been used to strangle her still knotted tightly around her neck.

Detectives went to tell Hunter the news, only to find him with his favourite twenty-two-year-old prostitute. A day later, the girl was dead. A friend said that she'd probably taken a deliberate overdose of heroin as, months before, Andrew had been complaining about Lynda and the girl had said lightly, "Why don't you just bump her off?" She had felt guilty when the older woman went missing, but others wondered if Hunter had been afraid of what she'd tell detectives and had given her the fatal dose.

The net closes in

Aware that Hunter was looking increasingly good for Lynda's murder, detectives were able to discredit his alibi. They'd found that it was possible to drive through the night to Manchester, return by train and still have twenty minutes to spare before going shopping for shoes.

On 1 April 1988 he was arrested. That summer he went on trial at Dundee's Bell Street court. The defence said that Hunter was a caring social worker who had lost his first wife to suicide and his second to murder. The prosecution countered that he was a coldblooded killer who cared only for himself.

Witnesses testified that Andrew had been violent towards Lynda on several occasions. She'd told a friend that he refused to stay home with her when she was pregnant and sometimes felt too ill to have sex.

Shep's collar also played an important part in the trial. Lynda always made sure that he never left home without it, yet it was found behind his basket, Andrew having thrown it there when he got home after abandoning the unfortunate dog. It meant that Hunter had been with his wife on her final car journey, a journey which resulted in her death.

The jury took less than two hours to find the thirty-seven-year-old guilty, and he was sentenced to life imprisonment. A subsequent appeal by the glib sociopath failed. For the next five years, Andrew Hunter served out his sentence in Perth Prison before dying there of a heart attack on 19 July 1993, aged forty-two.

CHAPTER TWENTY
MERCIFUL RELEASE

Most of the biological fathers in the previous chapters have killed their children out of madness or badness. But occasionally a father murders his offspring to prevent them suffering further. Most of these parents also kill themselves.

SONNIE GIGG

Sonnie and June Gigg dedicated their lives to their severely disabled fourth son, Lincoln – who had been born deaf, dumb and diabetic, as June had suffered from German measles during the pregnancy. Lincoln had the mental age of a three-year-old but the strength of an adult male. Though he went to a community centre near his home in Bristol during the day, the popular couple had no other respite care.

They would bathe, dress and feed Lincoln every morning, and give him his insulin injection. During the night they took turns keeping him company as he would walk around the house, unable to sleep. They also had to remain constantly vigilant to make sure that he didn't eat anything which would make his diabetes worse. Sonnie sometimes took Lincoln to the pub with him, but the younger man would often try to grab other people's beer and behave in an over-boisterous manner. The couple struggled to control their son, as he was very strong.

Sonnie, a civil engineer, took early retirement due to ill health at age sixty. He and June continued to nurse Lincoln. Though he couldn't express his feelings, they believed that he enjoyed spending time with his young nephew and nieces who were regular visitors.

In October 2007 June went into hospital for an operation. Though she at first appeared to be recuperating, the seventy-year-old died suddenly. Sonnie, also seventy, was understandably distraught. He and June were approaching their fiftieth wedding anniversary and had looked forward to many more years together. Equally overwhelming was the prospect of caring for Lincoln alone. The couple's other adult children and friends were happy to help, but Lincoln had always preferred being with his mum and dad. Now there would only be one person to sit up with the multiply-disabled man night after night.

The future looked bleak to Sonnie Gigg. On the evening after his wife's death, he put thirty-nine-year-old Lincoln and their two Yorkshire terriers in the car and deliberately drove it into the water at Sharpness Docks in Gloucester, drowning both of them and the two dogs. Friends and family later paid tribute to the Giggs through the local paper and on an internet tribute site.

ANDREW WRAGG

Andrew and Mary Wragg married in 1992. It was his first marriage and her second. They were a good-looking couple (she was a former teenage model), but the relationship was stormy from the start. He was twenty-five when they met, but had already travelled the world as a merchant seaman and had an exemplary record. His parents and siblings were all equally successful. Mary had a more difficult start in life, but had rallied after being adopted by a caring couple.

In 1993, when she was seven months pregnant, the foetus was diagnosed with Hunter Syndrome. When the baby was born, the couple called him Jacob. Unfortunately he suffered from the early-onset type of the syndrome, which meant that he wouldn't live beyond his teens. (Sufferers of late onset variety can live to anywhere from twenty to sixty, albeit with increasing medical problems, as a chemical build-up causes multiple organ failure and tissue damage.) By now,

Andrew had joined the army and was working in the SAS Signals to some acclaim.

Later, when Mary was seven months pregnant again, they discovered that this child would also have Hunter Syndrome, so medics advised her to have a late abortion. This involved stopping the foetus's heart in utero, after which Mary gave birth to it. This was an incredibly traumatic event and she would later say that she never fully recovered from it. Andrew was also deeply distraught and was given a compassionate discharge from the armed forces.

He set up a video business but this failed, leading to financial problems. Meanwhile, Mary had two miscarriages, though the couple had a healthy son in 1998 who they called George.

Meanwhile, as Jacob's disease progressed, he sometimes had breathing problems and almost died of pneumonia when he was six.

A failing marriage

In 2000, the Wraggs separated for the first time but reconciled within a year. They split up a second time and again reconciled. On one occasion, police were called and Andrew was cautioned for kicking the front door of the house where Mary was living with the children. He alleged that she'd slammed the door on him.

Meanwhile, Jacob's condition was worsening. When Andrew was away on security work, Mary was his main carer; it was a herculean task, especially as she was suffering from a kidney disorder and often felt unwell.

Whilst visiting Jacob in hospital, the Wraggs also saw various other child patients who were suffering and Andrew told another parent that, if Jacob ended up in unbearable pain, he would put a pillow over his head. Mary in turn told medics that, if Jacob died, they should not attempt to resuscitate him.

No hope

By the time that Jacob was ten years old he was deaf and mute, and could only stagger a few steps by standing on his toes, largely confined to a wheelchair. His hands had curled permanently into a claw-like shape, he was finding it increasingly difficult to breathe and his only way of communicating was by giving hugs.

On 19 July 2004 Andrew returned from a tour of duty in Iraq, during which he had witnessed various atrocities. He was shocked to see how much Jacob had deteriorated. His son's illness was terminal and it was likely that he would soon become doubly incontinent. His joint contracture would also escalate and he would deteriorate mentally.

On 24 July Andrew looked into his son's eyes and believed that Jacob wanted him to take action. (His mindset at this moment would be described during the trial as delusional.) After drinking heavily, the former SAS man told Mary to get their other son, George, out of bed and take him to her mother's. She put the child in his pyjamas and into the back of her car and drove to a lay-by, where she sat drinking wine from a bottle. Meanwhile, Andrew put a pillow over his sleeping son's head. He would later allege that he phoned Mary in tears and said, "I've done it."

When Mary returned to the Worthing bungalow, Andrew was lying next to Jacob, cuddling him. She said, "I hope you didn't hurt him," and he claimed he hadn't. He later added, "He's with Henry now, he's asleep." (Henry was the name that they'd given to their dead baby.) They toasted the idea that Jacob was at peace.

Afterwards, Andrew dialled 999 and said, "I've terminated my son's life . . . so arrest me." An ambulance arrived and took Jacob, who was still breathing, to hospital, but he died shortly afterwards.

Arrest

When police arrived, Andrew begged them not to judge him too harshly, saying that it had been a mercy killing. Interviewed, Mary admitted that, at times, she'd hated Jacob and wished that it was all over. She had the feelings of exhaustion and desperation that many fulltime carers share, and had been so fraught at one stage that she'd threatened to leave the boy on the steps of a residential care home if she wasn't given more help.

Police found that Andrew Wragg was three times over the drink driving limit and that Mary Wragg had amphetamines in her system. Cocaine was also found in the house. Both were arrested, but Mary was later released without charge.

Court

During Andrew Wragg's trial in February 2005, the jury was hopelessly deadlocked. A second trial took place in December that year at Lewes Crown Court. The prosecution alleged that Andrew Wragg had murdered Jacob for selfish reasons, because he no longer wanted to care for him. But the defence noted that he'd been a loving father, and witnesses backed this up.

By the time that the case went to trial, Mary had turned on Andrew. She told the court that he was a heavy drinker who avoided discussions about his son's future. Andrew admitted this but denied that he was embarrassed by Jacob. He said that his son was facing a painful and undignified end. Several witnesses echoed this theme, saying that Jacob was so traumatised by his illness that he looked like a zombie and had become little more than a shell. In contrast, Mary alleged that he had been happy and comparatively healthy on the day that he died. But a pathologist noted that Jacob's respiration was so poor that he could have died from a chest infection at any time. Indeed, the authorities would not have known that the boy had been suffocated if his father hadn't confessed to it.

Andrew Wragg took the stand and said that Mary had known he was about to put Jacob out of his misery, but Mary denied this. The judge believed Andrew's version of events, noting that it otherwise made no sense for her to take their son George out for a drive in his pyjamas in the middle of the night. (Mary had said that she and Andrew planned to have noisy sex, so she wanted seven-year-old George to stay at her mother's house.)

On 12 December 2005, the jury found the thirty-eight-year-old not guilty of murder but guilty of manslaughter. They recognised that he'd been shellshocked after returning from Baghdad and that this, plus his marital problems and the tragedy of his son's terminal illness, had led to a state of diminished responsibility.

The judge said that there was nothing to be gained from taking his liberty and gave him a two-year suspended sentence. Mary, now divorced from Andrew, said that she was incensed at the verdict. But Wragg's father, Bob, a retired policeman, asked that the family be allowed to grieve for the loss of Jacob, whom they had all loved.

DR ANTHONY PAUL
Seeing his family unravel due to chronic ill health, this American physician killed both them and himself.

Constant pain
Anthony was a respected cancer specialist who doted on his wife, a psychologist one year his junior. But, by the age of forty-three, she was in agony due to severe rheumatoid arthritis in her spine. He prescribed strong medication for her, but over the next few years the pain became unbearable due to nerve compression and her quality of life was very poor. Anthony Paul treated patients with intestinal cancer, and so he knew that painkilling medication could only do so much. To make matters worse, one of the couple's two children was severely brain damaged and, though she was a teenager, had the mental capacity of a one-year-old. This teenage daughter also had asthma and had to be given medication every six hours.

During the second week in July 1990, Mrs Paul's pain was so unrelenting that she didn't sleep for seven nights and tried to commit suicide. Unable to bear her suffering any longer, the doctor determined to put her and their retarded daughter out of their misery. Rather than spend the rest of his life in jail for their murders, he determined to also kill himself. More controversially, he also decided to kill his twelve-year-old son – a gifted child with no health problems – as otherwise the child would end up in a succession of foster homes, grieving for his family.

On Monday 16 July 1990, Dr Paul left his office, went home and gave his unsuspecting wife and children a drink laced with sedatives. They all curled up together on the same bed. When they were deeply asleep, he gave them an intravenous solution of lethal drugs then administered the same cocktail to himself. His secretary found his suicide note the following day and phoned the police, who arrived at the house to find the entire family dead.

Anthony Paul's heartfelt note read, "I am writing this so that no blame should fall on anyone except me. I cannot go on with the present situation. There's only one solution. It must end with my death." Later in the note, he gave details of the medication which his daughter required, lest she survive the murder attempt.

He continued: "I have no regrets. I have lived a good life. I have hurt nobody, I have loved my wife and children to the point that I am willing to sacrifice my career and my life for them."

Colleagues and former patients later paid homage to his selflessness and dedication to duty.

CHAPTER TWENTY ONE
CRUEL STEPFATHERS

An emotionally-immature man – particularly one who has endured an abusive childhood – is often incapable of bonding with a new lover's children. He sees them as a reminder of her previous marriage and, whilst he may be unkind to his own children, he scapegoats his stepchild and treats him or her with mounting severity.

Sadly, the biological mother – who is often from a similarly deprived background – may collude in the abuse, either actively hitting the child or turning a blind eye to the numerous beatings and emotional cruelties that her new partner is meting out.

In the following cases the stepfather was found guilty of murder or manslaughter, with the mother sometimes serving a lesser sentence. (The third section of this book is devoted to couples who jointly kill their children.)

WILLIAM KEPPLE

This man repeatedly brutalised his stepdaughter, Maria Colwell, who was also ill-served by the social workers who were supposed to protect her. There was a public enquiry after her death, aged seven, in 1973.

Maria was born on 26 March 1965 to Pauline and Raymond Colwell. She was the couple's fifth child, though Pauline had given birth to an illegitimate child by another man before she married, and had given this daughter up at birth.

Raymond left Pauline a month after Maria was born, and died of heart failure three months later. Pauline, who had already been an indifferent mother, sank into a deep depression and neglected all five of her offspring. They were taken into care for their own protection and Pauline lost touch with all of them (despite the fact that two of the children were fostered by her own mother) except for her youngest, Maria.

Maria was fostered by her father's sister and her husband, Doris and Bob Cooper, who loved the infant and gave her the same care as their own four children. Though she'd been underweight and listless when she arrived at their Sussex home, she soon began to thrive. Her mother took her back, but the National Society for the Prevention of Cruelty to Children were shocked at the way she was being underfed and neglected, and obtained a court order giving parental rights to East Sussex County Council. They, in turn, returned her to the loving home of the Coopers, who referred to her as their baby and were desperate to adopt her, although Pauline refused to let them.

Pauline Colwell continued to periodically disrupt her daughter's life. She insisted that the child be raised as a Catholic, her own religion, though she'd made no such stipulation about her other children. Each time she moved house or formed another brief liaison, she told the Coopers that she wanted Maria back. The little girl was terrified of this happening, as she loved her foster family and was afraid of her hatchet-faced mother. She tried to avoid her visits and was visibly relieved each time that the woman left. The constant fear of being snatched away from her caring foster family and siblings was so terrifying for Maria that she had nightmares and became clinically depressed.

Within a year of losing her first husband, Pauline had begun cohabitating with a heavy drinker called William Kepple, a confrontational man with a reputation for violence who occasionally worked as a labourer, but more often signed on the dole. She later married him and became Pauline Kepple. The couple had four children together in quick succession, with Pauline intermittently asking for Maria's return. The Kepples neglected all of their offspring and often went out drinking at night, leaving them to fend for themselves.

Returned to hell

When Maria was six the court decided that she should be returned to her biological mother, her social workers insisting that there was always a natural bond between mother and child. No one consulted Maria about whether this bond existed (it most definitely did not), and she was so distraught that she had to be removed by force on 22 October 1971 from the Coopers' home. They too were desolate at losing their beloved foster child.

Maria began her new life on a council estate in Brighton, with her inadequate mother and violent, unemployed stepfather. Kepple favoured his own children and would buy them treats, whilst leaving Maria to go without. He also forced her to do so many chores that she became exhausted and ill. A teenage babysitter saw Kepple slap Maria twice across the face for watching television, despite the fact that the babysitter had given her permission to do so. The child also tried to run away to a place of safety, but Pauline took the handle off Maria's bedroom door so that she was trapped.

Over the next few months the abuse escalated. William Kepple would often beat the seven-year-old and send her to bed early, whilst his biological children got to stay up and watch TV. He encouraged them to hit her – a relative saw one of Kepple's children repeatedly kicking Maria in Pauline's presence, but her mother refused to intervene. Kepple also increasingly withheld food from the little girl, and neighbours saw her scrabbling for scraps in the dustbins or eating bread which had been put out for the birds. But she turned down food from concerned adults, as she was terrified that her stepfather would find out.

Neighbours could see that the child was being ill-treated and was regressing. They made numerous calls to various agencies, including the police, the NSPCC and the local social work department. Her teachers also reported that she was losing weight and was often bruised. Educational welfare officers visited the home seventeen times to remind the Kepples that Maria must be sent to school, but again and again the couple kept her at home, doubtless to hide her many bruises and injuries.

Social workers called on a weekly basis at the house, but were afraid of the abusive William Kepple and accepted his reports that Maria was ill in bed and should not be disturbed. By the time she was seen by a social worker she weighed less than two-thirds of what a seven-year-old should weigh, but the woman reported that she was fine.

On 17 October 1972 Maria attended school for what would be the last time. That same month, Doris Cooper asked social workers if she might visit Maria, the child that she'd raised for six years and loved dearly. Her request was refused. The following month, police called following a complaint from the neighbours and found that the children had been left to fend for themselves. When the Kepples returned from the pub they told them that they couldn't abandon their youngsters in the evening. Thereafter, the couple often took their other children out with them, leaving Maria in her darkened bedroom with the door jammed shut.

Skeletal

The beatings continued apace and were doubtless more severe, now that the couple were keeping Maria permanently indoors and there was no one to look out for her. The school were so concerned that they made a medical appointment for her in December, but the Kepples didn't show up. A social worker saw her that month and failed to raise the alarm, though neighbours – who called everyone from the police to the housing association in their desperate attempts to get help for the seven-year-old – would later describe the little girl as a walking skeleton.

On Saturday 6 January 1973, William and Pauline Kepple came home from the pub to find Maria watching TV. Enraged that she wasn't in her room, her intoxicated stepfather beat her savagely. As usual, Pauline Kepple did nothing to help her child.

It's likely that they found the little girl dead the following morning. What's certain is that the Kepples left the house at 7:45am pushing a pram – but it was 10:35am before they wheeled it into Royal Sussex Country Hospital in Brighton. The pram contained the little girl's emaciated corpse. She had two black eyes, a fractured rib, internal injuries, massive bruising and brain damage. A previously fractured rib had been beginning to heal. An autopsy found that there was no food in her stomach, that she had been tearing the wallpaper from her bedroom walls and eating it in a last desperate effort to survive.

Pauline Kepple said that her daughter suffered from epileptic fits and had fallen down the stairs, but it was clear to the horrified medics that the child had been the victim of numerous assaults and that she was starving. They promptly called the police.

At Brighton police station, the bereaved mother stuck to her story for some time but eventually admitted that her husband had hit the child. He, in turn, confessed to striking Maria in the chest and stomach.

No justice

In April 1973, the stepfather from hell was convicted of manslaughter and sentenced to eight years. Incredibly, this was lessened on appeal to four years. After he went to prison, Pauline Kepple had a child by yet another man.

There was a public outcry about the way that so many agencies had failed Maria Colwell, and the authorities swore that it must never happen again. Sadly, there have been similar cases since.

Steve, one of Maria Colwell's older brothers, still puts flowers on his sister's grave. He and his wife have had five children and they have never hit them. Steve is understandably enraged that his mother was never charged with any offence relating to Maria's abuse and eventual death.

MAURICE BECKFORD

After Maria Colwell's appalling death in 1973, the authorities said that lessons had been learned. But, just over a decade later, Jasmine Beckford suffered a similarly cruel fate.

Maurice Beckford brutally assaulted one of his stepchildren and was found guilty, whereupon his older stepdaughter, Jasmine, was taken into care. She thrived in the two and a half years that she was with Brent social services, but eventually her biological mother got her back.

Beckford subjected the four-year-old to a catalogue of cruelty, burning her, cutting her and breaking her ribs. He locked her in a small room with bodybuilding weights attached to her broken legs so that she couldn't move about. He also withheld food and water from the brutalised child.

On 5 January 1984, she died. The pathologist said that it was the worst case of abuse that he had ever seen, for Jasmine weighed only one stone nine pounds, was covered in ulcers and injuries and "looked like a Belsen victim".

Maurice Beckford was sentenced to ten years for manslaughter, whilst her mother, Beverley Lorrington, got eighteen months for neglect.

NICHOLAS PRICE

Heidi Koseda, who died at age four, suffered similar prolonged abuse at the hands of her stepfather, Nicholas Price. Price dominated her mother, Rosemary, until her mental health broke down. He also isolated Heidi from her maternal grandmother and made excuses to health visitors about why they couldn't see her, when they called at the couple's home in Hillingdon, just outside west London.

New neighbours moved downstairs from the couple in August 1984. By now, Mrs Koseda (who already had a second child) was heavily pregnant with Price's baby but was refusing all medical attention. The new female neighbour heard banging and crashing followed by what sounded like a child's screams. Alarmed, she phoned the NSPCC on 3 September. She called again in October and November. During the latter month, a social services inspector failed to gain access to the flat but falsified his records to say that he'd made a successful visit. He was later sacked for this.

Meanwhile, Heidi was being starved by her stepfather as an alleged punishment for eating too many sweets during the summer. Eventually, she was so desperate for food that she ate part of a nappy and strips of wallpaper from the walls. In November or December he locked her in a room without food and water, and left her there until she died.

A police inspector, police constable and health visitor visited the flat on 27 December to enquire as to Heidi's wellbeing, but accepted Price's explanation that she was staying with friends. He barred them from entering Heidi's bedroom, saying that it was unsafe because it had been doused with chemicals to treat damp. If they *had* entered the tiny room, they would have found the four-year-old's decomposing corpse hidden at the back of a cupboard.

A neighbour phoned again in January, expressing fears that the children were being ill-treated. (The baby had been seen wearing only a vest, despite the freezing weather.) Finally, on 23 January 1985, police insisted on searching the entire flat, found the little girl's emaciated body and arrested Price. He was jailed for life, whilst her mother, Rosemary Koseda, was found guilty of manslaughter and sent to a psychiatric hospital.

NIGEL HALL

Two years later, in Greenwich, another stepfather similarly starved and fatally beat his partner's child. Nigel Hall met mother-of-four Pauline Carlile at a railway station. Her children had been in foster care, but she had succeeded in getting them back.

Hall ill-treated all of the children, but reserved the worst of his rage for Kimberley, who was a bedwetter. Social services became involved with the family again after the oldest boy, aged seven, admitted to his teacher that Nigel Hall was knocking him about. Neighbours also reported hearing children's screams and cries.

But Hall regularly refused social workers access to his home, determined that they wouldn't find out that he was regularly starving little Kimberley. Her mother was also assaulting her.

In the final hours of her life, Kimberley was so hungry that she ate her own faeces. In the same time period, Hall had held a cigarette against her spine in fifteen different places. She died, aged four, on 8 June 1986.

Hall was given a life sentence for her murder, whilst her mother was sentenced to twelve years for child cruelty.

COLIN SLEATE

Nottinghamshire social services were warned by little Leanne White's neighbours and grandmother that she was at risk from her stepfather, Colin Sleate. But they failed to properly follow up reports and he continued to ill-treat her, repeatedly torturing her and making her sleep on the floor. She was also abused by her mother, Tina. In the last few months of her life she suffered one hundred and seven external injuries.

During one beating on 15 November 1992, at their home in Hucknall, Sleate battered the three-year-old repeatedly in the stomach, causing severe internal injuries and a massive abdominal haemorrhage which proved fatal. The following year he was given a life sentence for her murder, whilst her mother, Tina, received ten years for manslaughter. Sleate was later informed that he'd become eligible for parole consideration in 2006.

PART THREE
HOMICIDAL COUPLES

CHAPTER TWENTY TWO
THE BABY BATTERERS

It's comparatively rare for a couple to both be charged with killing a child. As has been seen in earlier chapters, babies are most often murdered by a depressed or delusional mother, invariably when the husband is out at work, and older children are more likely to be killed by a vengeful father who knows that this destructive act will permanently wound his ex-wife.

Even if both parties *have* laid into the child with equal vigour, prosecutors will often encourage one to turn against the other – this tends to result in the woman testifying against her husband on the grounds that she will not be charged or will receive a lesser sentence. But occasionally a couple will admit to joint violence, or the evidence against them will be so overwhelming that they are both found culpable by the judiciary.

THE MOTHER/STEPFATHER OF BABY P

The suffering that some children endure was highlighted after the August 2007 murder of a male toddler, known only to the public as baby P. (He has since been identified only by his forename of Peter.) The authorities tend to withhold the child's name in such instances to hide the identities of other children in the same family.

Baby P was the fourth child of a married couple who had been together since the mother was seventeen. Shortly after his 1 March 2006 birth, she left her husband and took up with an illiterate skinhead, who was tattooed with Nazi emblems, worshipped Hitler and was obsessed with pain. The man, who suffered from mental health problems, had tortured small animals throughout his childhood. She, in turn, lacked parenting skills and rarely did any housework, so the family lived in squalor and the children were often left unattended and unfed.

The baby was seen with facial bruising and, later, with bruises to his buttocks and spine. His mother was arrested on two counts of abusing him. Health workers were concerned, so Peter was given to one of her friends to take care of. The woman received a generous fostering allowance for this, but the mother wasn't ultimately convicted of abusing the little boy. And so, in December 2006, when he was almost a year old, she was allowed to take him back. He now had less than eight months to live . . .

The chaotic household comprised the twenty-seven-year-old mother, her four children, her thirty-two-year-old skinhead boyfriend and his friend and lodger, thirty-six-year-old Jason Owen. The latter (who had three children from a previous relationship) soon moved in his fifteen-year-old girlfriend, who had run away from home. The skinhead stepfather also had a Rottweiler called Kaiser, which he terrorised, and two pet snakes which he fed on rats and rabbits, often leaving dead and dismembered animals in the kitchen for the snake's next meal. He was cruel to all of his stepchildren but reserved the worst of his wrath for Baby P, probably because his vulnerability reminded him of his own unmet needs. (He had been bullied throughout his childhood.)

The stepfather repeatedly beat the baby and tortured him by pulling out some of his fingernails, then smeared chocolate digestive biscuits over him to hide the bruises. His mother put her boyfriend first, and conspired to hide the child's condition from health and social workers. Every single one of his baby garments was stained with blood. The baby would only call for his mother for a moment or two, as he knew from experience that she would rarely comfort him. He was so terrified of his stepfather that he would tremble every time the man entered the room. Their teenage babysitter later admitted that the skinhead would often go into the toddler's nursery and shut the door, saying that he was trying to toughen the baby up. Meanwhile, his mother continued to neglect him and his siblings. As a result, both Baby P and one of her daughters were placed on Haringey's 'at risk' register.

Daily abuse

The stepfather taught the little boy and the Rottweiler to lower their heads submissively to the floor when he clicked his fingers. He also wrapped the child up in layers of blankets, so that he became seriously dehydrated, and, on other occasions, forced him to jump up and down until he was crying with exhaustion. The child's health deteriorated. He had an increasingly blank expression and sunken cheeks.

Social workers noticed that the baby was hungry, dirty and smelled of vomit, whilst a neighbour admitted that she'd seen him sitting in the front garden, eating earth. He also had areas of bruising which his mother said he'd accumulated whilst playing with an eighteen-month-old child, or when romping with the family dog. She understood how to deal with social workers as she'd encountered them throughout her own childhood, when they wanted to take her away from her alcoholic mother. (In the end the issue had been resolved by sending her to boarding school.)

The neglect and abuse of the little boy continued, with the stepfather warning others in the household that they mustn't comfort him or pick him up. The mother usually slept till lunchtime, which meant that her older children weren't taken to school. In the afternoons, she often went back to bed with her lover whilst the baby remained in his cot, unchanged and unfed. He had lice and developed a scab on his head, whereupon his stepfather shaved off his beautiful blonde hair.

Social workers visited the faeces-smeared and flea-ridden flat in Tottenham, north London, but failed to realise that the thirty-two-year-old boyfriend was living there. In eight months the family had sixty visits from doctors, social workers and police, but no one made the decision to take the terrorised toddler into care.

One of the beatings left the seventeen-month-old with a broken back, paralysed below the waist with eight broken ribs. But a paediatrician who examined him on 1 August 2007 failed to spot these injuries, after he was referred to her for examination by a social worker. Two days later, Peter was punched in the face and swallowed a tooth.

The following morning he was found dead in his bloodstained cot – and still his stepfather remained unconcerned. His mother was equally blasé; as paramedics, tried to rush her son to hospital, she asked them to wait whilst she found her cigarettes. Meanwhile, the stepfather and lodger are believed to have removed a bag of bloodstained baby clothes and bedding from the house to hide it. It has never been found.

At autopsy, the seventeen-month-old was found to have fifty distinct injuries, including severe head lacerations, a large gouge to his temple and a badly-split lip.

His mother, stepfather and the couple's lodger were all convicted of causing or allowing the boy's death. Chillingly, the mother gave birth again in prison and was originally given contact with her new daughter, the visits only stopping when she was moved to a segregation unit in Holloway Prison. Journalists warned that she might be reunited with the child on her release from jail.

When word of her actions got out, the prison was put into lockdown as many of the five hundred other female prisoners wanted to attack her. Prison officers posted comments on a Facebook page, saying what many other people were thinking – that she ought to be sterilised. A councillor dared to raise the same point, prompting such an outcry that he was forced to resign.

By early December, several members of Haringey council had resigned or been suspended as an inquiry by Ofsted, the Healthcare Commission and the Chief Inspector of Constabulary found that the council had failed to spot children at risk, there were significant weaknesses in its child-protection procedures and the council had failed to learn from the Victoria Climbie inquiry of 2003.

On 13 December 2008, campaigners marched through London to

hand in a petition to Downing Street calling for "urgent far-reaching changes" in Britain's child-protection laws.

LEANNE LABONTE/DENNIS HENRY

Physically, sexually and emotionally abused throughout her own childhood, Leanne Labonte gave birth to her first baby when she was only fifteen. Social services, who had previously monitored the parenting skills of her alcoholic mother, became involved when Leanne left the infant girl alone. She was also well-known to police, as she had several convictions for shoplifting.

At sixteen she became pregnant again but had an abortion. Shortly after this, in June 1998, she met Dennis Henry, who was more than twice her age and had a record for violence, criminal damage and living off immoral earnings. Three months later, she was pregnant with his child. Again, she considered having an abortion but changed her mind – though Henry would later say that she had further doubts about the pregnancy and tried to induce a miscarriage.

In June 1999 she gave birth to their daughter, Ainlee, but apparently rejected her at birth. The unfortunate child fared no better with her father, as Henry was using crack cocaine and hitting both Leanne and her firstborn daughter. Yet the couple swiftly went on to have another child.

A mother of three whilst still in her teens, Leanne increasingly took her rage out on Ainlee. She wrote in her diary that she hated her secondborn, and that the child was ruining her relationship with Dennis Henry. She also wrote that Dennis was always bathing Ainlee and said she believed he was interfering with the child. (The autopsy would show no signs of sexual abuse.)

Social services were involved in the first few months of Ainlee's life, and then the case was closed against the advice of health workers. A little over a year later it was reopened, though Leanne managed to create a smokescreen by claiming Ainlee's surname was Walker rather than Labonte. The couple also stole medical notes from the child's file. A doctor who attended to the family asked for police protection during their visits, as they were so intimidating. Social workers were also terrified, as they were frequently attacked by both Henry and Labonte.

In the eighteen months before Ainlee's death police visited her home on fifty-three occasions, often to deal with reports of domestic violence.

Meanwhile, social workers repeatedly failed to gain access to the couple's home in Plaistow, east London. Behind closed doors they repeatedly hit and nipped the toddler, scalded her with hot water and burned her with cigarettes. They also starved her to half of her optimum bodyweight.

On 5 and 6 January 2002 Ainlee's parents refused to give her anything to eat, despite the fact that there was food in the house and they had fed her two siblings. On the 7th she died, and the couple belatedly phoned an ambulance. Paramedics arrived to find the two-year-old lying on a kitchen table. She had sixty-four contusions on her emaciated body – some new, some healing – and it was later established that she had been abused almost from birth. She weighed only twenty-one pounds.

Labonte and Henry were arrested at the hospital. In custody, they soon resorted to blaming each other. Leanne Labonte said that she hadn't been in contact with Ainlee for a week, had only seen her injuries on the day of her death and was horrified, but too afraid to contact the authorities. Dennis Henry also claimed that he had no idea that his daughter was being abused.

Whilst on remand, Leanne sent him a love letter saying that she missed him and wanted to give him a blowjob. She added that she missed her two surviving children and blamed social services for sending her and Dennis to jail.

The couple – she aged twenty, he aged thirty-nine – were found guilty of manslaughter at the Old Bailey in September 2002. She was sentenced to ten years, with an eight-year sentence for cruelty to run concurrently. He was sentenced to twelve years, with a nine-year sentence for cruelty also to run concurrently. Leanne was given the lesser sentence because of her youth.

Afterwards, the chief executive of the NSPCC, Mary Marsh, said that the number of child killings in Britain were a national outrage. She called for greater integration between agencies – but, as the subsequent cases show, it was a call which remained unheard.

By June 2007, Leanne Labonte had been moved to an open prison in Surrey and was working in a tearoom on a day-release scheme. But, after a tabloid newspaper revealed her whereabouts, she was moved to a Lincoln jail and given work within the prison unit. Having served half of her sentence, she is likely to be paroled soon.

ANDREW LLOYD/REBECCA LEWIS

Aaron Gilbert, murdered at thirteen months, suffered terribly during the last eight weeks of his life. His mother, Rebecca Lewis, stood by as her new boyfriend, Andrew Lloyd, swung the child around by his ears, bit his face and punched him in the head and body. He died of brain damage on 5 May 2005, after Lloyd had battered him against the wall.

Just another sad case of cruelty to children, you might say. But this case made legal history because his mother was the first woman in Wales to be convicted of familial homicide. Prior to this law, women like Rebecca Lewis were not held accountable for letting their partner abuse their child.

As is usual in such cases, many adults in the vicinity knew that something was wrong. Aaron was seen to be badly bruised within days of twenty-three-year-old Lloyd moving in with twenty-one-year-old Lewis, and neighbours soon noticed that the baby was terrified of the heavy-drinking man. A family friend heard Lloyd screaming, "Fucking shut up!" at Aaron and saw him blow cannabis smoke into the infant's face.

Lloyd – who had suffered severe physical abuse during his own childhood and who had made two suicide attempts the previous year – clearly hated the baby. The National Health Service knew that he'd been violent towards a previous partner's child, the prison and probation services knew that he'd served a jail sentence for grievous bodily harm, and social workers were tipped off that Aaron was covered in bruises. A total of seven agencies were involved with Andrew Lloyd, but they didn't share information and most didn't know that he was living with Rebecca Lewis and her baby son.

When social workers received a phone call from a female cousin of Rebecca's, stating that Aaron was being abused, they decided that the call could be malicious and so opted not to visit the house. Three days later they wrote a letter to Rebecca, but they'd been given the wrong address so the letter didn't reach her. She took her young son to the Accident & Emergency department of her local hospital, after Lloyd damaged Aaron's arm, but ran out when questioned by doctors as to how he had sustained the injury. A member of staff planned to carry out a home visit but it was called off because of ill health. Rebecca's cousin phoned again, telling social workers that Andrew Lloyd took drugs and that he'd been seen out with the baby at 2am. Again, they failed to react appropriately. Aaron now had eight days left to live.

Shortly afterwards, neighbours noted that the baby's face and body were so swollen that he resembled the Elephant Man. He had over fifty injuries on his tiny body. And still Rebecca Lewis did nothing to help her terrorised son.

On 4 May 2005 she went out shopping, leaving her baby with Lloyd. He picked Aaron up and swung him violently against the wall. When Lewis returned, Lloyd was attempting to give the child CPR. For the next eighteen hours doctors battled to save the infant, but he had suffered massive brain damage and could not be revived.

Andrew Lloyd admitted Aaron's murder and was jailed for twenty-four years. But Rebecca Lewis denied familial homicide and was tried at Swansea Crown Court in December 2006. The jury heard that she'd done nothing to prevent her boyfriend's attacks on her baby. They found her guilty and she was jailed for six years. The judge told her: "You put your own interests first, and above and beyond that of your vulnerable child. You could have stopped the violence that Lloyd was subjecting Aaron to. You could so easily have got the authorities to stop it."

Afterwards, the Welsh division of the NSPCC stated, "Without this new law it is likely that Rebecca Lewis and Andrew Lloyd would have joined a long list of couples who have been acquitted or not even brought to trial for murdering a child."

JODIE TAYLOR/PAUL O'NEIL

Jodie gave birth to her first child at age fourteen but proved unable to look after it. By twenty, she had convictions for battery and robbery. Her boyfriend, Paul O'Neil, was unemployed and had been brutal towards the five children he had by two different women.

In November 2004, Taylor gave birth to O'Neil's son and they called him Aaron. But O'Neil bitterly resented the attention that his girlfriend paid to their child. Over the next few weeks, he hit his baby son repeatedly, battered him against the furniture and kicked him, breaking both of his legs and his collarbone, and fracturing his ribs in twelve places. Social workers called repeatedly at the couple's Kenton, Newcastle home to see the infant, but the pair refused to answer the door.

On 6 February of the following year, O'Neil pressed the baby's face against a gas fire until the skin blistered, causing agonising burns. He did the same to Aaron's hands. But Taylor still didn't take her infant to a doctor – she merely applied cream to the baby's wounds.

Four days later, when Taylor was out, O'Neil battered ninety-two-day-old Aaron about the head, fracturing his skull and causing his death.

On 23 February 2006, the couple appeared at Newcastle Crown Court. Thirty-three-year-old Paul O'Neil admitted cruelty but denied murder, whilst twenty-one-year-old Jodie Taylor admitted cruelty by neglect as she'd failed to seek medical attention for her son's burns.

O'Neil was jailed for life with the recommendation that he serve at least twenty-two years, whilst Taylor got three and a half years for failing to protect her child.

Lessons unlearned

John G. Howells, former director of the Institute of Family Psychiatry, has written, "Behind the battered child is an army of deprived children. They are surging into the future to make more disturbed families. Unhappiness feeds on unhappiness. The spiral of emotional deprivation must be halted. It can be halted."

These well-meaning words were written in 1974, after the horrors of Maria Colwell's death at the hands of her stepfather, William Kepple. Sadly, the phenomenon of damaged adults going on to brutalise their babies has continued unabated, with overburdened social services letting cases slip below their radar, or ideological young social workers foolishly giving an abusive parent one last chance.

Though governments and social-service departments promise new initiatives after such horrific murders, babies and older children are still starved, neglected and beaten at the hands of a hopeless underclass. Given money from the welfare state for each child – with additional payments if the child has certain medical problems – they view their offspring as little more than cash cows and resent spending time or effort on them.

Ironically, many of these children are on the 'at risk' register from birth, so authorities know that they are likely to suffer. Someone then decides *how much* suffering is *too much*. But, short of giving each of these babies a live-in carer from birth, they are destined to have a painful and frightening start to their lives.

It's a sizeable problem, with one in ten children – a million a year – being badly treated, abused or neglected in Britain today, according to a 2008 *Lancet* report.

CHAPTER TWENTY THREE
CHASING DEMONS

In the previous chapter, several of the couples shared a belief in excessive and repeated corporal punishment, indifferent to the fact that their behaviour was both counterproductive and illegal. In this chapter, the couples shared a religious mania and took it out on their progeny with equally fatal results . . .

ANGELA CAMACHO/JOHN ALLEN RUBIO

Twenty-three-year-old Angela Camacho and her twenty-two-year-old common-law husband, John Rubio, lived in a rundown apartment in Brownsville, Texas. Their living quarters were cramped, filthy, cockroach-ridden, strewn with dirty laundry and unwashed dishes, conditions which meant that their three children were frequently unwell. The family got most of their meals from soup kitchens as Rubio preferred to spend their welfare money on cans of spray paint, inhaling five such cans a day. Social workers became so concerned at the emaciated state of the children that they enrolled the hapless couple in parenting classes. Both Camacho and Rubio complied with this. (Rubio had fathered the two youngest children whilst three-year-old Julissa, the eldest, was from one of his common-law wife's previous relationships.)

Like many uneducated people, they believed that a supernatural being would save them from poverty if they could only find the right words or actions. As such, they set up a black-magic shrine in their rat-infested lounge and spent some of their welfare money on witchcraft paraphernalia rather than on food.

John, who had grown up in a superstitious household, told a family member that he kept hearing the voices of their dead relatives, and that they sometimes spoke to him through his unfortunate offspring. He added that the children were possessed. He later told police that his wife had asked him to kill the babies because they were evil and wouldn't get to Heaven.

On 10 March 2003 he battered the children's pet hamsters with a hammer then poured bleach on them in a bizarre exorcism, before turning his attention to the children themselves. He suffocated three-year-old Julissa for four minutes, telling his wife that the struggling little girl had the Devil in her, which was why she didn't want to die. He then stabbed the child twenty times and beheaded her, by sawing through her tiny neck with his knife; then he and Angela had sex, rolling around in the toddler's blood.

Next, John Rubio suffocated, stabbed and beheaded his two-month-old baby daughter, Mary Ann, after which the couple had sex again. Finally, he murdered one-year-old John Junior in the same way.

The couple had a bath, put their bloodstained clothing into the water to soak and had sex for a third time, as they knew they wouldn't have the opportunity once they were arrested. Later, they put the severed heads of their three children into a rubbish bag, leaving John Junior's decapitated body at the end of the bed.

A day after the triple murder, John's brother visited the tiny apartment and was sickened to find it covered in blood, with John Junior's headless corpse still propped up in the bedroom. He raced out and flagged down a passing police car, and officers found the three mutilated corpses. Angela told one of the horrified policemen that they'd killed the children because they couldn't afford to feed them – but John's wallet was found to contain $146. In custody she admitted that the motive had been religious, saying that someone had put an evil spell on the children and that they'd had to be killed brutally in order to cast the evil out. John –

who believed that his late mother and grandmother had both been witches – told the same story, explaining that the children were possessed.

Rubio's trial

The couple were tried separately, with John Rubio pleading not guilty by reason of insanity. After eight hours of deliberation the jury rejected his insanity plea and found him guilty of the triple homicide. He asked for the death penalty, saying that God had forgiven him and that he wanted to be with his children in Heaven. The jury granted his wish; he was sent to Death Row to await his date with a lethal injection. But this ruling was later reversed by the Texas Court of Criminal Appeals in September 2007, on the grounds that his defence lawyers hadn't been given the opportunity to cross-examine his common-law wife during his trial.

After mental health tests, Rubio was told that he was competent for a retrial. In June 2008 he was told that this new trial would be held at Cameron County, a venue he objected to. At the time of writing he has yet to be retried, though prosecutors hope to start proceedings by summer 2009.

Camacho's sentence

Angela Camacho pleaded guilty to three counts of capital murder to avoid the death penalty, and was given three consecutive life sentences. She will be eligible for parole in forty years.

STUART & LESLIE GREEN

In October 1982 the Greens were living in Stonegate, a fundamentalist Christian household near Charleston, West Virginia. Along with other Christian parents, they occupied a twenty-seven-roomed house run by the group's leader, Dorothy McClellan, and her accountant husband, John. For years the McClellans had been taking in troubled teenagers, often drug addicts, and persuading them to live a religious life. It was often a struggle, with the communal families surviving by farming and construction work.

Dorothy McClellan's ethos was that children should be subjected to corporal punishment to enforce obedience, and each parent had their own monogrammed paddle which they carried around with them. These were used frequently, and with severity – on one occasion in September 1982, McClellan beat her grandson, Daniel, for four hours.

On 5 October 1982, the Greens' twenty-three-month-old son, Joseph, hit another child (the way that he'd seen adults treat children) and refused to apologise; whereupon the Stonegate community formed a circle around the boy as his twenty-five-year-old mother, Leslie, began to beat him on the buttocks with a paddle. Later, his father Stuart, aged twenty-eight, took over the paddling whilst both parents ordered him to say sorry to the other child.

After two hours of intermittent beating and demands that he apologise, Joseph went pale – he had gone into shock. One of the fundamentalists fetched the group leader, McClellan, who told the parents to halt the paddling and administered first aid. But it was too late for the not-quite-two-year-old, who died in hospital from loss of blood. The Stonegate community tried to pass the death off as an accident, but the child's internal injuries revealed exactly what had taken place.

The couple were convicted of involuntary manslaughter. Both served a year in jail and paid a $1,000 fine. Controversially – given that she hadn't even been in the room whilst Joseph was being beaten – the religious group's leader, Dorothy McClellan, was also found guilty of causing the boy's death. Stuart Green spoke out against her in court, saying that she had encouraged parents to beat their children until the little ones apologised. His wife, Leslie, had joined McClellan's household when she was only fifteen and so was very much under the older woman's spell. After their release from prison, the Greens left the religious community and set up home together in Baltimore.

The judge said that Dorothy McClellan was a strong-willed and manipulative woman, who instituted a policy of discipline which led to Joseph Green's terrifying ordeal and untimely demise. She was convicted of involuntary manslaughter in 1985. Her 1987 appeal against conviction was turned down.

CHAPTER TWENTY-FOUR
MEDICAL NEGLECT

In 2008 a woman complained to the British Medical Council that she had been given a blood transfusion whilst unconscious, and that the transfusion was against her Jehovah's Witness religion. Surgeons responded that the transfusion had been necessary to save her life. In principle, an adult should be allowed to refuse treatment and live – or not – with the consequences, but it should surely be illegal for a parent to withhold vital treatment from a child. Yet several American states still have a religious exemption clause, allowing parents to put their sick children through agonising days or weeks, followed by an entirely-preventable death.

DAVID & GINGER TWITCHELL

Two-year-old Robyn Twitchell became ill in 1986, screaming and vomiting. He'd developed a twisted bowel, which would have been easily corrected in hospital. But his parents were Christian Scientists, bound to a religion which believes that only prayer should be used to heal.

By the second day of Robyn's illness he was in such pain that the Twitchells, who lived near Boston, phoned the worldwide public relations manager of the Christian Science Church for advice. He assured them that solely using prayer to treat symptoms was permissible, both morally and under the law. The suffering child was attended to by a Christian Science nurse (surely a contradiction in terms), who must have noted signs that he was becoming seriously dehydrated and that acid from his vomit had stripped the skin from his lips and chin, leaving it bright red. By now his screams were so loud and disturbing that the next-door neighbours closed their window to shut out the sound.

On the fourth day, Robyn was still in agony and unable to eat, but the Christian Science nurse force-fed him and ordered his mother to give him food every half-hour. By now, three wounds had appeared on his thigh, possibly suggesting septicaemia (blood poisoning).

By day five, his scrotum had blackened where the blood supply had been cut off and he began to vomit excrement. Later that same day, he died. Christian Scientists believe in resurrection, so the Twitchells waited patiently by their son's corpse, expecting him to come back to life again. Rigor mortis had set in by the time they finally admitted defeat and called the emergency services.

The couple were charged with manslaughter, with Massachusetts prosecutors alleging that they were guilty of child neglect and the defence countering that the Twitchells had a right under the First Amendment to treat their son's illness solely with prayer. The Christian Science nurse said that she'd healed Robyn, and that he'd been playing with his cat a mere fifteen minutes before he died. But an autopsy had shown this was impossible, as the child's intestines were jet black and ruptured; he would have been in such agony that he'd have tried to avoid any movement at all.

The couple were sentenced to ten years' probation, but this was overturned on a technicality in 1993. Thankfully, due to a public outcry over Robyn's protracted suffering and unnecessary death, the Massachusetts legislature repealed the religious exemption in their criminal code.

WILLIAM & CHRISTINE HERMANSON

1986 also saw a similarly-preventable death in Sarasota, Florida, when seven-year-old Amy Hermanson began to lose weight and became increasingly lethargic. She had developed diabetes but her Christian Scientist parents refused to seek medical care. A neighbour saw Amy crawling on her hands and knees, too weak to walk, and begged her mother to take her to a doctor but she refused. Amy was seen by an aunt the day before she died, and the woman observed that the seven-year-old had become incoherent and could no longer focus her eyes.

After her death, her parents were convicted of felony child abuse and third-degree murder. However, in 1992 the Florida Supreme Court overturned their convictions because of a religious exemption clause in Florida's legal code.

The death toll mounts

Parents who live in a religious commune can find it almost impossible to seek medical aid for their child, as the group reinforces their already rigid anti-interventionist belief system. Fifty-two people in the Faith Assembly communes have died, most of them children, as the group professes that "only God can heal". One woman begged to see a doctor as she lay writhing in agony, but the group refused and continued their ostensibly-healing prayers until her death.

Unwanted children

In the aforementioned cases, the parents killed out of a misguided belief system. Alhough their children suffered terribly as the result of their inaction, they didn't actually want them to die. But in the following case the couple didn't refuse medical aid out of some confused religiosity. Instead, they just didn't care.

ROBERT & SABINA HIRST

Three-year-old Tiffany Hirst had a nursery place, but her twenty-two-year-old mother, Sabina, and fifty-four-year-old stepfather, Robert, couldn't be bothered to take her there. Instead, they locked her up for days on end in her bedroom above the pub that they ran in Upperthorpe, Sheffield. Passersby often saw her thin, unsmiling face at the window, but apparently didn't realise that she was half-starved. The Hirsts mostly ignored the child, who was covered in insect-bites as the filthy room was infested with beetles. They also neglected and locked up a one-year-old child who cannot be identified for legal reasons.

The couple kept their dogs in another room which was covered in faeces and urine. (The stench was appalling.) The first-floor flat was also a potential deathtrap for children, with live wires protruding from the walls.

The Hirsts apparently started locking Tiffany in her room on a regular basis in August 2006, though a health visitor saw her in February 2007 and said that she was happy and healthy. But the lock-ins continued, as did periods when the couple failed to provide the child with adequate food or water. By mid-2007, the three-year-old weighed the same as a two-year-old. In September she developed pneumonia, but her mother and stepfather were too busy to notice, let alone to seek medical assistance. When they found her body in October, she had already been dead for up to two days. They phoned paramedics, who arrived to find what looked like a porcelain doll lying amongst filthy bedclothes. When they picked her up they were shocked by her low bodyweight.

An autopsy revealed abnormalities in her bones, showing that she'd been given so little food at times that she'd stopped growing. At other times she had been fed and her body had responded with a growth spurt. Pneumonia, brought on by a lack of food and water, was the cause of death.

The couple were initially charged with murder, but Robert Hirst's lawyer pointed out that he had recently started a new job which took him away from the pub for thirteen or fourteen hours a day, so it was up to Mrs Hirst to care for her daughter during these hours. (Apparently she *had* cared for Tiffany until meeting Robert.) His charge was then changed to one of neglect. Sabina Hirst's charge was also reduced, in her case from murder to manslaughter. Whilst awaiting trial, the couple moved to Barnsley and began to run another pub.

At Sheffield Crown Court in June 2008, Robert Hirst pleaded guilty to neglecting Tiffany, whilst Sabina Hirst pled guilty to her daughter's manslaughter. They were remanded in custody. Later that month, she was sentenced to twelve years for manslaughter and he to five for cruelty, with Judge Alan Goldsack describing Tiffany's pitiful end as "about as bad a case of child manslaughter as there can be".

PART FOUR
REALITY CHECK

CHAPTER TWENTY-FIVE
SAVING LIVES

A s the previous chapters have shown, parents kill for a wide variety of reasons. Whilst some of these killers are arguably untreatable, such as psychopathic parents who kill for the insurance money, others could have been prevented from harming their children or, indeed, from having children at all.

NOT EVERYONE IS PARENT MATERIAL

In an ideal world, every baby would be a wanted one, born to emotionally-mature parents who can cope with eighteen years (or more, if the child has to be supported through college) of enormous personal sacrifice. The reality is very different – the more intelligent a couple are, the less likely they are to procreate.

Our society is culpable in promoting the myth that everyone is parental material. Soap operas and other simplistic television programmes give the impression that a baby will bring a straying boyfriend back to the fold. In truth, he's more likely to flee into the arms of an unencumbered girlfriend who is free to party.

On Britain's sink estates (and in American ghettoes) it's not unusual for a man to have fathered children with half a dozen women, each of whom has convinced herself that a baby will glue together an unstable relationship. Many muddle through, but a significant percentage take their anger, loneliness and frustration out on the child with sometimes fatal results – more than one child a week (seventy a year) in Britain is murdered by its parent, and, in under-fives, this parent is usually the mother. Uneducated teenage girls with a poor support network are especially likely to abuse their child.

Sadly, though a young woman may be beating or abusing her toddler she often goes on to have another baby. Such women love their children when they are infants, but become enraged or withdrawn when they grow into small children with their own personal likes and dislikes. They feel rejected – and can become violent – if the child refuses food or wants to spend time with anyone else.

Even if the man does stay around, the partnership doesn't return to its pre-baby level of happiness until the children have left home. In a survey of six hundred parents in the UK, conducted by *Home Start*, only four percent said that child-rearing had lived up to their expectations. When *Good Housekeeping* magazine questioned a thousand of their readers in 2003, sixty-one percent of mothers admitted that their family life had been damaged by having a baby, sixty percent had lost friendships and twelve percent found that having a baby had led to separation or divorce. An American survey conducted in the mid-1970s went further, asking the question, "If you'd known what parenthood was going to be like, would you have had children?" A resounding seventy percent said no.

There is surely scope for a social-care programme which takes babies into schools on a regular basis, to show teenagers just how demanding childcare is. At the moment modified versions of this exist, where children are given a bag of flour and told to carry it around for a week, and to arrange for a babysitter whenever they want to go out. But a bag of flour doesn't cry all night, defecate, urinate or vomit on its carer, involuntary acts which immature parents often misinterpret as deliberate wickedness on the part of the child.

Good contraceptive advice is also vital, as is free contraception – there have been instances of boys in their early teens using chocolate-bar wrappers in place of condoms because they didn't have access to the latter. Puritans may argue that these teenagers are too young to have sex, but – hormones and emotions being what they are – some teens will become sexually active before it's legal. Surely it's better that they use a sheath rather than create a tell-no-one baby, or a neglected and abused child?

A SAFE HAVEN

But let's assume that the worst happens, that a young woman gives birth alone and feels she has no option but to dispose of the child. In an effort to cut down on infanticide, America has made its fire stations available to new mothers. A girl can safely leave her newborn at any of these buildings, knowing that he or she will receive immediate care.

Germany has instigated a similar system whereby there is a flap on the outside wall of many hospitals, which opens to reveal an insulated box. The mother can place her baby into this warm environment and leave, with no questions asked, whilst an alarm alerts staff to the fact that a baby has been left inside.

Mothers can reclaim their infant within the next eight weeks without fear of legal reprisals, after which the baby is put up for adoption. Germany currently has at least eighty hatches and Pakistan has over three hundred, saving many newborn lives.

France's system is even better for the tell-no-one mother, as it is legal for a woman to give birth anonymously in hospital and leave her baby there.

HORMONAL HELP

Unfortunately, even babies who are planned and brought into a stable marriage can be at risk from a mother suffering from post-natal depression, or who has an episode of post-natal psychosis. These women often tell doctors, spouses and friends that they hate the baby, but are told that it's just the baby blues, that they'll soon be fine. As a society, we need to listen to these deeply-distressed women and encourage them to seek medical intervention – be it chemical, therapeutic or a combination of the two – before the situation becomes critical. A clinically-depressed woman should not be left alone with her infant, as she is potentially a danger to both the child and herself.

THE 'STOP AT TWO' CAMPAIGN

Whilst many women can cope with one or two children, their emotional resources become stretched at three or four. Andrea Yates, a deeply religious woman living in Texas, had four children in quick succession – whom she named after saints – after which she had a nervous breakdown. In hospital, she told her doctors that every child was a gift from God and that He would care for them. (A ten-second look at any Third World country, where huge numbers of babies die of starvation, would have disabused her of this belief.) Two months after her therapy ended, the registered nurse became pregnant again and, on 30 November 2000, gave birth to her fifth child, Mary. By the following spring she was rehospitalised for depression, but allowed home to be cared for by her husband and mother-in-law. That June, she drowned all five of her children – ranging from seven years to six months – in the bath.

Her plight is echoed elsewhere in this book, where mothers coped with a first and perhaps a second child, but went to pieces when overburdened with caring for a third or subsequent child.

In July 2008, a group of leading doctors concerned about Britain's increasing overcrowding problem suggested that couples should restrict themselves to a maximum of two children. Noting that we are now more overcrowded than China – and that England is the fourth most densely populated country in the world – the Optimum Population Trust's policy director, Rosamund McDougall, said, "With the UK population growing by more than 350,000 a year, it's hard to understand why it's so controversial to suggest we need solutions to our over-population crisis."

At the time of writing, in 2009, Britain's population is just over sixty million and the country is struggling to provide enough accommodation, social services and energy supplies. That number is projected to swell to seventy-seven million by 2050 – but, if people restrict themselves to two children, the number may fall to fifty-five million and our resources become less overstretched.

RETHINK THE WELFARE SYSTEM

Unless we are willing to remove babies from grossly inadequate parents within the first month of life, they are destined to suffer. Some of these parents, part of Britain's growing underclass, see each child in terms of further cash for themselves. Karen Matthews – found guilty in December 2008 of kidnap and false imprisonment for financial gain of her own daughter, Shannon – had seven children to five different fathers and lived entirely off the state. One of these fathers admitted that she was only interested in the child benefit payments, which she spent on partying and cigarettes. The children were repeatedly abused and neglected, and Shannon had been on the at-risk register. Her twelve-year-old brother was so unhappy that he had started to run away from home.

In November 2008 an incestuous Sheffield father went to jail for twenty years for impregnating his two daughters a total of nineteen times between the late 1980s and early 2000s – all because he wanted the various housing and welfare handouts, including child benefit of £31.25 a week per child. (Because of congenital abnormalities in the foetuses, the young women had multiple miscarriages and abortions and only seven children survived. It was still enough to net him thousands of pounds in benefits, allowing him to spend his days in the pub and his nights watching TV.)

Baby P's mother also netted a considerable sum for her four children, allowing her to spend her days gambling online, smoking and drinking vodka. As is typically the case in such families, the children benefited little from the money and were left hungry, dirty and afraid.

A study by Libertad Gonzalez, *The Effect of Benefit on Single Motherhood in Europe*, showed that, as benefits rise, so does single motherhood. The fathers, equally feckless, have often moved on before the child is even born. These children are disproportionately likely to end up in special needs schools, or to require child psychology services, at further cost to society. Our welfare state, intended as a backup in times of need, has increasingly become a meal ticket for life for Britain's work-shy. Correspondingly, their children may suffer or sometimes even die at their hands.

In 2007, UNICEF published a report which analysed forty indicators of children's well-being in twenty-one developed countries between 2000 and 2003. Britain came at the bottom of the league when it came to child welfare, with broken families identified as putting children at risk. As the report said, "The true measure of a nation's standing is how well it attends to its children – their health and safety, their material security, their education and socialisation and their sense of being loved, valued and included in the families and societies into which they are born."

ZERO TOLERANCE

Ten percent of British children are born into homes in which they are abused either physically, sexually or emotionally. If we are serious about protecting children we must ban corporal punishment. This has already been achieved in Austria, Bulgaria, Croatia, Cyprus, Denmark, Finland, Germany, Greece, Hungary, Iceland, Italy, Latvia, the Netherlands, Norway, Portugal, Romania, Spain, Sweden and Ukraine. But Britain and America still take a punitive stance, despite numerous studies linking such punishment with depression, alcoholism and criminality.

Many children are being hit at nine months old by their parents, who are ignorant regarding the options of positive parenting. When the slaps don't have the desired effect these parents tend to hit harder, with occasionally fatal results.

British law on this subject is significantly confused, and it is left to the courts to determine, retrospectively, exactly what 'reasonable' punishment is.

THE VENGEFUL SPOUSE

It's difficult to protect children on an hourly basis from a former spouse intent on revenge, especially when a court has given him or her private access visits. It's far easier to avoid creating children with an unstable partner by examining their past history, current behaviour and personality traits. Are they pushing for an especially speedy marriage? This suggests a level of insecurity which may cause problems in the future. Have they a history of physically attacking their partners, or even their own parents? Why did their previous love affairs end?

Have they a history of suicide attempts or self-harming? For now, they may be turning their anger inwards – but if they externalise it, you or any future children may become the targets.

In March 2002, a government amendment to the Adoption & Children Bill said that domestic violence should be taken into account when court orders granted parents access to their children. The move came about after fifteen children from different families were killed by non-custodial parents who had a history of violence.

But, clearly, some cases are still falling through the cracks. Viviane Gamor was given unsupervised access to her children – after shaving off half of her baby's hair and attacking her half-sister with a knife – despite their father begging the legal system and social services to maintain supervision. (Gamor, who features in Chapter Three, killed both of her children during their third unsupervised visit.)

A SURE START IN LIFE

Many parents benefit from regular short breaks from their children. Three- or four-year-olds who adapt to nursery also tend to find starting school less stressful than children who have been at home fulltime, with only their mothers for company. At the time of writing, all three- and four-years-olds are entitled to twelve and a half hours of free education per week in a Sure Start centre for thirty-eight weeks of the year. Sure Start centres also offer antenatal checks, healthcare advice and parenting classes, as well as information about training opportunities and work.

For details of free nursery places under the Sure Start scheme, visit www.surestart.gov.uk/surestartservices/settings/fundedsettings or telephone 0800 2 346 346.

CONCLUSION

By bringing babies into schools and showing how much work they really entail – and by encouraging young women to have aspirations beyond motherhood – we can lessen the number of tell-no-one babies which are murdered. Hospital hatches, where girls can leave their newborns without fear of reprisals, would also cut down on such unnecessary deaths.

Many hormonally-triggered murders could also be prevented if GPs, psychiatrists and the general public were better educated about the signs of post-natal depression. We have to start supporting mothers who have the courage to admit that they aren't coping, rather than blandly reassuring them that all will be fine.

We should also be more open to the idea that, if the mother has addiction problems or mental health issues, the father may make the better custodial parent. At present, a man has only a three percent chance of gaining custody of his child.

But if we are really serious about child care, then we have to make it illegal for parents to hit their offspring. Our current legalised violence inhibits child protection and breeches children's fundamental human rights. As Professor Paulo Pinheiro, independent expert for the UN Secretary General's study on violence against young people, has said, "We cannot draw lines and try and define acceptable ways of hitting children. There can be no compromise, any more than we compromise in challenging all violence against women."

By modernising the law on assault to give children the same protection as adults, we would take a huge step towards becoming a peaceful and loving society.

APPENDIX

RESOURCES

Preventing teenage pregnancies:
www.likeitis.org Part of Marie Stopes International, this site offers sexual health information for young people.

Ending pressure on women to have children:
www.nokidding.net International online group for the happily childfree.

Avoiding cot death:
www.fsid.org.uk Internet home of the Foundation for Sudden Infant Death, the UK's leading baby charity. Their free booklet, *Reduce the Risk of Cot Death*, can be ordered online or by telephoning 020 7222 8001. Alternatively, send a cover note requesting the free booklet to them at FSID, Artillery House, 11-19 Artillery Row, London SW1P 1RT. For the helpline, phone 020 7233 2090.

Advice on positive discipline:
www.childrenareunbeatable.org.uk To join the campaign for a zero-tolerance approach to parents hitting children, contact: Children Are Unbeatable, 94 White Lion Street, London N1 9PF.

To order a parenting pack of six leaflets (including *Keeping Your Cool*, *Listening to Children* and *Encouraging Better Behaviour*), send an A4 stamped addressed envelope with five first class stamps to: 'Parenting Pack', NSPCC, Weston House, 42 Curtain Road, London EC2A 3NH.

Or download them on:
www.nspcc.org.uk/html/Home/Informationresources/forparentscarers.htm

For a single copy of the leaflet *The No Smacking Guide To Good Behaviour* by Penelope Leach, send a C5 stamped addressed envelope with one second class stamp to: APPROACH Ltd, 94 White Lion Street, London N1 9PF.

For a single copy of the A4 poster *Think Before You Smack*, send an A4 envelope with a second class stamp (remember that A4 envelopes need a 'large-size' second-class stamp) to: APPROACH at the above address.

Early child education:
To find out if there is a Sure Start Children's Centre in your area, telephone the Families Information Service on 0800 2 346 346.

SELECT
BIBLIOGRAPHY

Bagby, David *Dance with the Devil* Key Porter Books, 2007

Begg, Paul & Fido, Martin *Great Crimes and Trials of the Twentieth Century* Carlton/Simon & Schuster, 1993

Busby, Sian *The Cruel Mother* Short Books, 2004

Campbell, Duncan *A Stranger and Afraid: The Story of Caroline Beale* Macmillan, 1997

Carrere, Emmanuel *The Adversary* Bloomsbury, 2000

Defago, Nicki *Childfree and Loving It* Fusion Press, 2005

Englade, Ken *Murder in Boston* Angus & Robertson, 1990

Finkel, Michael *True Story* HarperCollins, 2005

Firstman, Richard & Talan, James *The Death of Innocents* Bantam Books, 1998

Francis, Monte *By Their Father's Hand: The True Story of the Wesson Family Massacre* Harper, 2007

Furneaux, Rupert *Famous Criminal Cases 6* Odhams Press Ltd, 1960

Howells, John G. *Remember Maria* Butterworths, 1974

Johnson, Steven, McCoy, Heath, Muchnick, Irwin & Oliver, Greg *Benoit* ECW Press, 2007

Long, Steven *Every Woman's Nightmare* St Martin's Press, 2006

McGregor, Alexander *The Law Killers* Black & White Publishing, 2005

McPhee, Michele R. *Heartless* St Martin's Paperbacks, 2008

Millen, Paul *Crime Scene Investigator* Constable, 2008

O'Brien, Darcy *Murder in Little Egypt* New American Library, 1989

O'Malley, Suzanne *Are You There Alone?* Pocket Star Books, 2005

Olsen, Gregg *Cruel Deception* St Martin's Paperbacks, 1995

Peyser, Andrea *Mother Love, Deadly Love: The Susan Smith Story* HarperPaperbacks, 1995

Randazzo, Matthew *Ring of Hell* Phoenix Books, 2008

Reder, Peter & Duncan, Sylvia *Lost Innocents* Routledge, 1999

Smith, Carlton *Love, Daddy* St Martin's Paperbacks, 2003

Smith, David *Beyond All Reason* Pinnacle Books, 1995

Stowers, Carlton *To the Last Breath* St Martin's Paperbacks, 1999

Tullett, Tom *Clues to Murder* The Bodley Head, 1986

FILMOGRAPHY

Dateline: Inside the Murder Trial of Neil Entwistle (online transcript) by Dennis Murphy, aired *Dateline*, NBC on 27 June 2008.

Honour Kills, produced by BBC Manchester, aired BBC3 in October 2007.

Tonight: 'My Greek Tragedy' (John Hogan case), aired ITV1 on 21 January 2008.

MAGAZINES AND NEWSPAPERS

'Babies' Bodies Found in Box' by Jan Disley, *Daily Mirror*, 13 May 2008.

'Bipolar Disorder and Childbirth: The Importance of Recognising the Risk' by Ian Jones & Nick Craddock, *British Journal of Psychiatry*, 2005.

'Catalogue of Cruelty' by David Batty, *The Guardian*, 27 January 2003.

'City Executive Alberto Izaga Charged with Murder of Daughter, 2' by Helen Nugent, *The Times*, 13 September 2007.

'Couple Behead Their Three Children', *True Detective Spring Special*, 2008.

'Couple Found Guilty Over Toddler Abuse Death', *The Guardian*, 3 August 2007.

'Couple Who Starved and Killed Girl, 2, Are Jailed' by Tania Branigan & Audrey Gillan, *The Guardian*, 21 September 2002.

'Drugs Kill Baby as Mum Smokes' by John Coles, *The Sun*, 27 June 2008.

'Drunk Father "Smothered Sick Son in Mercy Killing"' by Arifa Akbar, *The Independent*, 1 May 2005.

'Executive Gets Life Term for Killing of His Family', *New York Times*, 7 February 1993.

'Face of a Monster' by Marion Scott, *Sunday Mail*, 23 November 2008.

'Father's Grief over Wife and Murdered Sons' by Graham Duffill, *The Times*, 4 March 2007.

'Father Killed Son, 4, after Wife Jilted Him' by Paul Jeeves, *Daily Express*, 26 February 2008.

'How a Little Boy's Sad Death Has Left a Family in Shreds' by Phil Mills, *The Argus*, 14 December, 2005.

'Husband Guilty of Family Murder' by James Bone, *The Times*, 26 June 2008.

'Iraq Girl Murdered by Dad for Loving a British Squaddie' by Victoria Ward, *Daily Mirror*, 28 April 2008.

'It's Horrible to Think that It's Happening Again' by Maria Colwell's brother, *The Argus*, 24 March 2000.

'Lauren Wright Case: Tragic Tale of a Child Unwanted from Day of Her Birth' by Terri Judd, *The Independent*, 2 October, 2001.

'Mother Jailed after Bristol Child's Drug Death', *Bristol Evening Post*, 27 June 2008.

'Mother Who Killed Her Own Baby by Throwing Him to the Ground Walks Free from Court', *Daily Mail*, 14 July 2008.

'Oh No, Not Again!' by Gary Fox, *Master Detective*, July 2006.

'Should Parents Stop at Two Children?' by Damien Fletcher, *Daily Mirror*, 25 July 2008.

'Should We Condemn the Mum Who Drowned Her Daughter?' by Claire Bates, *Bella* issue 41, October 2008.

'The 26-Year Secret' by Mark Randall, *True Detective Spring Special*, 2008.

'Tiffany Hirst: The Toddler Left to Die Alone and Unloved' by Lucy Bannerman, *The Times*, 13 June 2008.

'Timeline of the Christopher Foster Mansion Murders' by Gordon Rayner, *Daily Telegraph*, 3 September 2008.

'Tribute Paid to Tragic Sharpness Docks Pair', *Gloucestershire Echo*, 11 October 2007.

'Violent Parents Will Lose Access', *The Independent*, 17 March 2002.

'Who'd Want to Kill My Baby?' by Robert Gallon, as told to Angela Wormald and Claire Stretton, *Real People*, 5 October 2006.

'Woman Who Pleaded "Baby Blues" in Infant Case Now Says She's Sane' by Larry Welborn, *Orange County Register*, 30 May 2008.

'Why I Burnt My Baby to Death' by Danielle Wails, *Love It!* issue 43, November 2006.

'You Are My Best Friend: Last Words of Ellie, 3, to Mother', *Daily Mirror*, 7 October 2008.